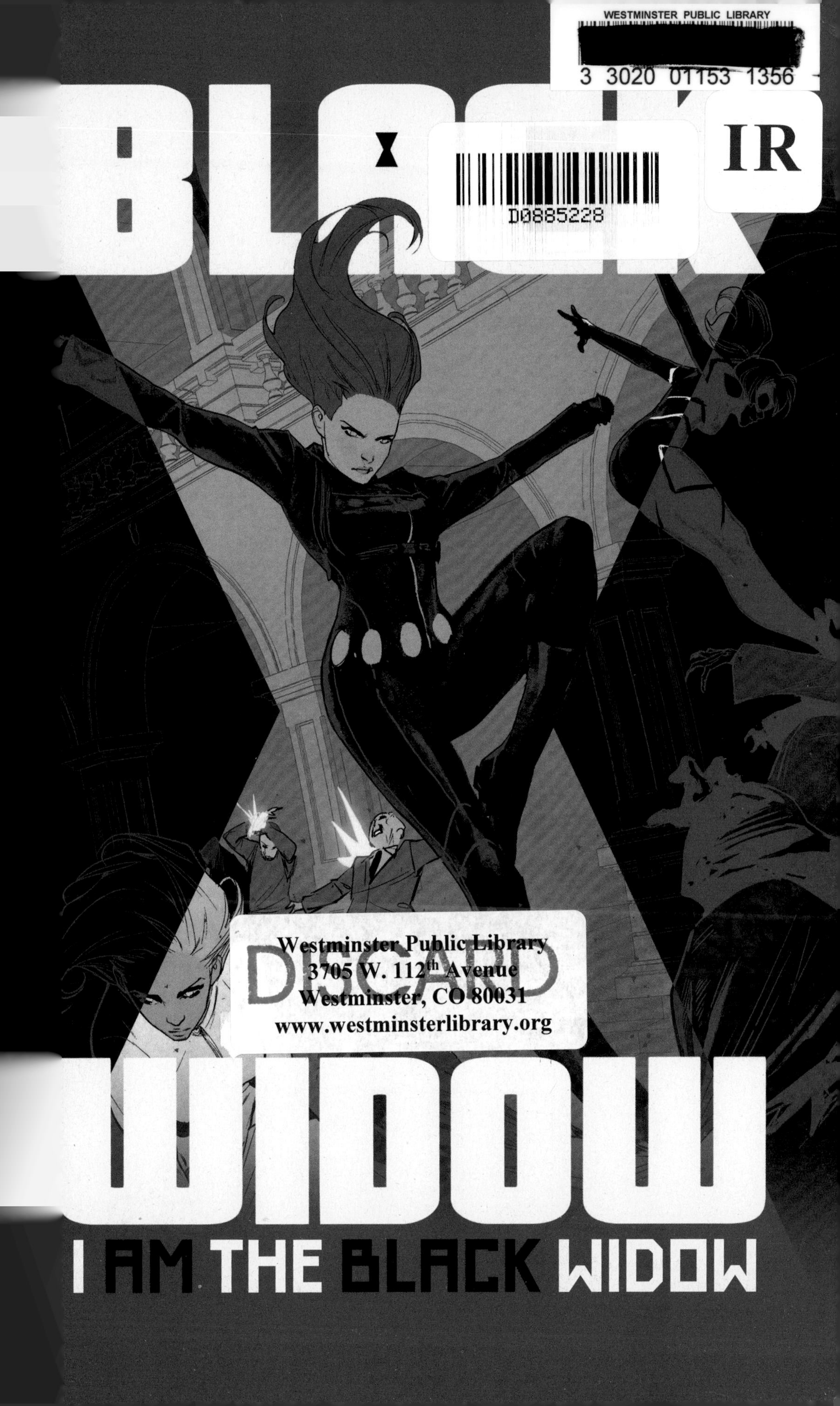
BLACK
WIDOW
I AM THE BLACK WIDOW

The world's greatest superspy has a broken heart. Kidnapped and brainwashed by a cadre of her greatest enemies, **Natasha Romanoff**, A.K.A. the **Black Widow**, spent months believing she was an architect in San Francisco. With a beautiful husband and perfect baby boy — her actual genetic son — life looked good...for perhaps the first time ever. When the dream dissolved, Natasha sent James and Stevie far away, where not even she could find them again. They are alive...they are safe...but gone forever. Alone again, Natasha invited **Yelena Belova** to stay and help her build something new. Now the Widows set out to remake themselves yet again in the heart of San Francisco.

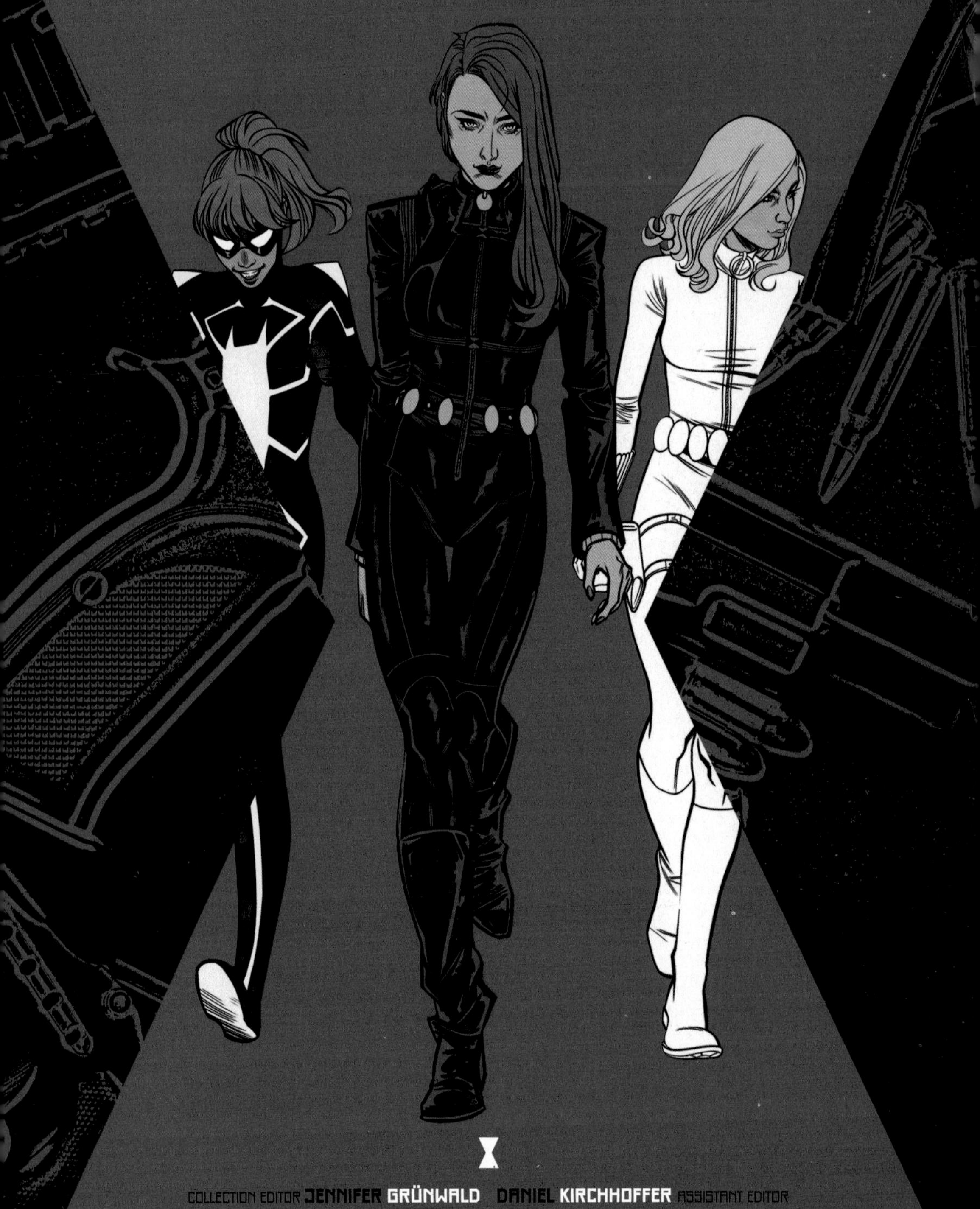

COLLECTION EDITOR **JENNIFER GRÜNWALD**
ASSISTANT MANAGING EDITOR **MAIA LOY**
VP PRODUCTION & SPECIAL PROJECTS **JEFF YOUNGQUIST**
SVP PRINT, SALES & MARKETING **DAVID GABRIEL**

DANIEL KIRCHHOFFER ASSISTANT EDITOR
LISA MONTALBANO ASSISTANT MANAGING EDITOR
ADAM DEL RE WITH **JAY BOWEN** BOOK DESIGNERS
C.B. CEBULSKI EDITOR IN CHIEF

BLACK WIDOW BY KELLY THOMPSON VOL. 2: I AM THE BLACK WIDOW. Contains material originally published in magazine form as BLACK WIDOW (2020) #6-10. First printing 2021. ISBN 978-1-302-93013-4. Published by MARVEL WORLDWIDE, INC., a subsidiary of MARVEL ENTERTAINMENT, LLC. OFFICE OF PUBLICATION: 1290 Avenue of the Americas, New York, NY 10104.

Printed in Canada. KEVIN FEIGE, Chief Creative Officer; DAN BUCKLEY, President, Marvel Entertainment; JOE QUESADA, EVP & Creative Director; DAVID BOGART, Associate Publisher & SVP of Talent Affairs; TOM BREVOORT, VP, Executive Editor; NICK LOWE, Executive Editor, VP of Content, Digital Publishing; DAVID GABRIEL, VP of Print & Digital Publishing; JEFF YOUNGQUIST, VP of Production & Special Projects; ALEX MORALES, Director of Publishing Operations; DAN EDINGTON, Managing Editor; RICKEY PURDIN, Director of Talent Relations; JENNIFER GRÜNWALD, Senior Editor, Special Projects; SUSAN CRESPI, Production Manager; STAN LEE, Chairman Emeritus. For information regarding advertising in Marvel Comics or on Marvel.com, please contact Vit DeBellis, Custom Solutions & Integrated Advertising Manager, at vdebellis@marvel.com. For Marvel subscription inquiries, please call 888-511-5480. **Manufactured between 8/13/2021 and 9/14/2021 by SOLISCO PRINTERS, SCOTT, QC, CANADA.**

10 9 8 7 6 5 4 3 2 1

BLACK

I AM THE BLACK WIDOW

KELLY THOMPSON
WRITER

RAFAEL DE LATORRE
(#6, #8-10) &
ELENA CASAGRANDE
(#7-10)
PENCILERS

RAFAEL DE LATORRE
(#6, #8-10),
ELENA CASAGRANDE
(#7) &
ELISABETTA D'AMICO
(#7-10)
INKERS

JORDIE BELLAIRE
COLOR ARTIST

VC's CORY PETIT
LETTERER

ADAM HUGHES
COVER ART

KAT GREGOROWICZ
ASSISTANT EDITOR

SARAH BRUNSTAD
EDITOR

WIL MOSS
SENIOR EDITOR

TOM BREVOORT
EXECUTIVE EDITOR

WIDOW

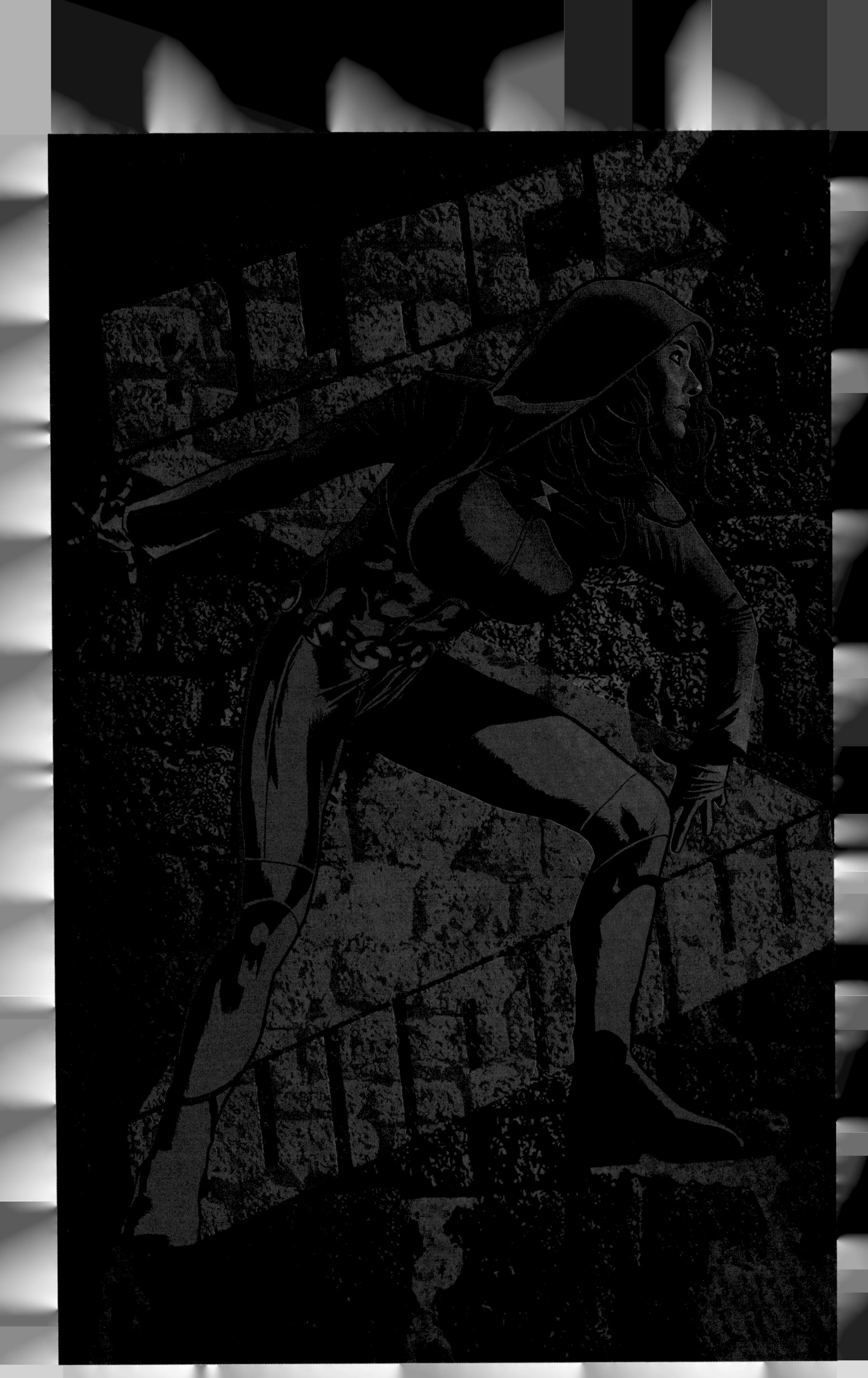

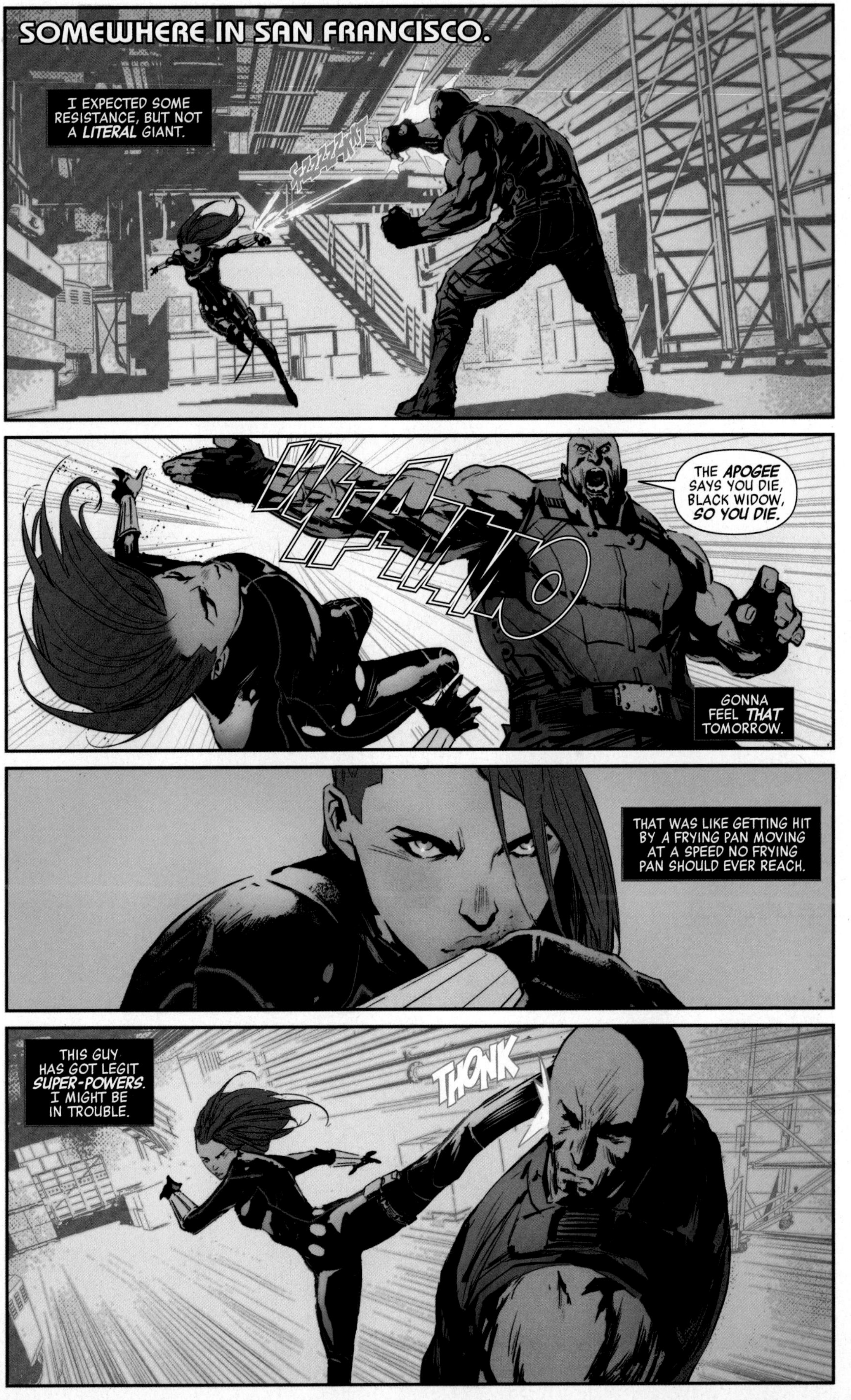
SOMEWHERE IN SAN FRANCISCO.
I EXPECTED SOME RESISTANCE, BUT NOT A LITERAL GIANT.
THE APOGEE SAYS YOU DIE, BLACK WIDOW, SO YOU DIE.
GONNA FEEL THAT TOMORROW.
THAT WAS LIKE GETTING HIT BY A FRYING PAN MOVING AT A SPEED NO FRYING PAN SHOULD EVER REACH.
THIS GUY HAS GOT LEGIT SUPER-POWERS. I MIGHT BE IN TROUBLE.
THONK

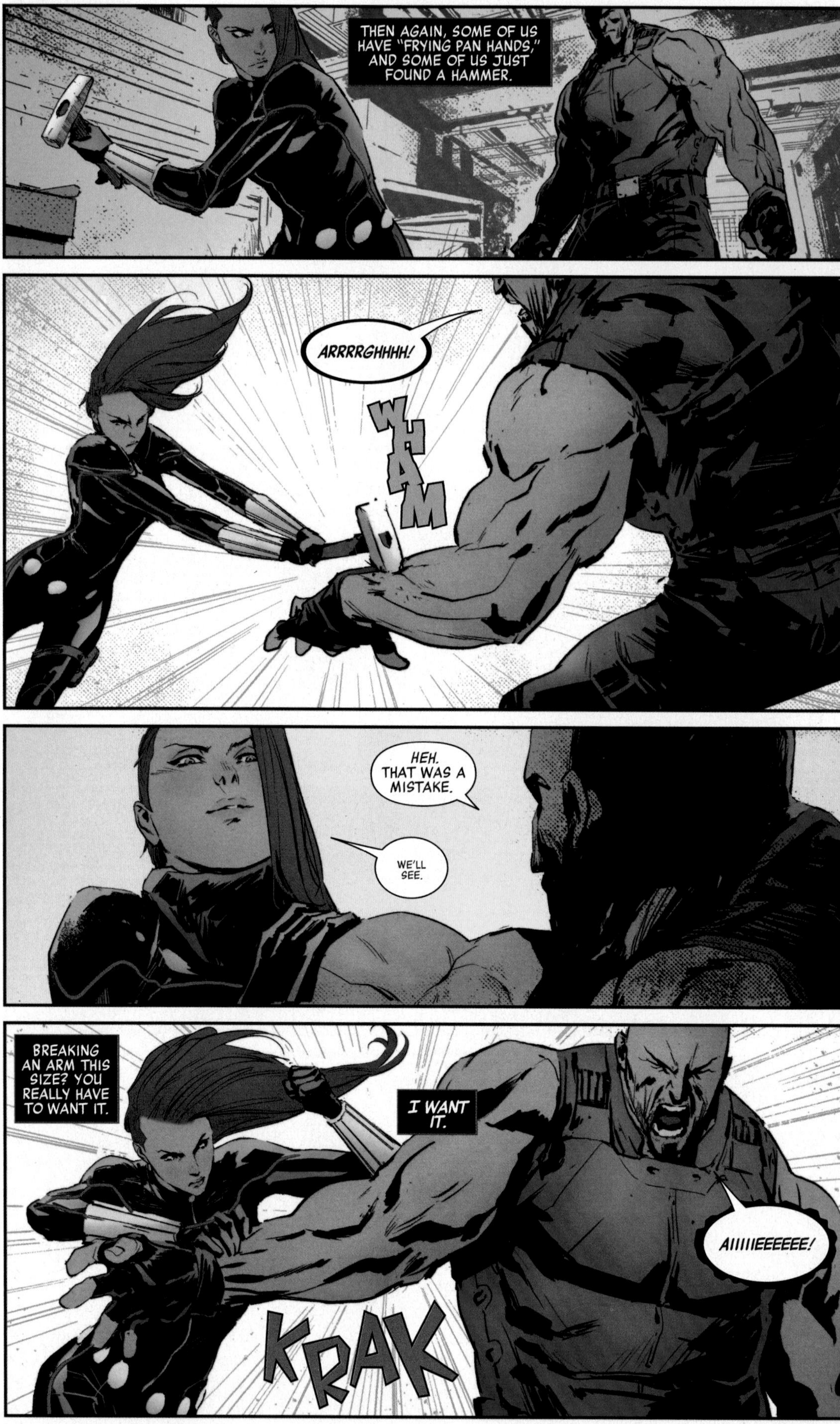
THEN AGAIN, SOME OF US HAVE "FRYING PAN HANDS," AND SOME OF US JUST FOUND A HAMMER.
ARRRRGHHHH!
WHAM
HEH. THAT WAS A MISTAKE.
WE'LL SEE.
BREAKING AN ARM THIS SIZE? YOU REALLY HAVE TO WANT IT.
I WANT IT.
AIIIIEEEEEE!
KRAK

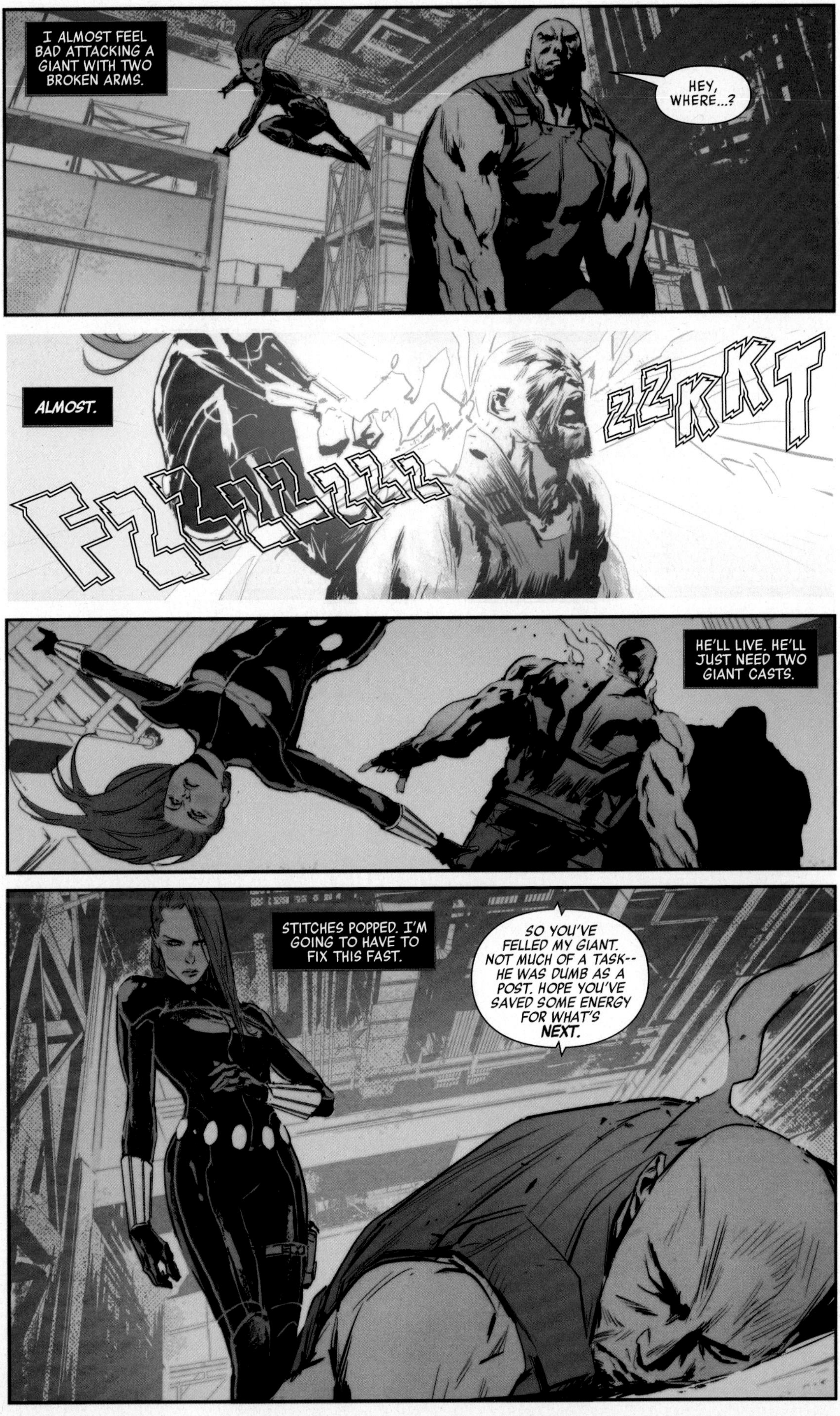

I ALMOST FEEL BAD ATTACKING A GIANT WITH TWO BROKEN ARMS.
HEY, WHERE...?
ALMOST.
FZZZZZZZ
ZZKKT
HE'LL LIVE. HE'LL JUST NEED TWO GIANT CASTS.
STITCHES POPPED. I'M GOING TO HAVE TO FIX THIS FAST.
SO YOU'VE FELLED MY GIANT. NOT MUCH OF A TASK-- HE WAS DUMB AS A POST. HOPE YOU'VE SAVED SOME ENERGY FOR WHAT'S **NEXT**.

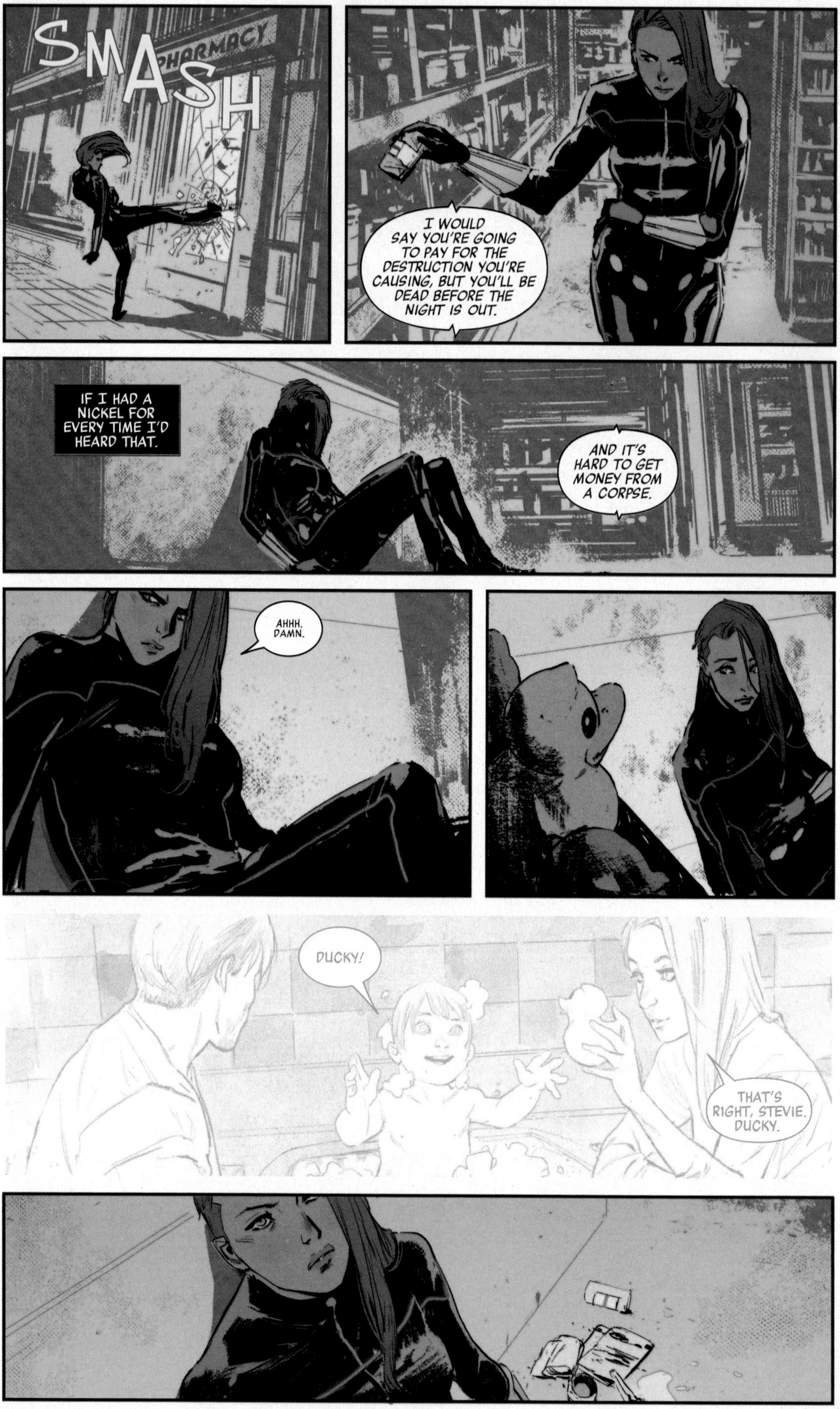
SMASH
PHARMACY
I WOULD SAY YOU'RE GOING TO PAY FOR THE DESTRUCTION YOU'RE CAUSING, BUT YOU'LL BE DEAD BEFORE THE NIGHT IS OUT.
IF I HAD A NICKEL FOR EVERY TIME I'D HEARD THAT.
AND IT'S HARD TO GET MONEY FROM A CORPSE.
AHHH. DAMN.
DUCKY!
THAT'S RIGHT, STEVIE. DUCKY.

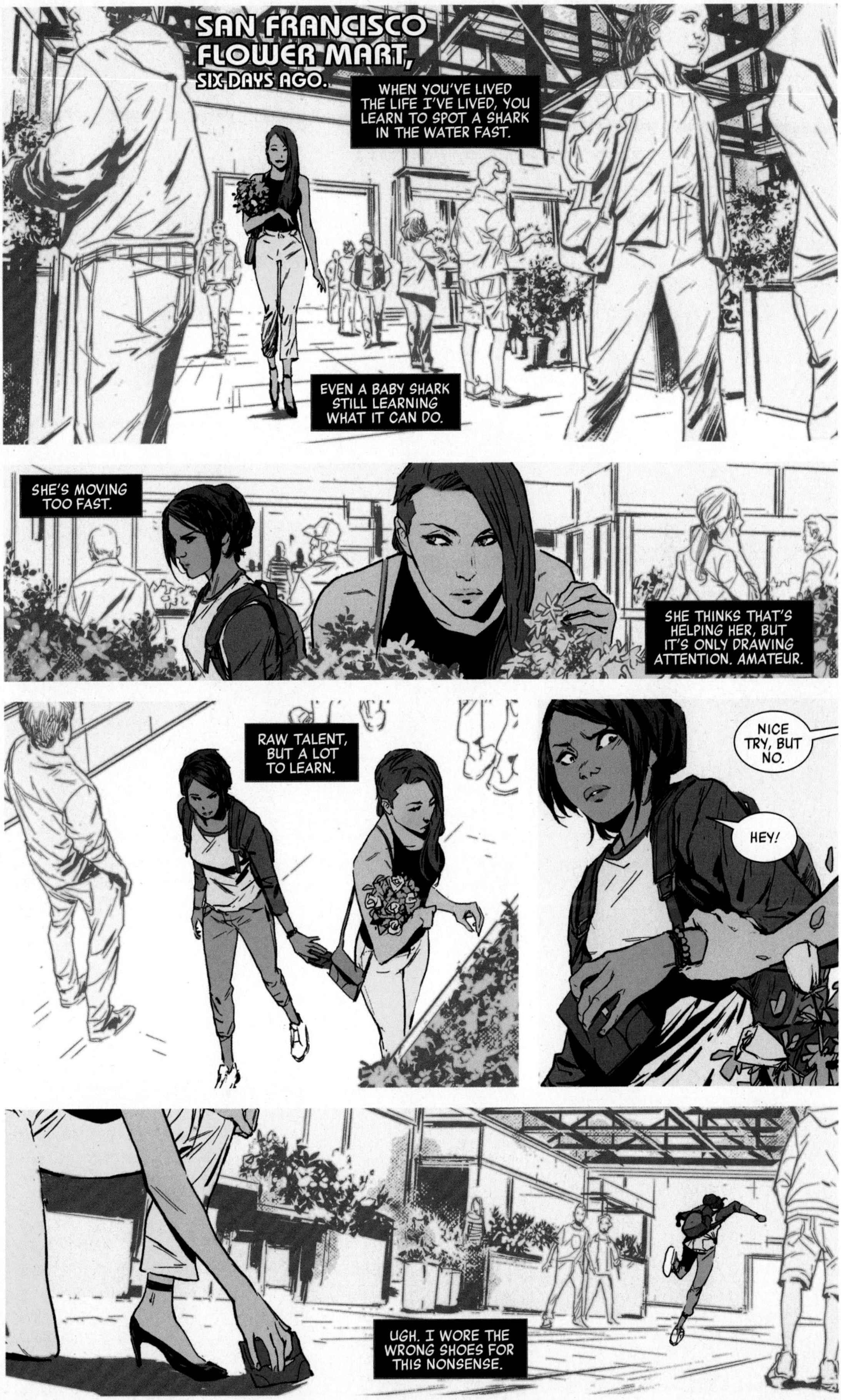
SAN FRANCISCO FLOWER MART,
SIX DAYS AGO.
WHEN YOU'VE LIVED THE LIFE I'VE LIVED, YOU LEARN TO SPOT A SHARK IN THE WATER FAST.
EVEN A BABY SHARK STILL LEARNING WHAT IT CAN DO.
SHE'S MOVING TOO FAST.
SHE THINKS THAT'S HELPING HER, BUT IT'S ONLY DRAWING ATTENTION. AMATEUR.
RAW TALENT, BUT A LOT TO LEARN.
NICE TRY, BUT NO.
HEY!
UGH. I WORE THE WRONG SHOES FOR THIS NONSENSE.

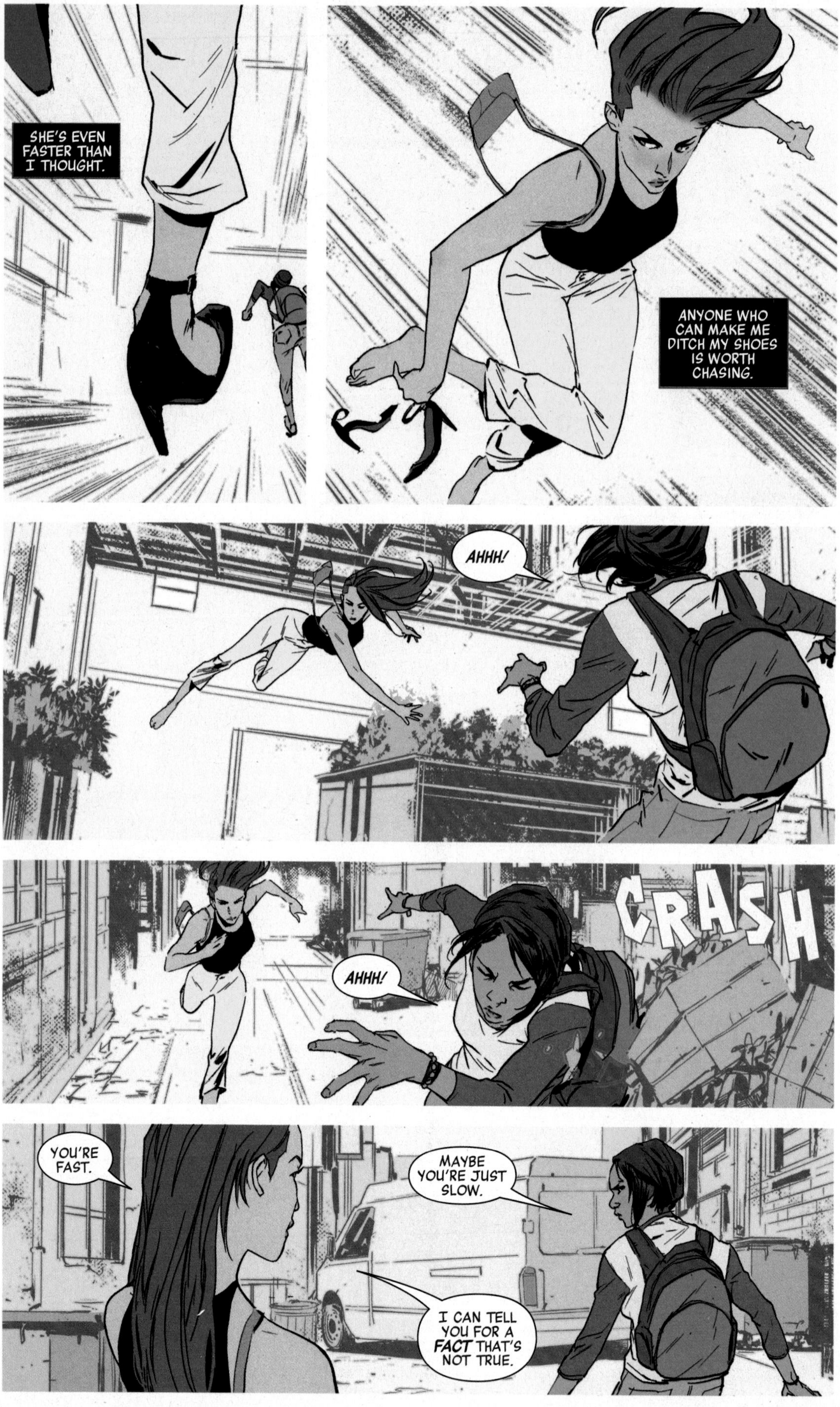

SHE'S EVEN FASTER THAN I THOUGHT.
ANYONE WHO CAN MAKE ME DITCH MY SHOES IS WORTH CHASING.
AHHH!
CRASH
AHHH!
YOU'RE FAST.
MAYBE YOU'RE JUST SLOW.
I CAN TELL YOU FOR A FACT THAT'S NOT TRUE.

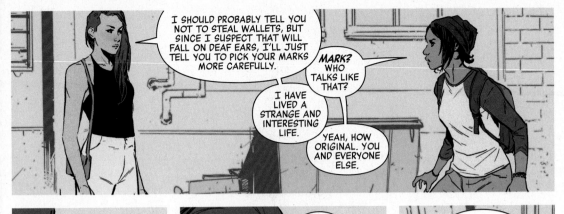

I SHOULD PROBABLY TELL YOU NOT TO STEAL WALLETS, BUT SINCE I SUSPECT THAT WILL FALL ON DEAF EARS, I'LL JUST TELL YOU TO PICK YOUR MARKS MORE CAREFULLY.

I HAVE LIVED A STRANGE AND INTERESTING LIFE.

MARK? WHO TALKS LIKE THAT?

YEAH, HOW ORIGINAL. YOU AND EVERYONE ELSE.

WHAT'S YOUR NAME?

MARIGOLD.

WELL, THAT'S A LIE.

NO $#@%, LADY. YOU THINK I'M TELLING YOU MY NAME?

FAIR ENOUGH.

TELL YOU WHAT--I'LL TRADE YOU MY WALLET FOR HOWEVER MANY YOU'RE HOLDING RIGHT NOW.

WHY WOULD I DO THAT?

SO THAT I LET YOU GO WITHOUT CALLING ANY COPS.

DAMMIT.

IT'S NOT SO BAD. MY WALLET MIGHT IMPRESS YOU.

IT WON'T BE ENOUGH.

FOR WHAT?

NONE OF YOUR BUSINESS. IT'S MY PROBLEM.

MAYBE I COULD HELP?

BECAUSE YOU'VE BEEN SO HELPFUL SO FAR?

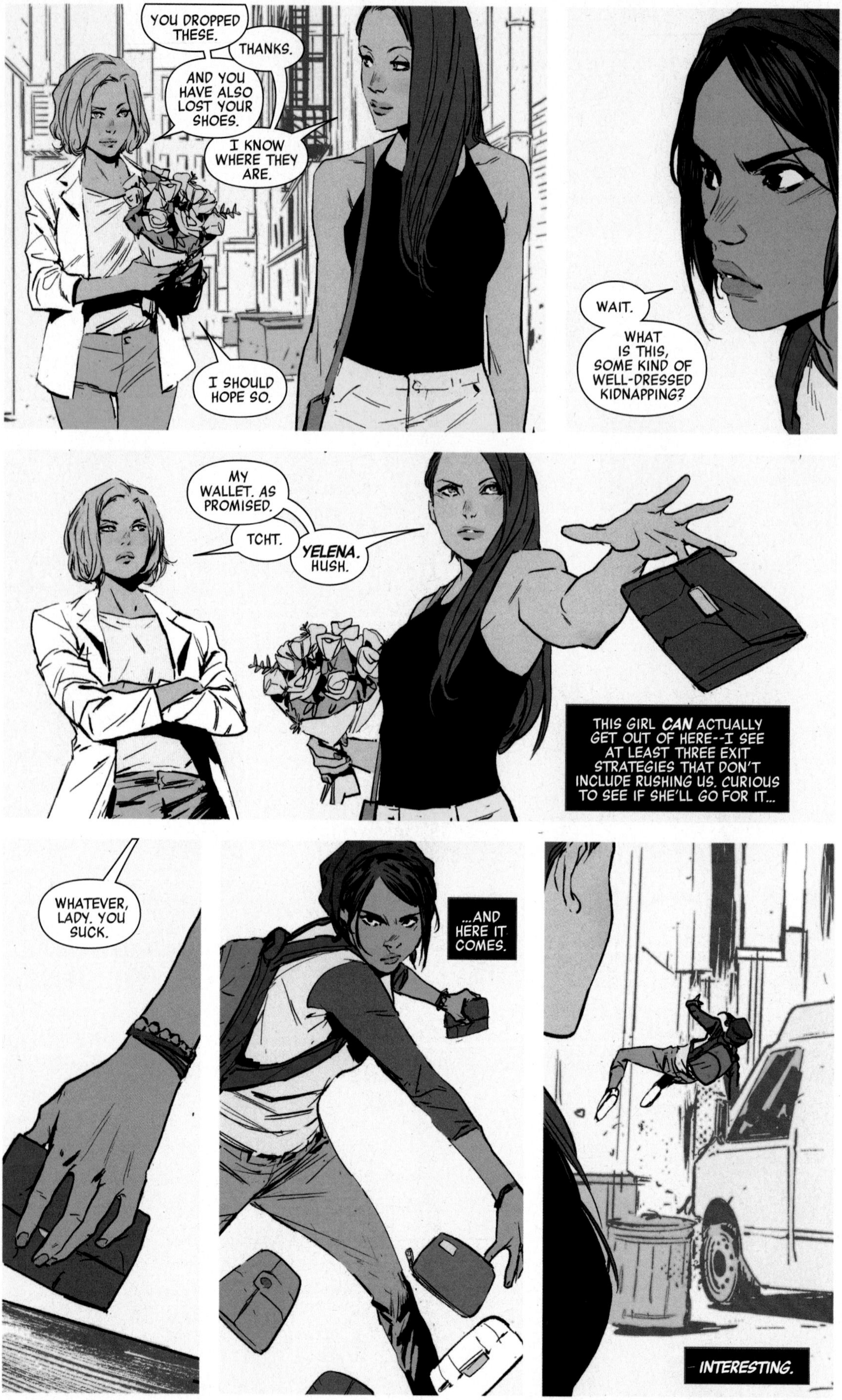
YOU DROPPED THESE.
THANKS.
AND YOU HAVE ALSO LOST YOUR SHOES.
I KNOW WHERE THEY ARE.
I SHOULD HOPE SO.
WAIT.
WHAT IS THIS, SOME KIND OF WELL-DRESSED KIDNAPPING?
MY WALLET. AS PROMISED.
TCHT.
YELENA. HUSH.
THIS GIRL CAN ACTUALLY GET OUT OF HERE--I SEE AT LEAST THREE EXIT STRATEGIES THAT DON'T INCLUDE RUSHING US. CURIOUS TO SEE IF SHE'LL GO FOR IT...
WHATEVER, LADY. YOU SUCK.
...AND HERE IT COMES.
--INTERESTING.

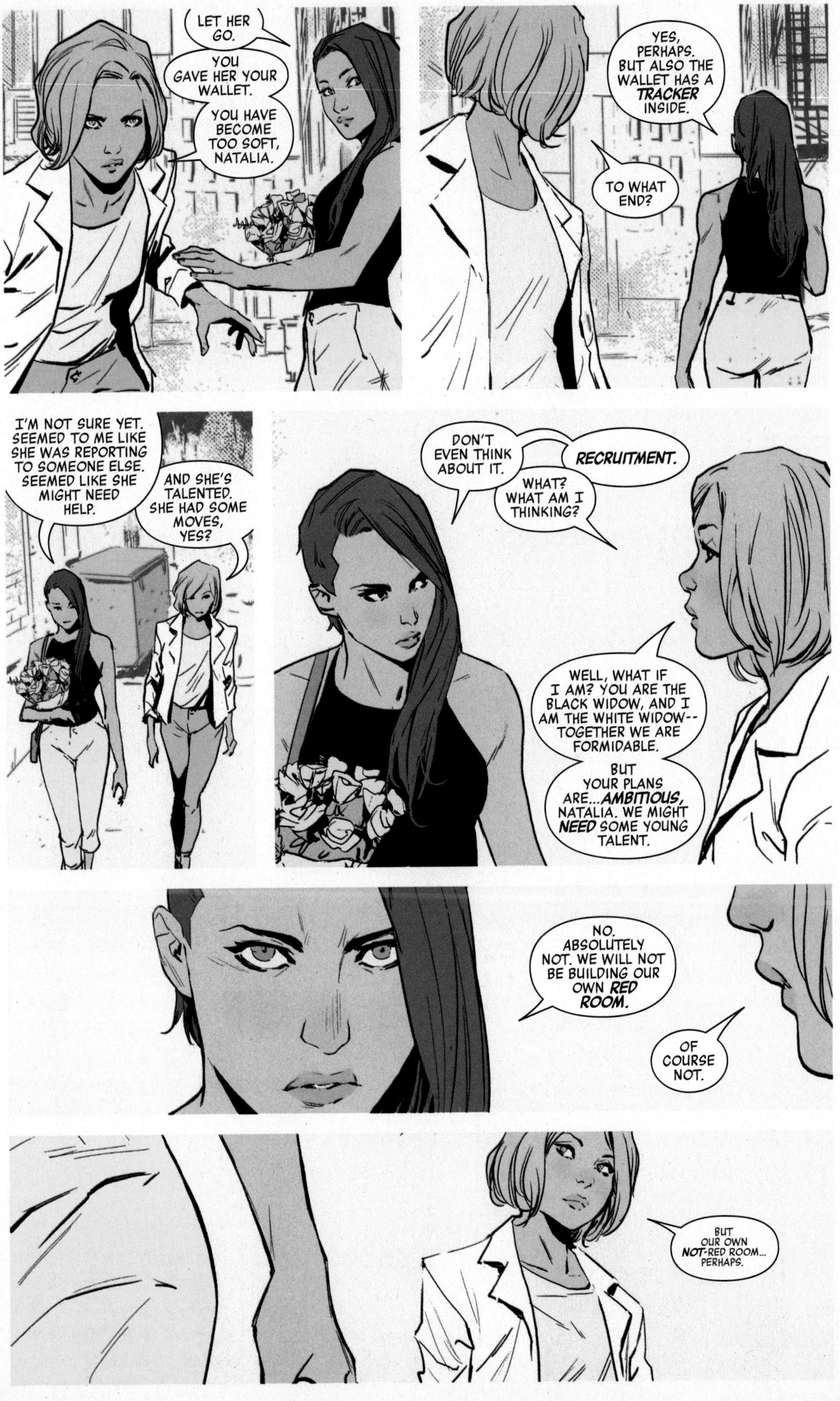
LET HER GO.
YOU GAVE HER YOUR WALLET.
YOU HAVE BECOME TOO SOFT, NATALIA.
YES, PERHAPS. BUT ALSO THE WALLET HAS A TRACKER INSIDE.
TO WHAT END?
I'M NOT SURE YET. SEEMED TO ME LIKE SHE WAS REPORTING TO SOMEONE ELSE. SEEMED LIKE SHE MIGHT NEED HELP.
AND SHE'S TALENTED. SHE HAD SOME MOVES, YES?
RECRUITMENT.
DON'T EVEN THINK ABOUT IT.
WHAT? WHAT AM I THINKING?
WELL, WHAT IF I AM? YOU ARE THE BLACK WIDOW, AND I AM THE WHITE WIDOW-- TOGETHER WE ARE FORMIDABLE.
BUT YOUR PLANS ARE...AMBITIOUS, NATALIA. WE MIGHT NEED SOME YOUNG TALENT.
NO. ABSOLUTELY NOT. WE WILL NOT BE BUILDING OUR OWN RED ROOM.
OF COURSE NOT.
BUT OUR OWN NOT-RED ROOM... PERHAPS.

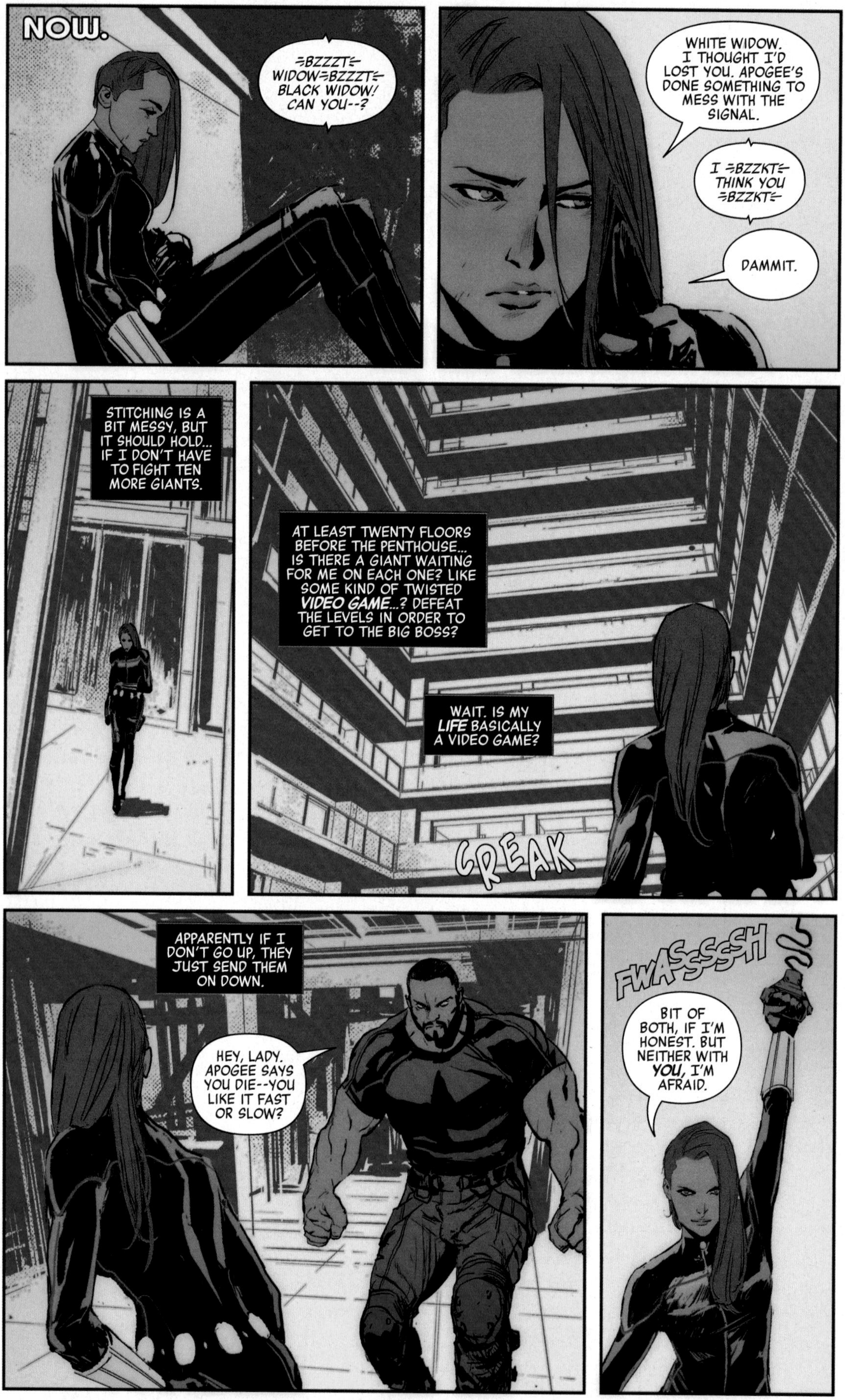
NOW.
=BZZZT= WIDOW=BZZZT= BLACK WIDOW! CAN YOU--?
WHITE WIDOW. I THOUGHT I'D LOST YOU. APOGEE'S DONE SOMETHING TO MESS WITH THE SIGNAL.
I =BZZKT= THINK YOU =BZZKT=
DAMMIT.
STITCHING IS A BIT MESSY, BUT IT SHOULD HOLD... IF I DON'T HAVE TO FIGHT TEN MORE GIANTS.
AT LEAST TWENTY FLOORS BEFORE THE PENTHOUSE... IS THERE A GIANT WAITING FOR ME ON EACH ONE? LIKE SOME KIND OF TWISTED VIDEO GAME...? DEFEAT THE LEVELS IN ORDER TO GET TO THE BIG BOSS?
WAIT. IS MY LIFE BASICALLY A VIDEO GAME?
CREAK
APPARENTLY IF I DON'T GO UP, THEY JUST SEND THEM ON DOWN.
HEY, LADY. APOGEE SAYS YOU DIE--YOU LIKE IT FAST OR SLOW?
FWASSSSH
BIT OF BOTH, IF I'M HONEST. BUT NEITHER WITH YOU, I'M AFRAID.

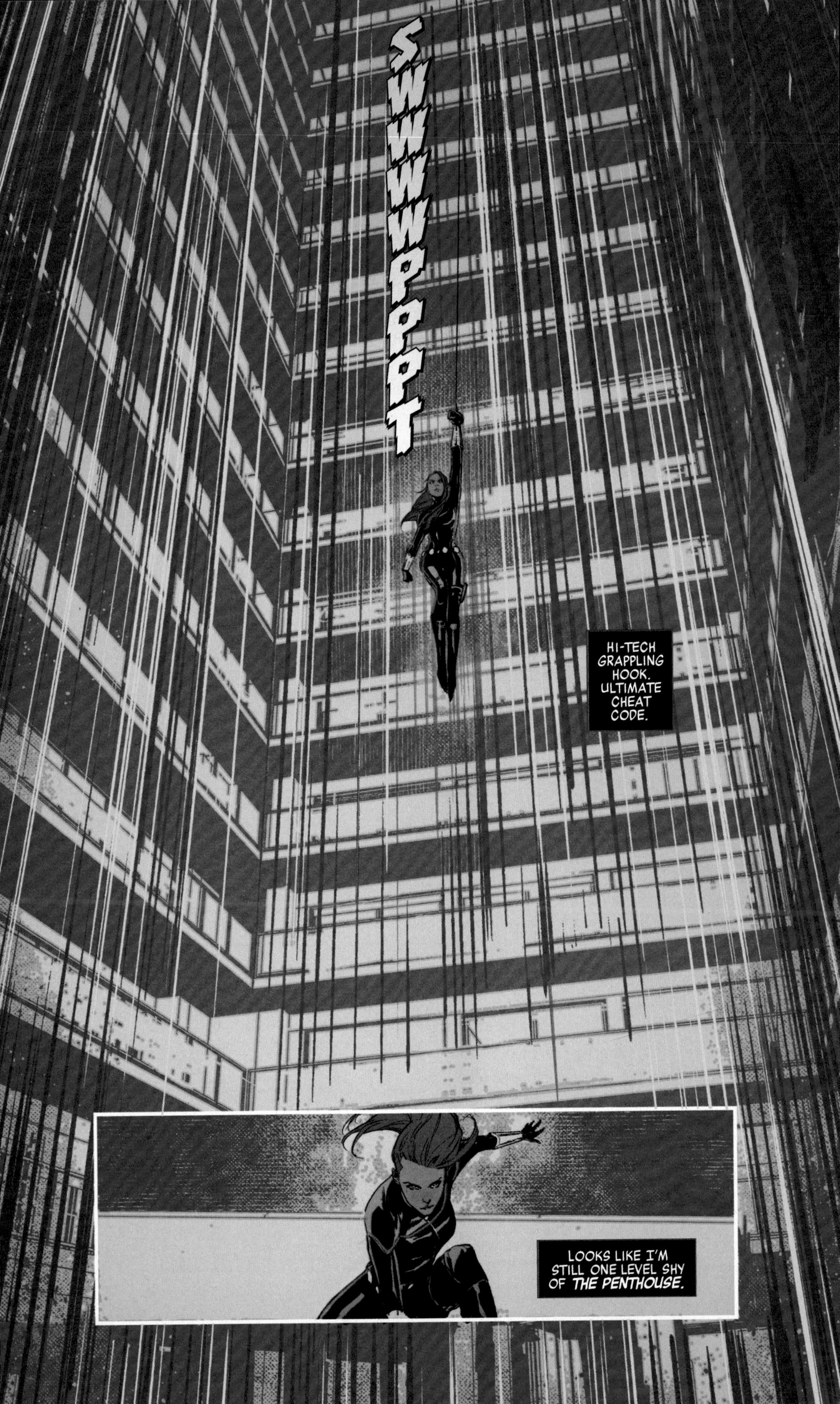
SWWWPPPT
HI-TECH GRAPPLING HOOK. ULTIMATE CHEAT CODE.
LOOKS LIKE I'M STILL ONE LEVEL SHY OF THE PENTHOUSE.

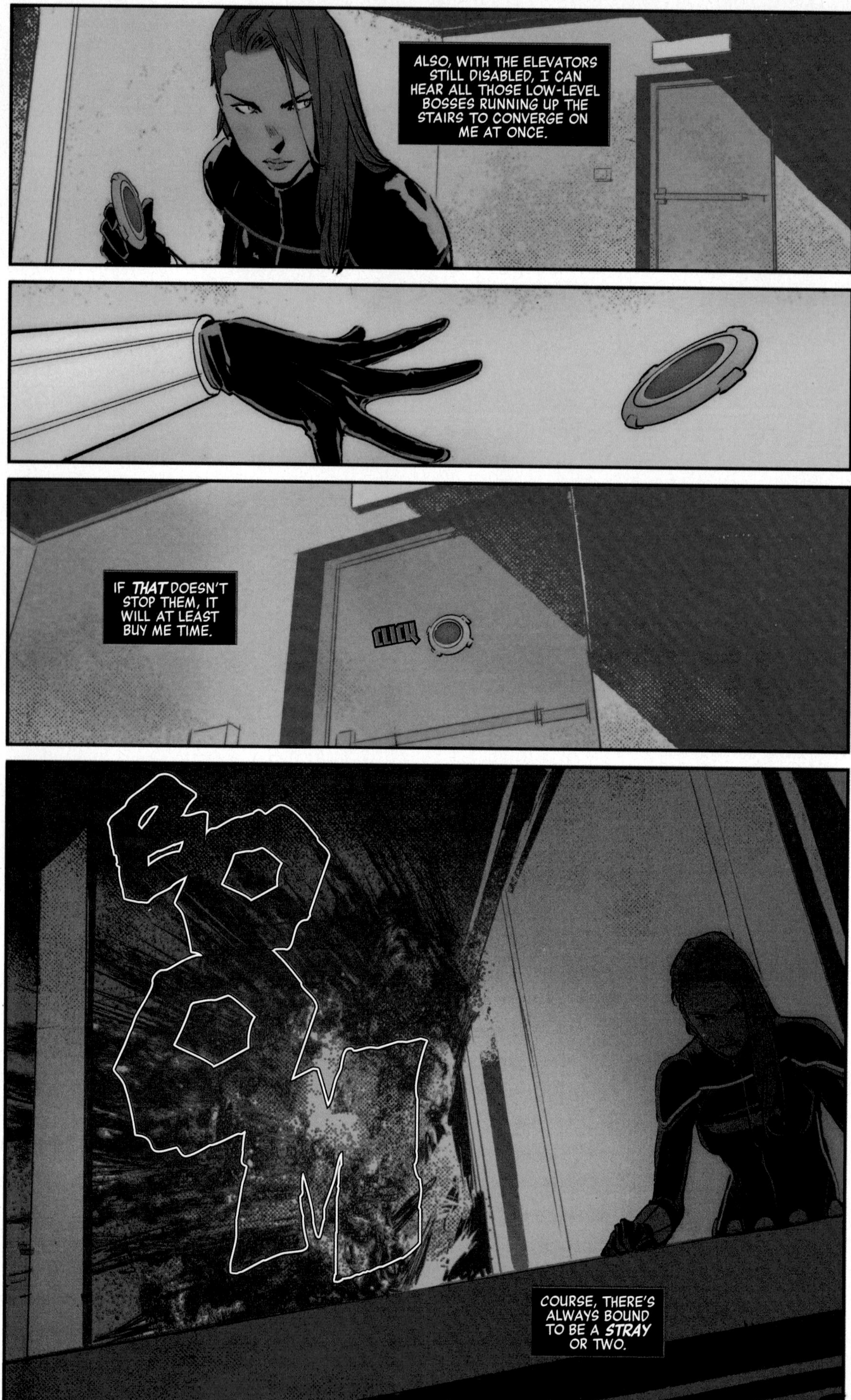
ALSO, WITH THE ELEVATORS STILL DISABLED, I CAN HEAR ALL THOSE LOW-LEVEL BOSSES RUNNING UP THE STAIRS TO CONVERGE ON ME AT ONCE.
IF THAT DOESN'T STOP THEM, IT WILL AT LEAST BUY ME TIME.
CLICK
BOOM
COURSE, THERE'S ALWAYS BOUND TO BE A STRAY OR TWO.

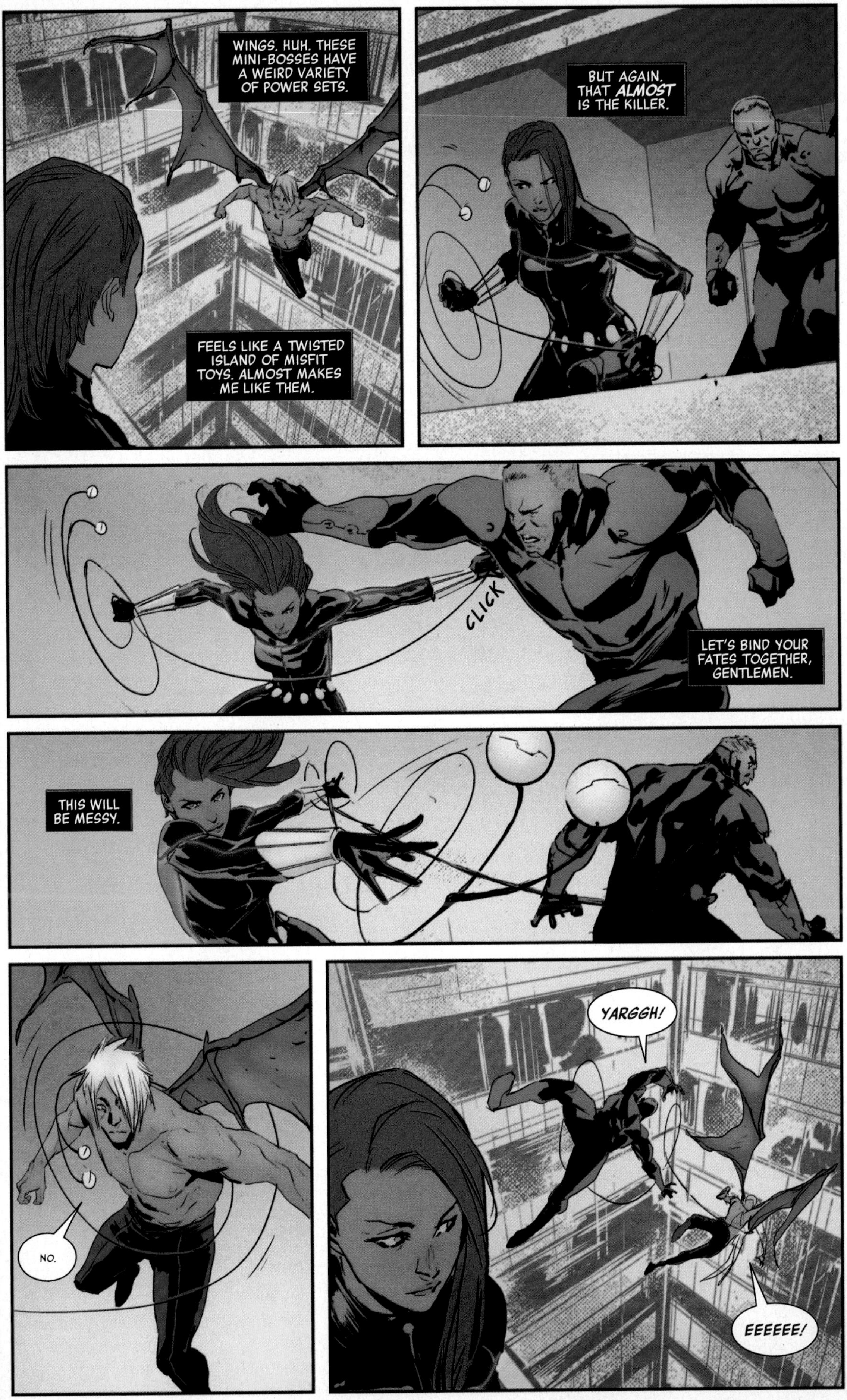

WINGS. HUH. THESE MINI-BOSSES HAVE A WEIRD VARIETY OF POWER SETS.
FEELS LIKE A TWISTED ISLAND OF MISFIT TOYS. ALMOST MAKES ME LIKE THEM.
BUT AGAIN. THAT ALMOST IS THE KILLER.
CLICK
LET'S BIND YOUR FATES TOGETHER, GENTLEMEN.
THIS WILL BE MESSY.
NO.
YARGGH!
EEEEEE!

THEY HIT A LOWER FLOOR...THEY'LL LIVE, BUT THEY'RE OUT OF *THIS* FIGHT.

SSPINNNGG

SURPRISE, SURPRISE, THE PENTHOUSE LEVEL DOESN'T HAVE OPEN RAILINGS... IT'S NOT EXPOSED LIKE THE REST.

IT WILL TAKE SOMETHING STRONGER TO BREAK THROUGH HERE.

CLICK

HUH. SO THE *FINAL BOSS* NEEDS SOME HELP, DOES HE?

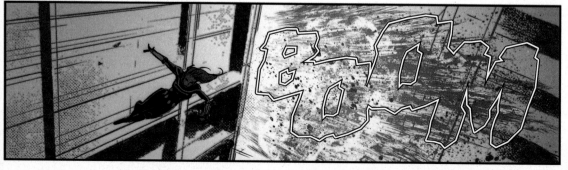

BOOM

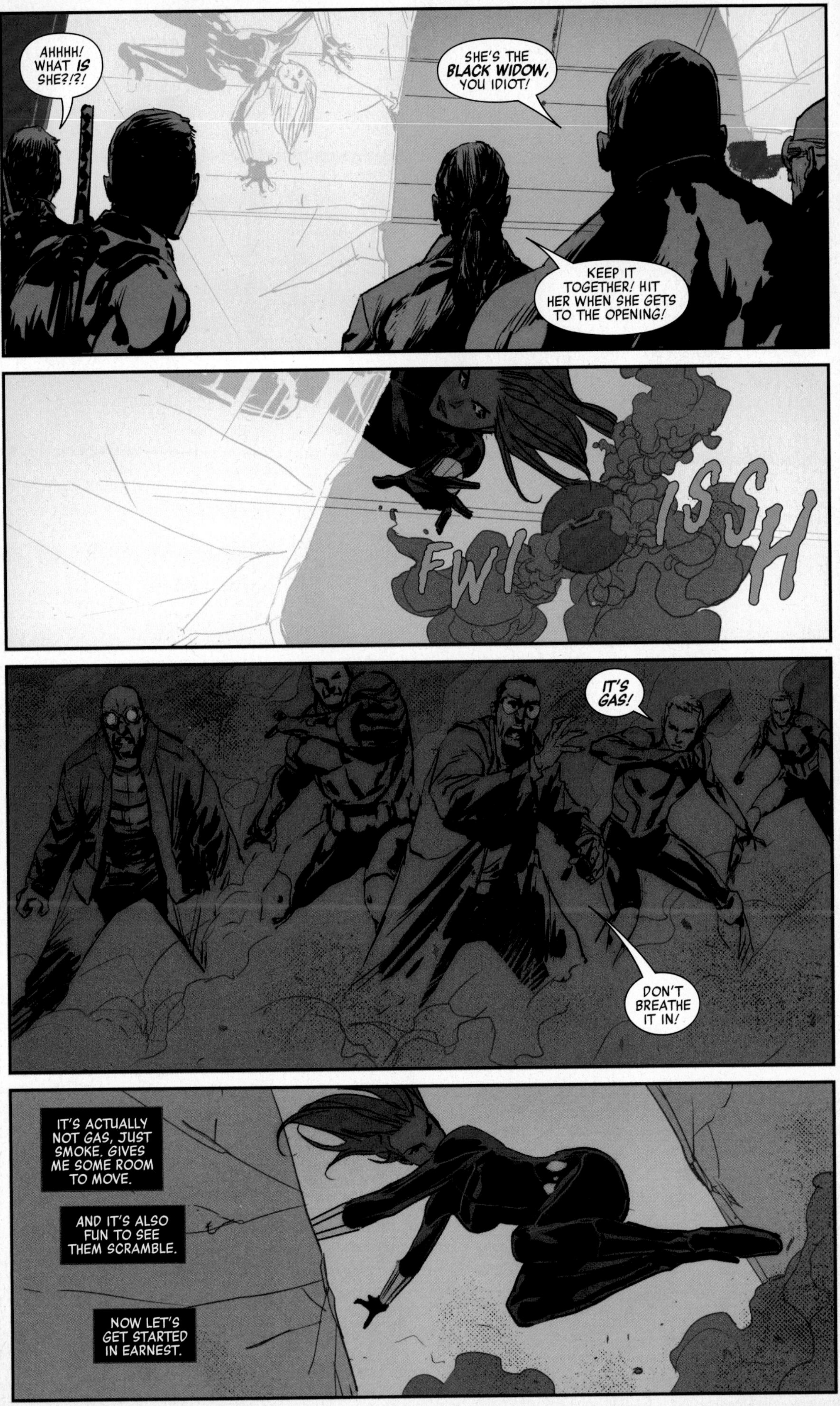
AHHHH! WHAT IS SHE?!?!
SHE'S THE BLACK WIDOW, YOU IDIOT!
KEEP IT TOGETHER! HIT HER WHEN SHE GETS TO THE OPENING!
FWIISSH
IT'S GAS!
DON'T BREATHE IT IN!
IT'S ACTUALLY NOT GAS, JUST SMOKE. GIVES ME SOME ROOM TO MOVE.
AND IT'S ALSO FUN TO SEE THEM SCRAMBLE.
NOW LET'S GET STARTED IN EARNEST.

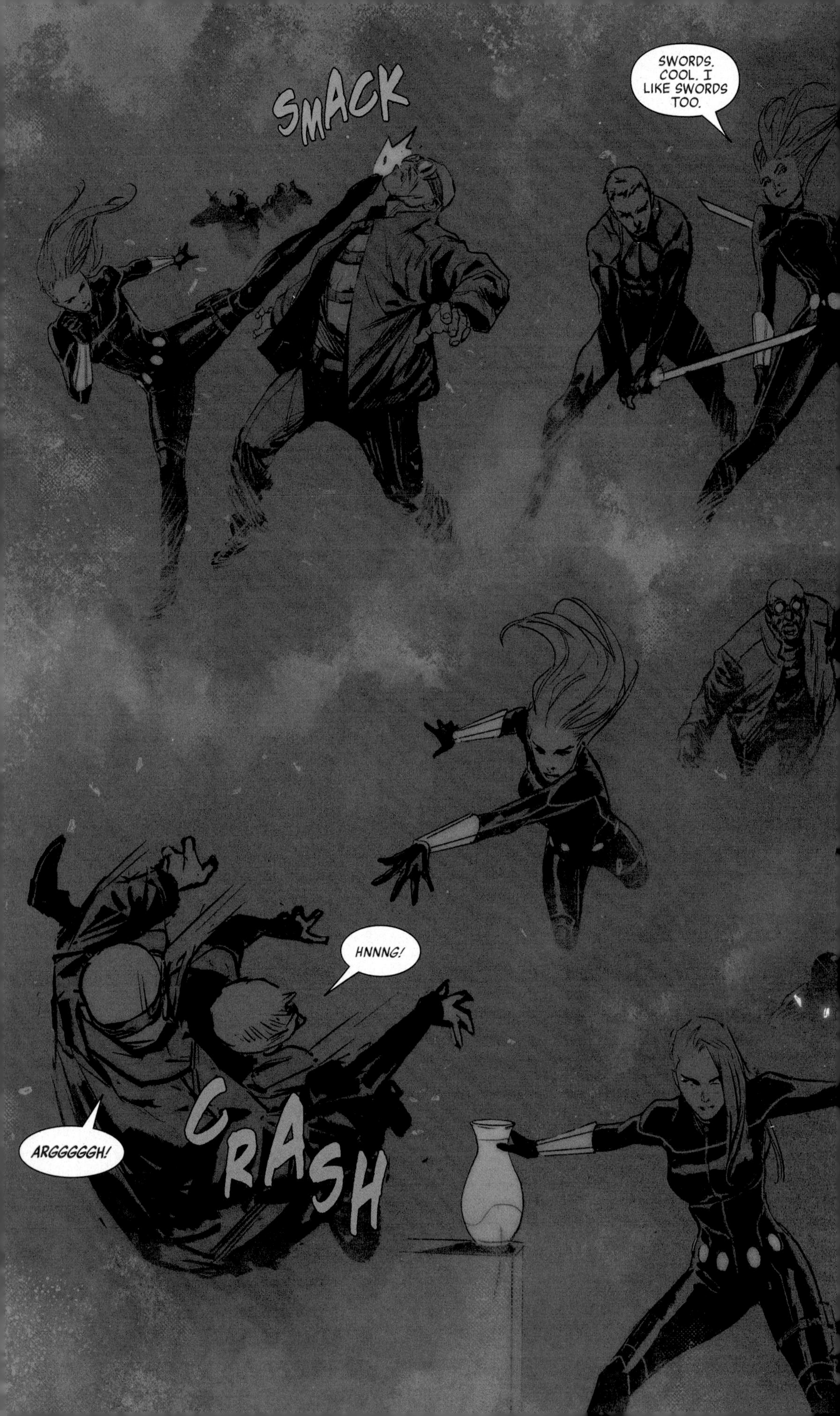
SMACK
SWORDS. COOL. I LIKE SWORDS TOO.
HNNNG!
ARGGGGGH!
CRASH

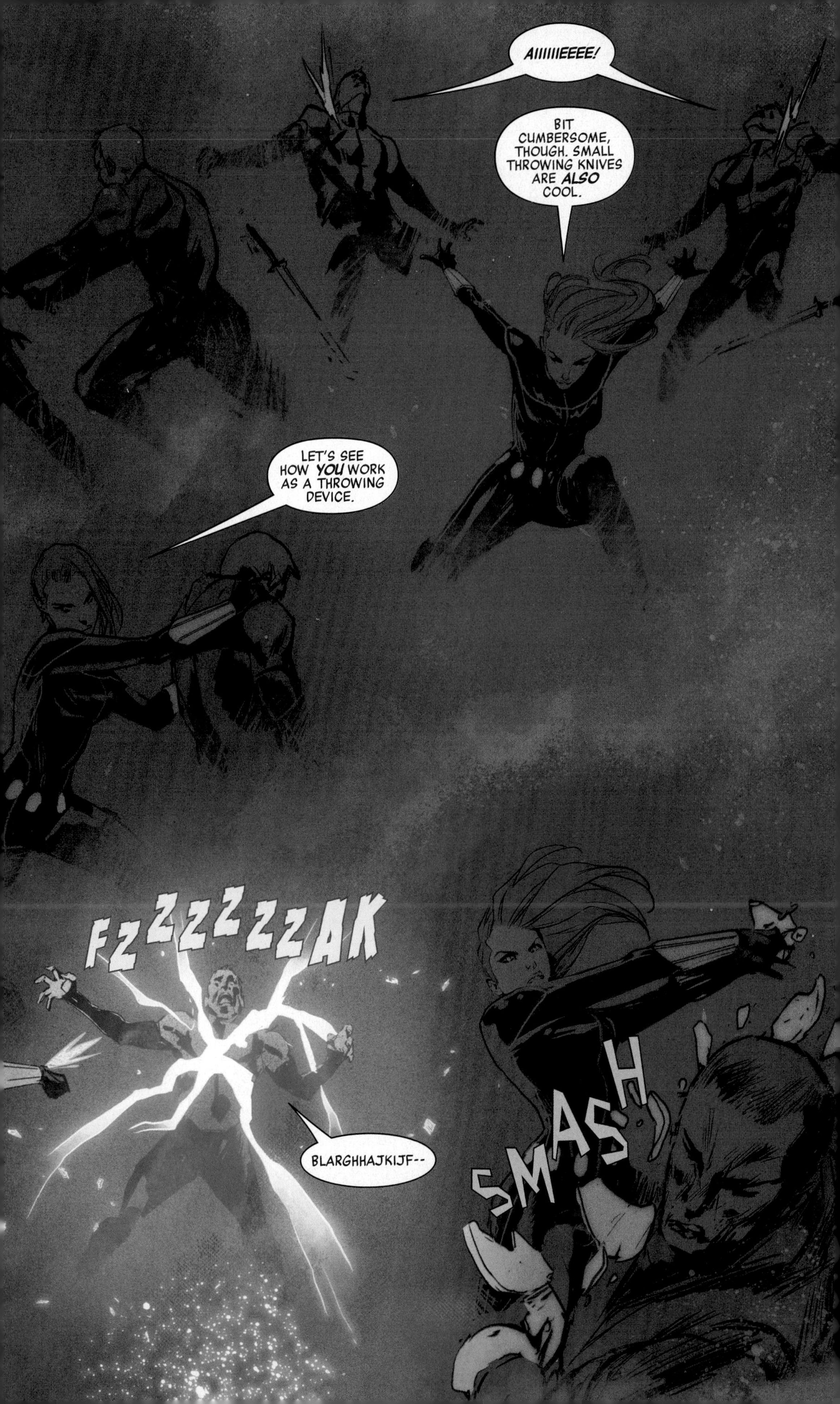
AIIIIIIEEEE!
BIT CUMBERSOME, THOUGH. SMALL THROWING KNIVES ARE *ALSO* COOL.
LET'S SEE HOW *YOU* WORK AS A THROWING DEVICE.
FZZZZZZZAK
BLARGHHAJKIJF--
SMASH

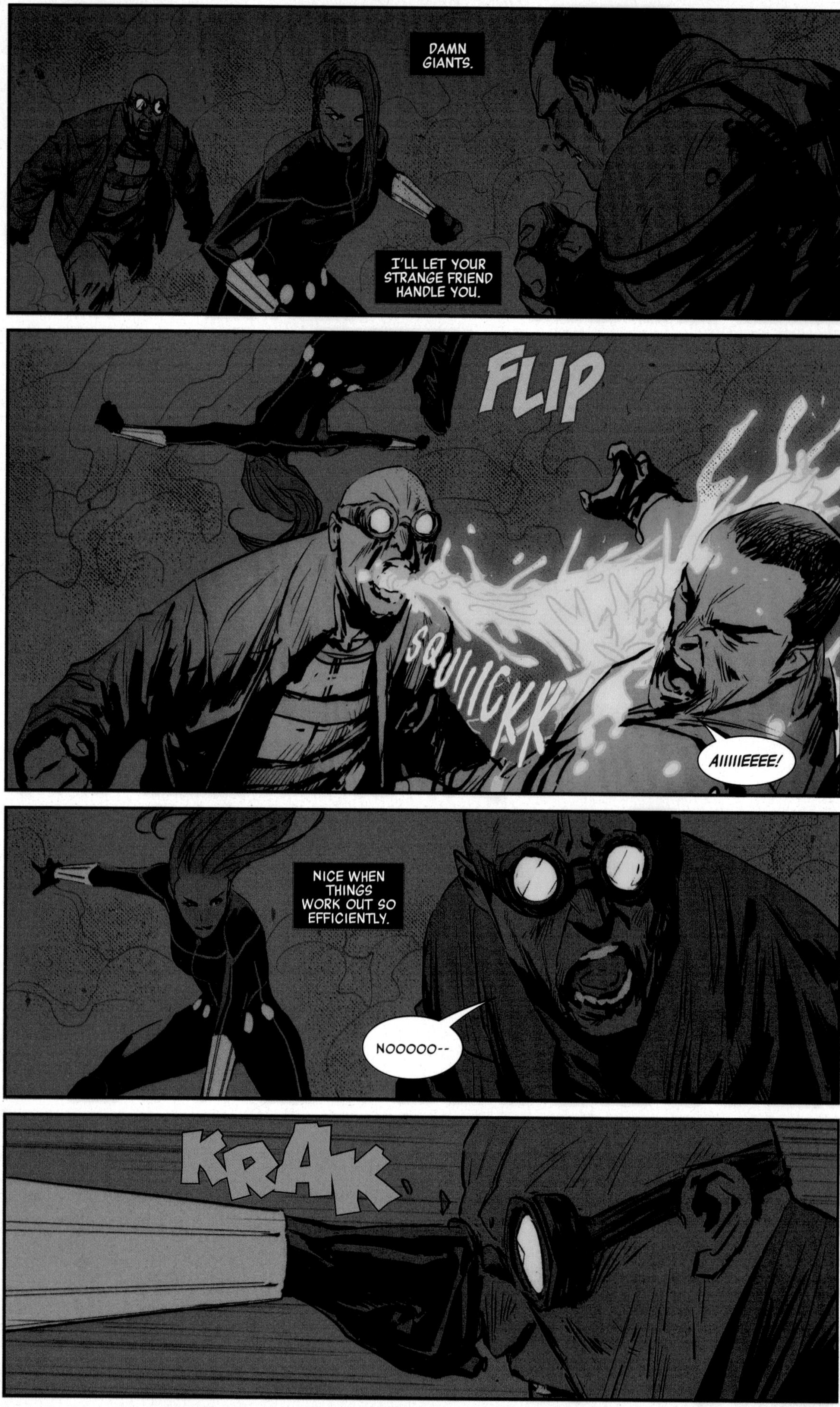
DAMN GIANTS.
I'LL LET YOUR STRANGE FRIEND HANDLE YOU.
FLIP
SQUIIICKK
AIIIIIEEEE!
NICE WHEN THINGS WORK OUT SO EFFICIENTLY.
NOOOOO--
KRAK

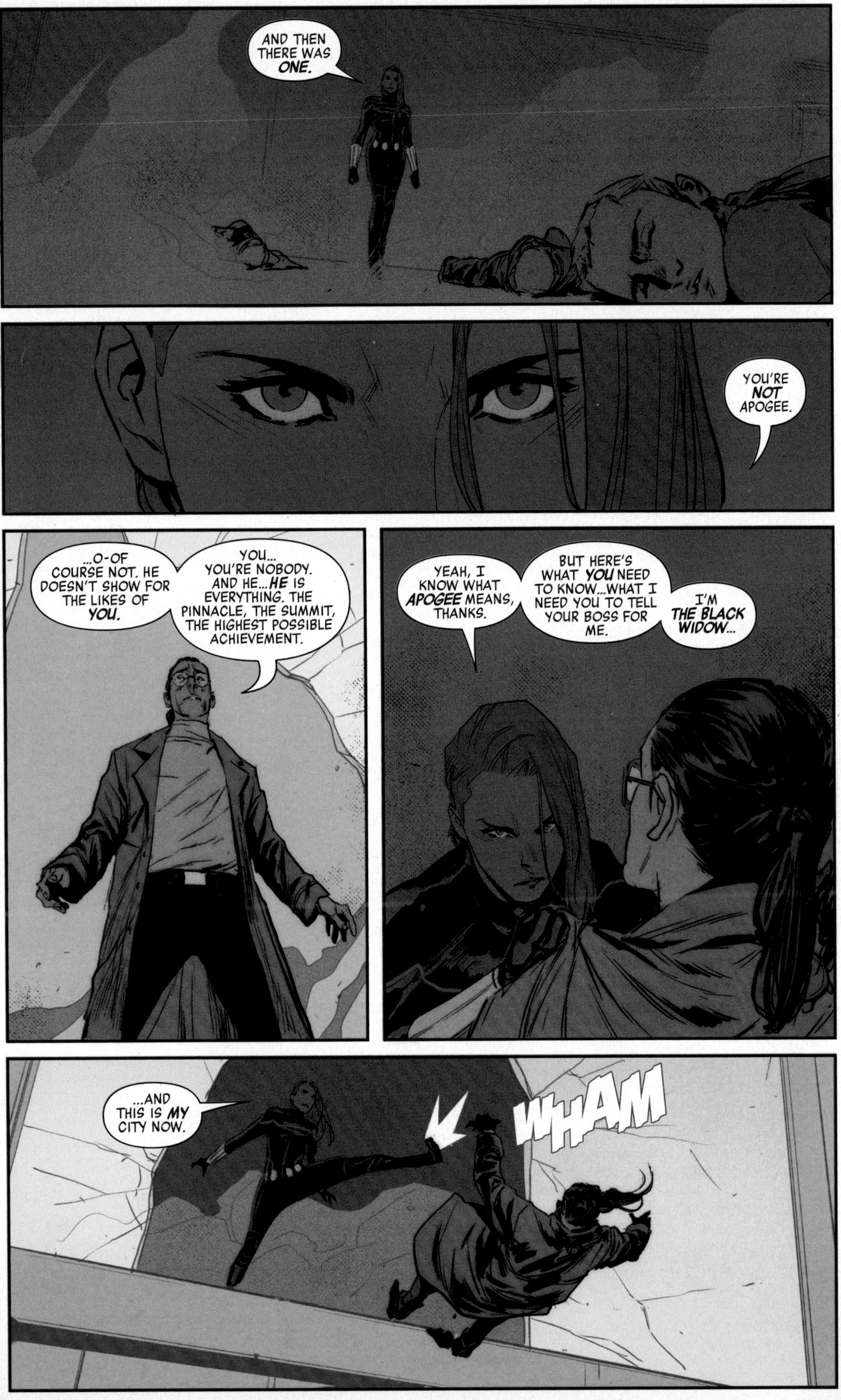
AND THEN THERE WAS ONE.
YOU'RE NOT APOGEE.
...O-OF COURSE NOT. HE DOESN'T SHOW FOR THE LIKES OF YOU.
YOU... YOU'RE NOBODY. AND HE...HE IS EVERYTHING. THE PINNACLE, THE SUMMIT, THE HIGHEST POSSIBLE ACHIEVEMENT.
YEAH, I KNOW WHAT APOGEE MEANS, THANKS.
BUT HERE'S WHAT YOU NEED TO KNOW...WHAT I NEED YOU TO TELL YOUR BOSS FOR ME.
I'M THE BLACK WIDOW...
...AND THIS IS MY CITY NOW.
WHAM

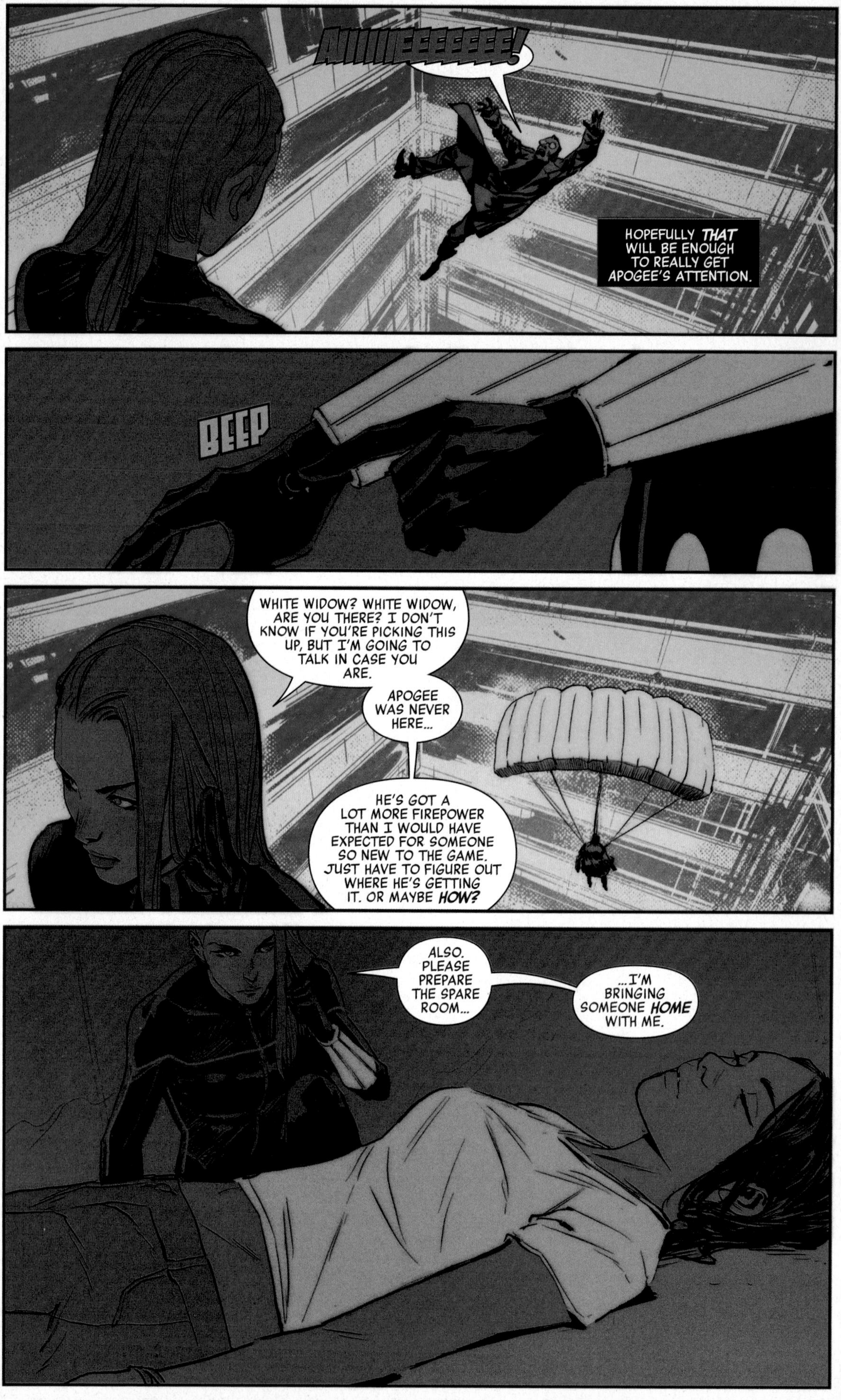
AIIIIIEEEEEEEE!
HOPEFULLY THAT WILL BE ENOUGH TO REALLY GET APOGEE'S ATTENTION.
BEEP
WHITE WIDOW? WHITE WIDOW, ARE YOU THERE? I DON'T KNOW IF YOU'RE PICKING THIS UP, BUT I'M GOING TO TALK IN CASE YOU ARE.
APOGEE WAS NEVER HERE...
HE'S GOT A LOT MORE FIREPOWER THAN I WOULD HAVE EXPECTED FOR SOMEONE SO NEW TO THE GAME. JUST HAVE TO FIGURE OUT WHERE HE'S GETTING IT. OR MAYBE HOW?
ALSO. PLEASE PREPARE THE SPARE ROOM...
...I'M BRINGING SOMEONE HOME WITH ME.

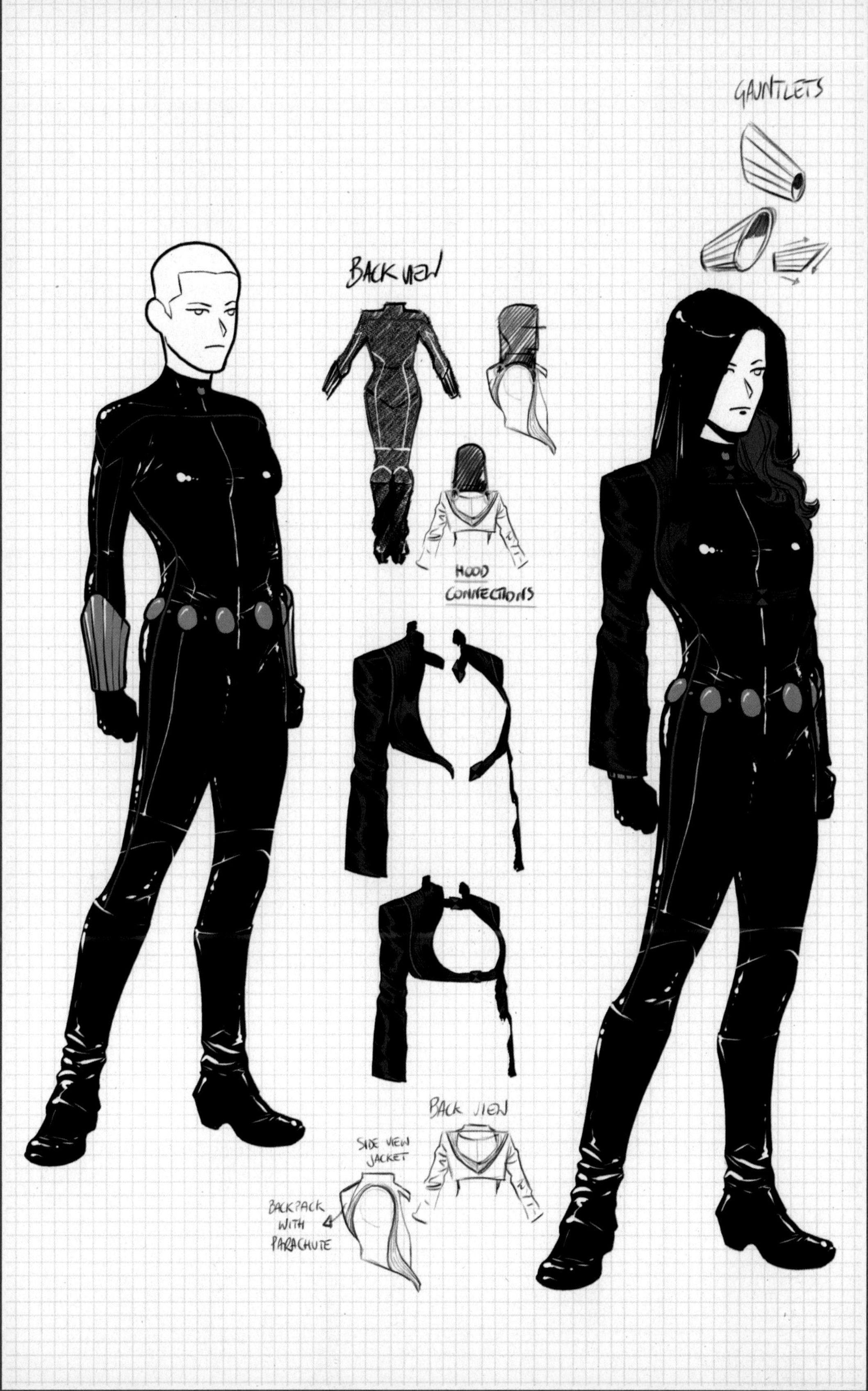
GAUNTLETS
BACK VIEW
HOOD CONNECTIONS
BACK VIEW
SIDE VIEW JACKET
BACKPACK WITH PARACHUTE

#6 DESIGN VARIANT BY ELENA CASAGRANDE

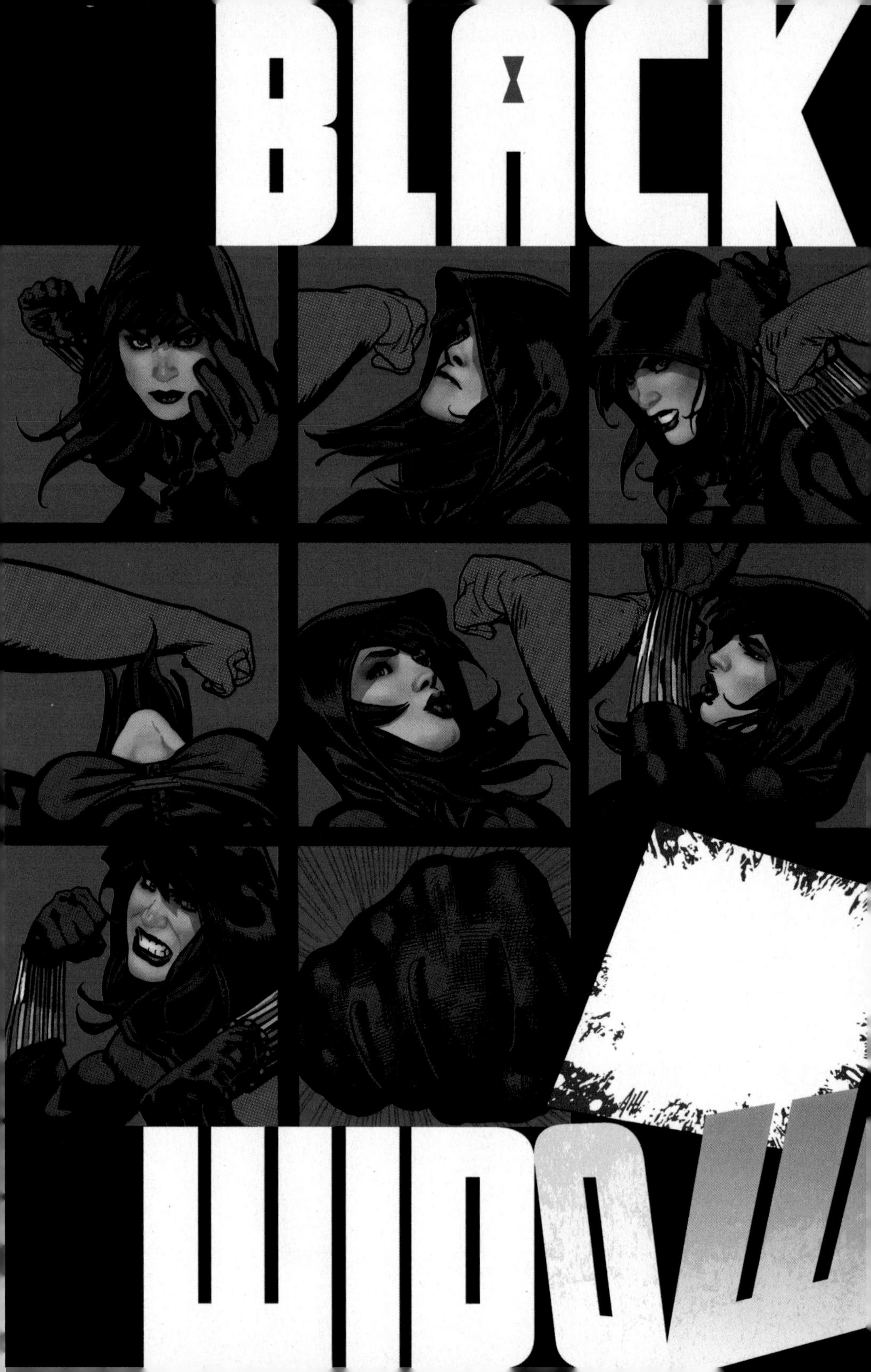
BLACK
WIDOW

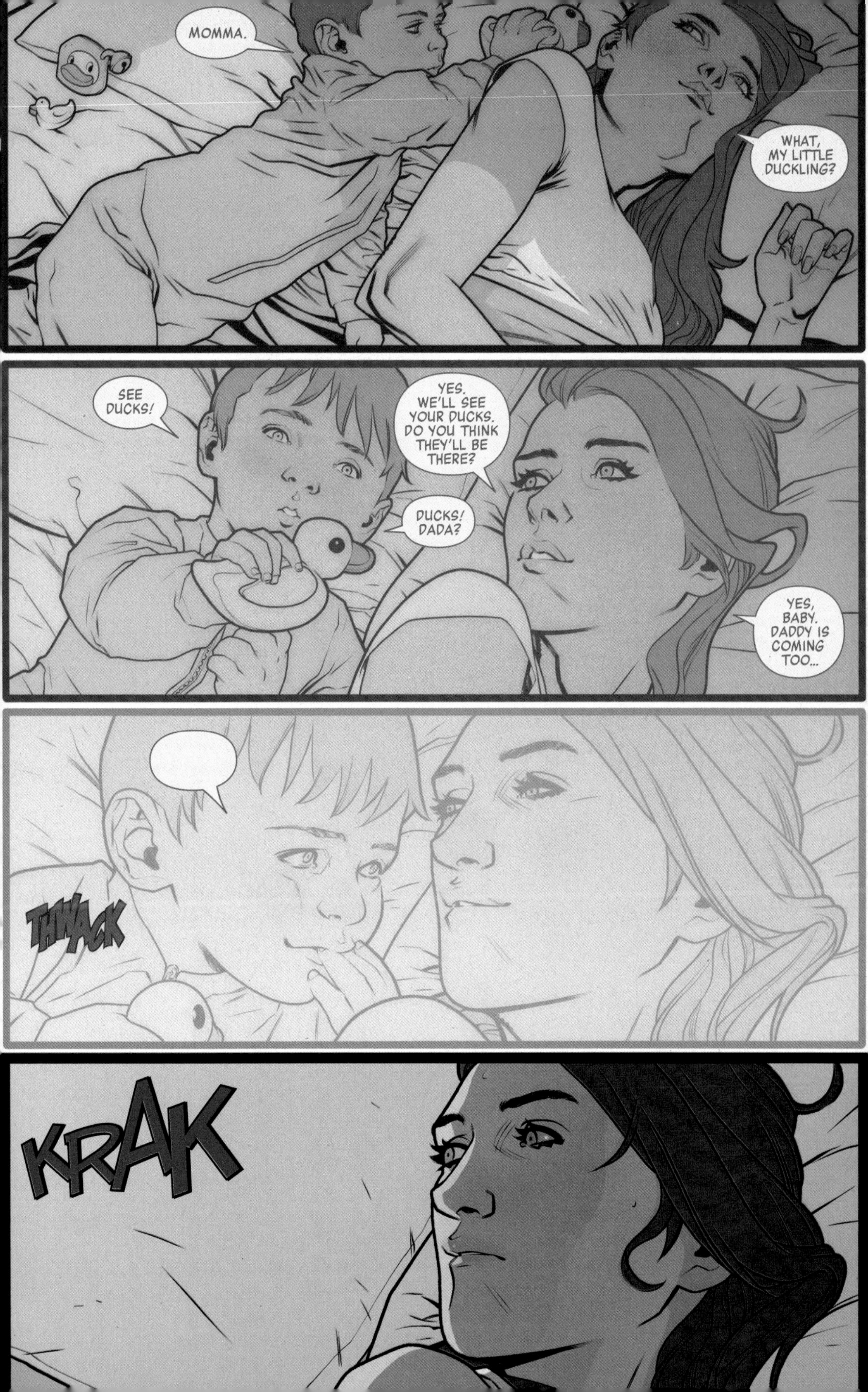
MOMMA.
WHAT, MY LITTLE DUCKLING?
SEE DUCKS!
YES. WE'LL SEE YOUR DUCKS. DO YOU THINK THEY'LL BE THERE?
DUCKS! DADA?
YES, BABY. DADDY IS COMING TOO...
THWACK
KRAK

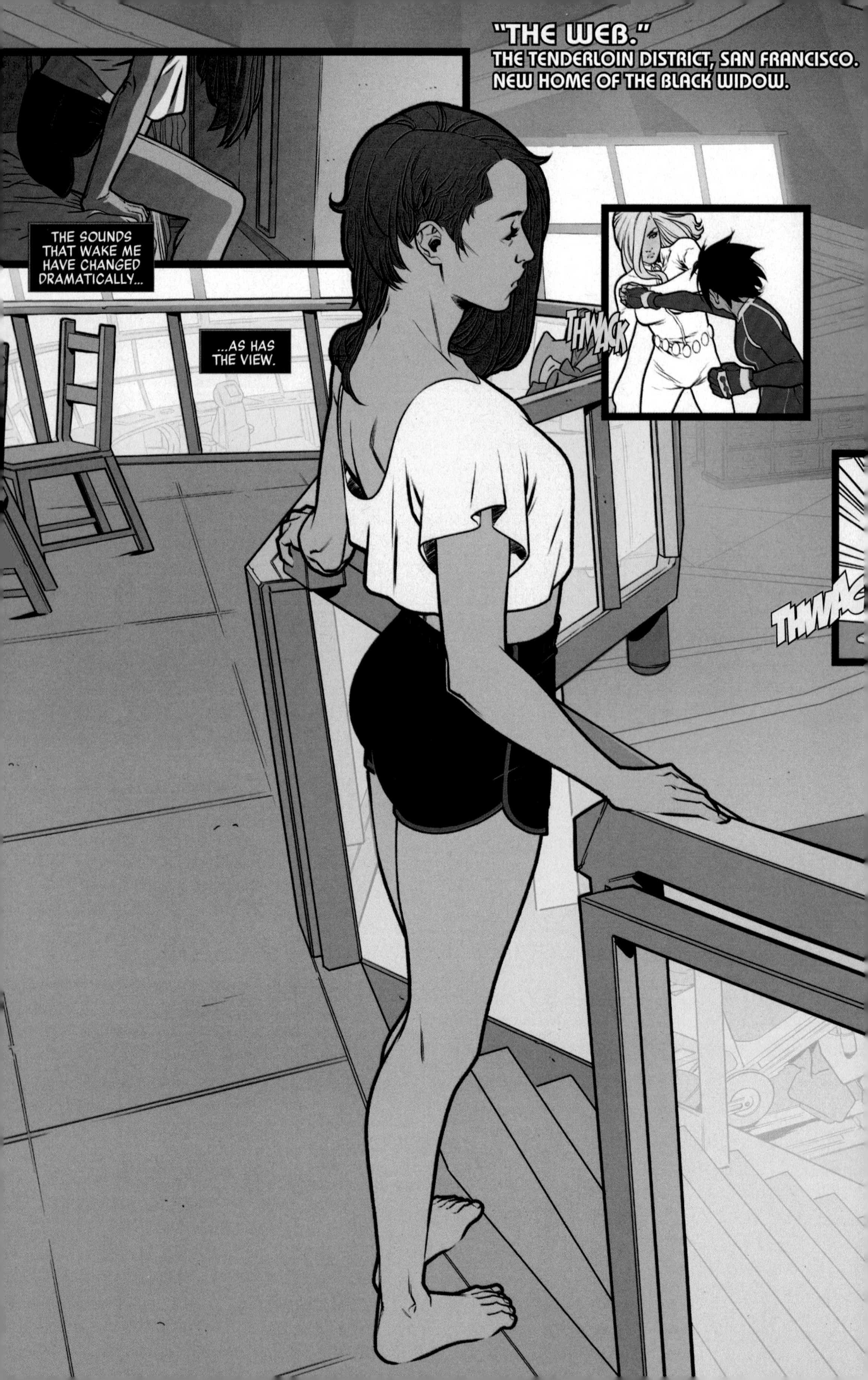
"THE WEB."
THE TENDERLOIN DISTRICT, SAN FRANCISCO.
NEW HOME OF THE BLACK WIDOW.
THE SOUNDS THAT WAKE ME HAVE CHANGED DRAMATICALLY...
...AS HAS THE VIEW.
THWACK
THWAC

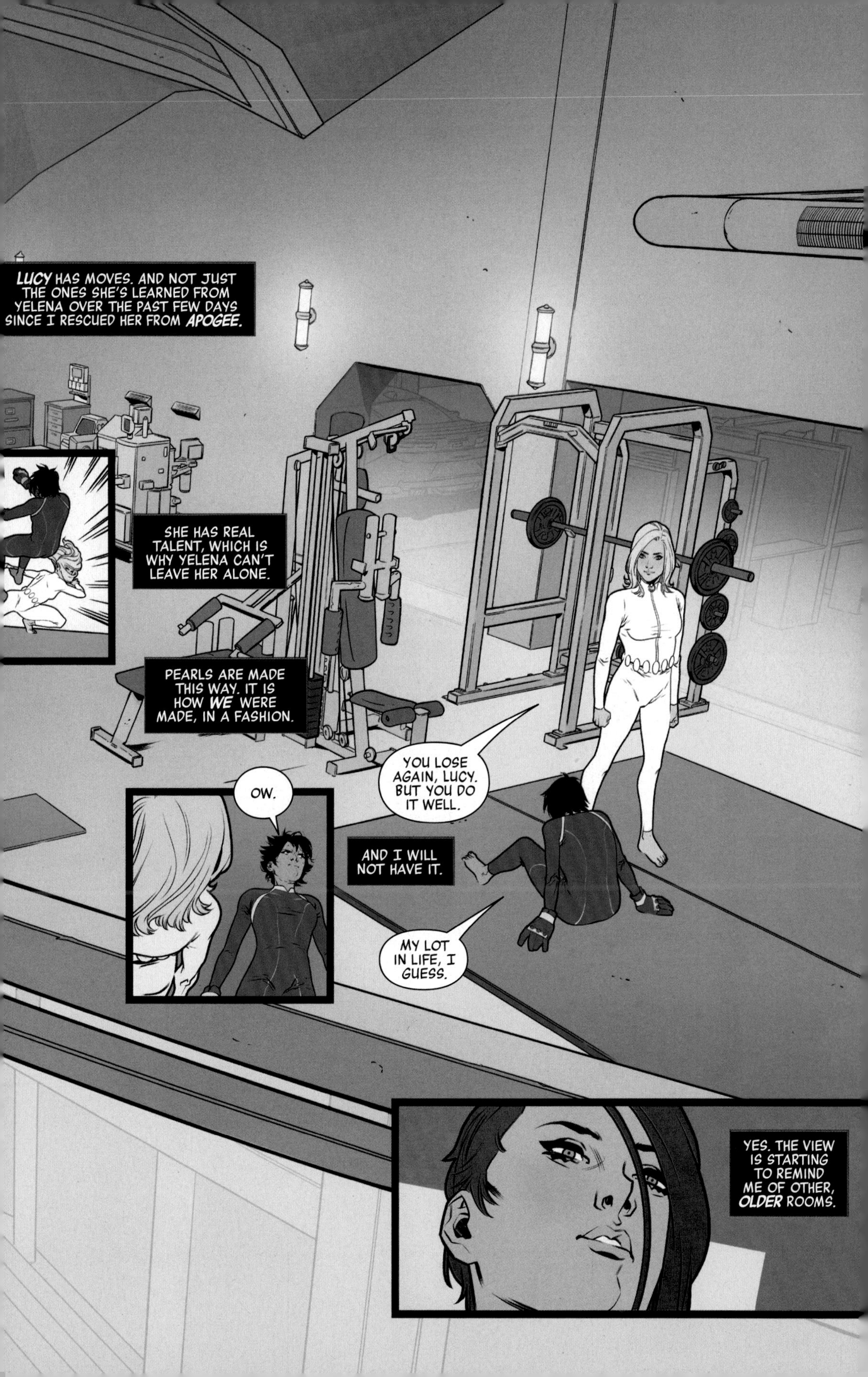
LUCY HAS MOVES. AND NOT JUST THE ONES SHE'S LEARNED FROM YELENA OVER THE PAST FEW DAYS SINCE I RESCUED HER FROM APOGEE.
SHE HAS REAL TALENT, WHICH IS WHY YELENA CAN'T LEAVE HER ALONE.
PEARLS ARE MADE THIS WAY. IT IS HOW WE WERE MADE, IN A FASHION.
YOU LOSE AGAIN, LUCY. BUT YOU DO IT WELL.
OW.
AND I WILL NOT HAVE IT.
MY LOT IN LIFE, I GUESS.
YES. THE VIEW IS STARTING TO REMIND ME OF OTHER, OLDER ROOMS.

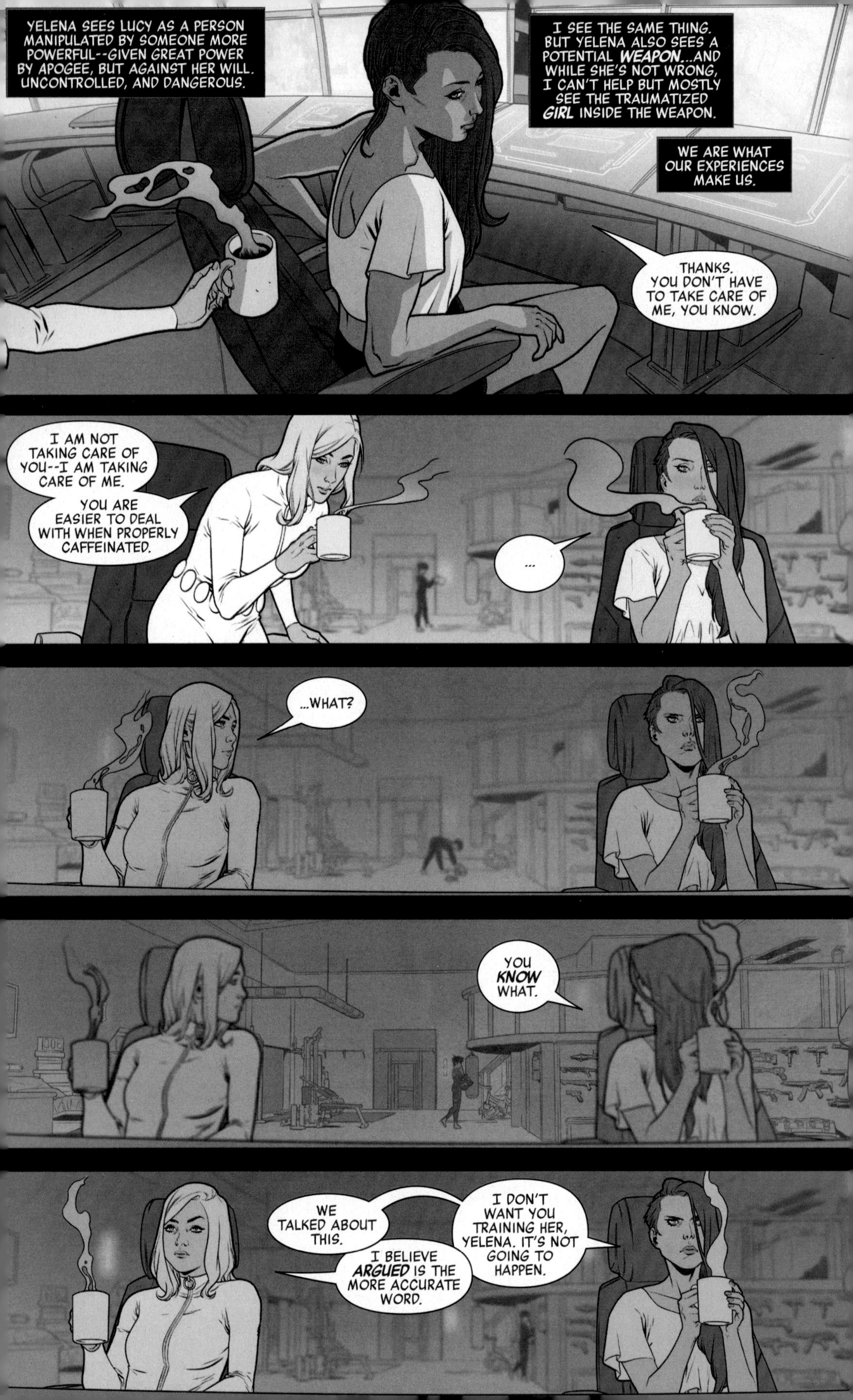
YELENA SEES LUCY AS A PERSON MANIPULATED BY SOMEONE MORE POWERFUL--GIVEN GREAT POWER BY APOGEE, BUT AGAINST HER WILL. UNCONTROLLED, AND DANGEROUS.
I SEE THE SAME THING. BUT YELENA ALSO SEES A POTENTIAL WEAPON...AND WHILE SHE'S NOT WRONG, I CAN'T HELP BUT MOSTLY SEE THE TRAUMATIZED GIRL INSIDE THE WEAPON.
WE ARE WHAT OUR EXPERIENCES MAKE US.
THANKS. YOU DON'T HAVE TO TAKE CARE OF ME, YOU KNOW.
I AM NOT TAKING CARE OF YOU--I AM TAKING CARE OF ME.
YOU ARE EASIER TO DEAL WITH WHEN PROPERLY CAFFEINATED.
...
...WHAT?
YOU KNOW WHAT.
I DON'T WANT YOU TRAINING HER, YELENA. IT'S NOT GOING TO HAPPEN.
WE TALKED ABOUT THIS.
I BELIEVE ARGUED IS THE MORE ACCURATE WORD.

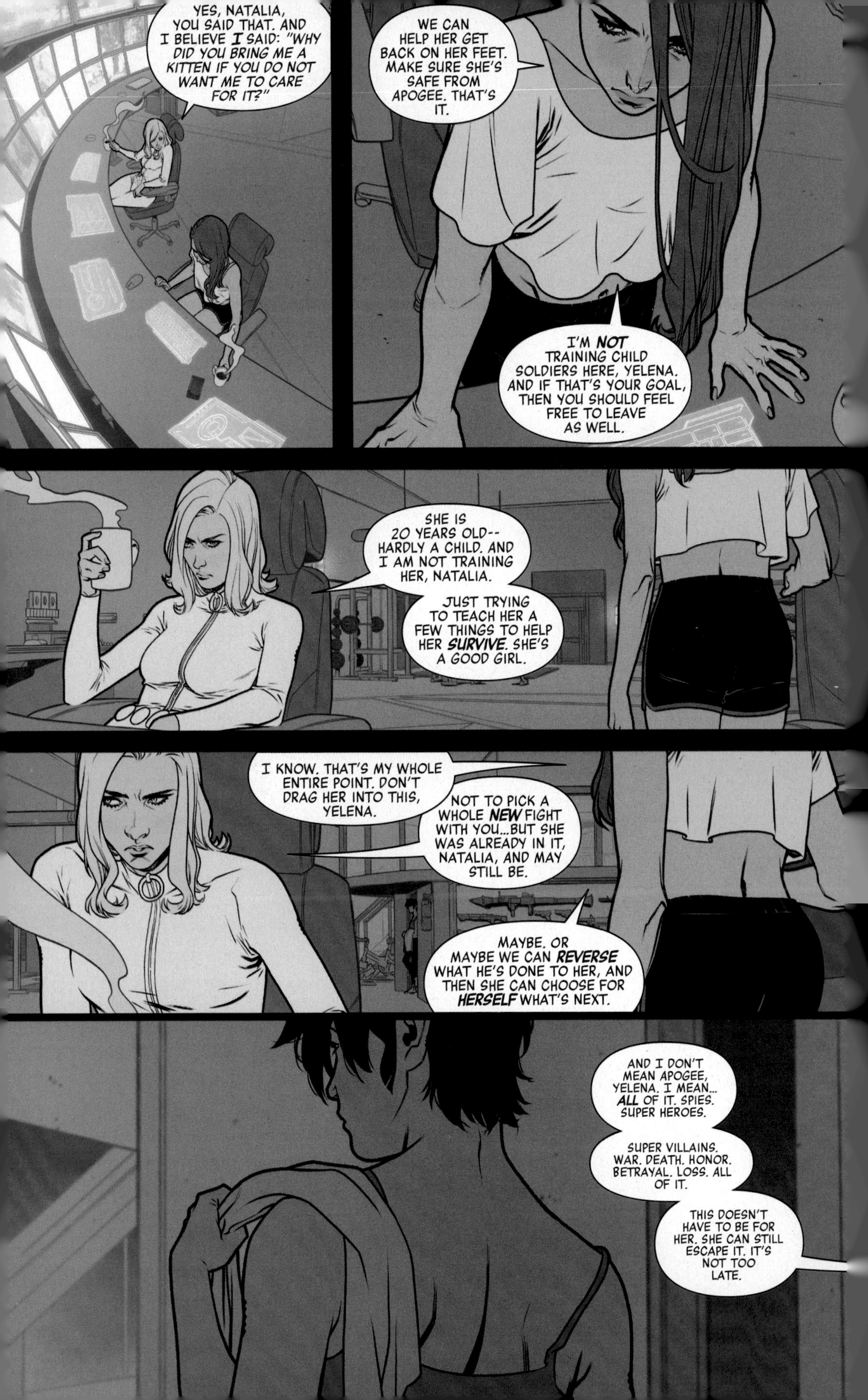
YES, NATALIA, YOU SAID THAT. AND I BELIEVE I SAID: "WHY DID YOU BRING ME A KITTEN IF YOU DO NOT WANT ME TO CARE FOR IT?"
WE CAN HELP HER GET BACK ON HER FEET. MAKE SURE SHE'S SAFE FROM APOGEE. THAT'S IT.
I'M NOT TRAINING CHILD SOLDIERS HERE, YELENA. AND IF THAT'S YOUR GOAL, THEN YOU SHOULD FEEL FREE TO LEAVE AS WELL.
SHE IS 20 YEARS OLD-- HARDLY A CHILD. AND I AM NOT TRAINING HER, NATALIA.
JUST TRYING TO TEACH HER A FEW THINGS TO HELP HER SURVIVE. SHE'S A GOOD GIRL.
I KNOW. THAT'S MY WHOLE ENTIRE POINT. DON'T DRAG HER INTO THIS, YELENA.
NOT TO PICK A WHOLE NEW FIGHT WITH YOU...BUT SHE WAS ALREADY IN IT, NATALIA, AND MAY STILL BE.
MAYBE. OR MAYBE WE CAN REVERSE WHAT HE'S DONE TO HER, AND THEN SHE CAN CHOOSE FOR HERSELF WHAT'S NEXT.
AND I DON'T MEAN APOGEE, YELENA. I MEAN... ALL OF IT. SPIES. SUPER HEROES.
SUPER VILLAINS. WAR. DEATH. HONOR. BETRAYAL. LOSS. ALL OF IT.
THIS DOESN'T HAVE TO BE FOR HER. SHE CAN STILL ESCAPE IT. IT'S NOT TOO LATE.

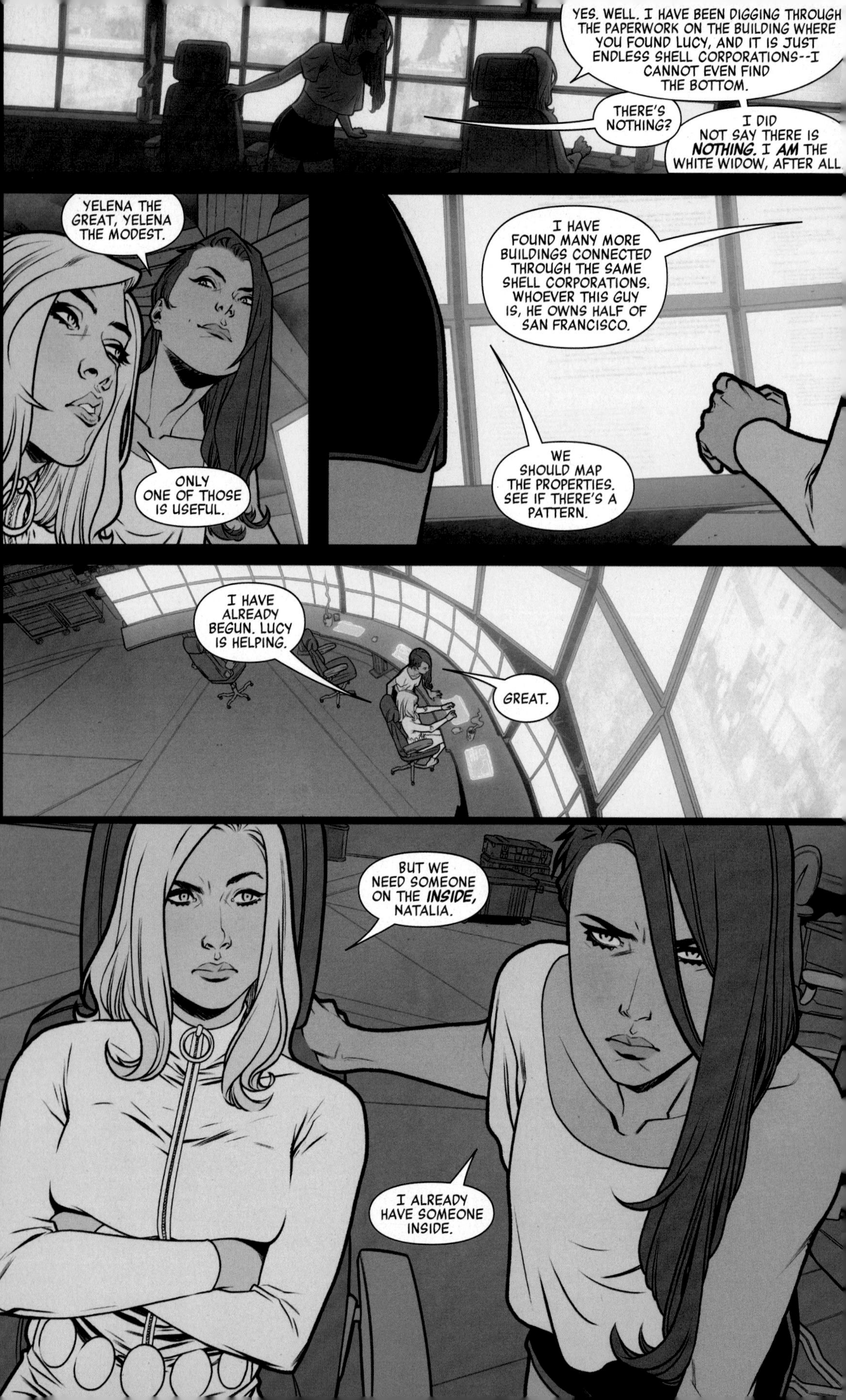
YES. WELL. I HAVE BEEN DIGGING THROUGH THE PAPERWORK ON THE BUILDING WHERE YOU FOUND LUCY, AND IT IS JUST ENDLESS SHELL CORPORATIONS--I CANNOT EVEN FIND THE BOTTOM.
THERE'S NOTHING?
I DID NOT SAY THERE IS ***NOTHING.*** I ***AM*** THE WHITE WIDOW, AFTER ALL
YELENA THE GREAT, YELENA THE MODEST.
ONLY ONE OF THOSE IS USEFUL.
I HAVE FOUND MANY MORE BUILDINGS CONNECTED THROUGH THE SAME SHELL CORPORATIONS. WHOEVER THIS GUY IS, HE OWNS HALF OF SAN FRANCISCO.
WE SHOULD MAP THE PROPERTIES. SEE IF THERE'S A PATTERN.
I HAVE ALREADY BEGUN. LUCY IS HELPING.
GREAT.
BUT WE NEED SOMEONE ON THE ***INSIDE,*** NATALIA.
I ALREADY HAVE SOMEONE INSIDE.

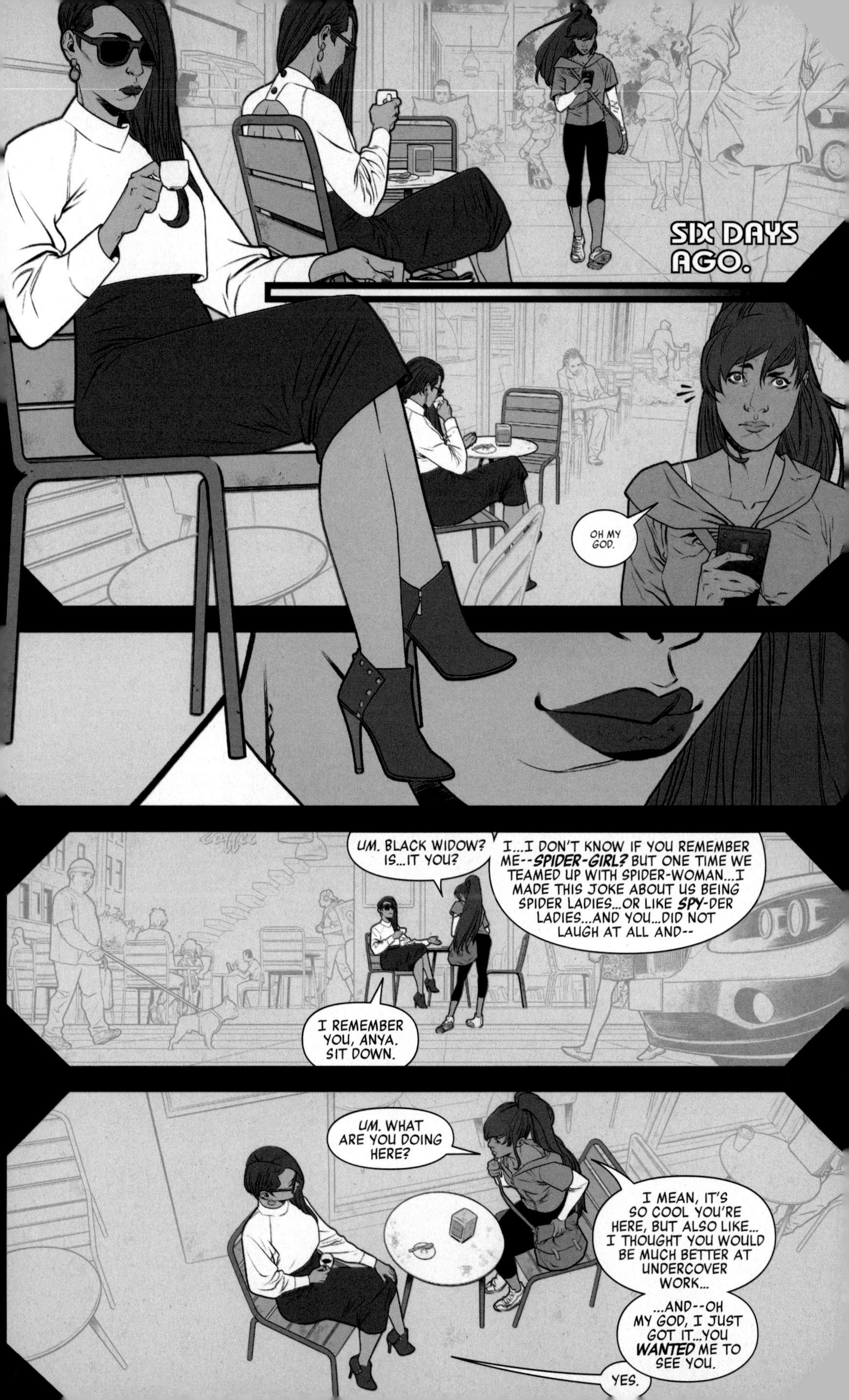
SIX DAYS AGO.
OH MY GOD.
UM. BLACK WIDOW? IS...IT YOU?
I...I DON'T KNOW IF YOU REMEMBER ME--SPIDER-GIRL? BUT ONE TIME WE TEAMED UP WITH SPIDER-WOMAN...I MADE THIS JOKE ABOUT US BEING SPIDER LADIES...OR LIKE SPY-DER LADIES...AND YOU...DID NOT LAUGH AT ALL AND--
I REMEMBER YOU, ANYA. SIT DOWN.
UM. WHAT ARE YOU DOING HERE?
I MEAN, IT'S SO COOL YOU'RE HERE, BUT ALSO LIKE... I THOUGHT YOU WOULD BE MUCH BETTER AT UNDERCOVER WORK...
...AND--OH MY GOD, I JUST GOT IT...YOU WANTED ME TO SEE YOU.
YES.

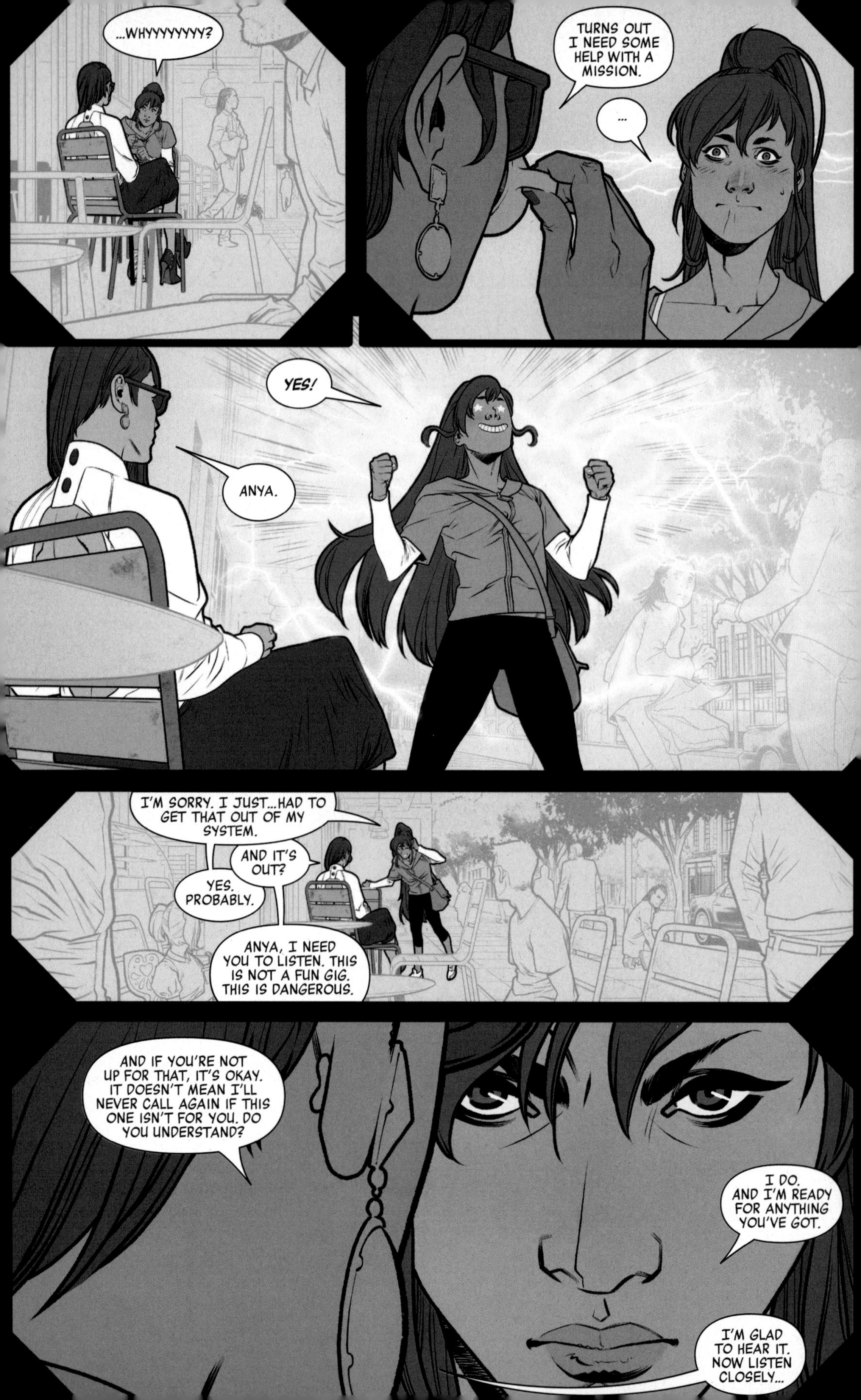
...WHYYYYYYYY?
TURNS OUT I NEED SOME HELP WITH A MISSION.
...
YES!
ANYA.
I'M SORRY. I JUST...HAD TO GET THAT OUT OF MY SYSTEM.
AND IT'S OUT?
YES. PROBABLY.
ANYA, I NEED YOU TO LISTEN. THIS IS NOT A FUN GIG. THIS IS DANGEROUS.
AND IF YOU'RE NOT UP FOR THAT, IT'S OKAY. IT DOESN'T MEAN I'LL NEVER CALL AGAIN IF THIS ONE ISN'T FOR YOU. DO YOU UNDERSTAND?
I DO. AND I'M READY FOR ANYTHING YOU'VE GOT.
I'M GLAD TO HEAR IT. NOW LISTEN CLOSELY...

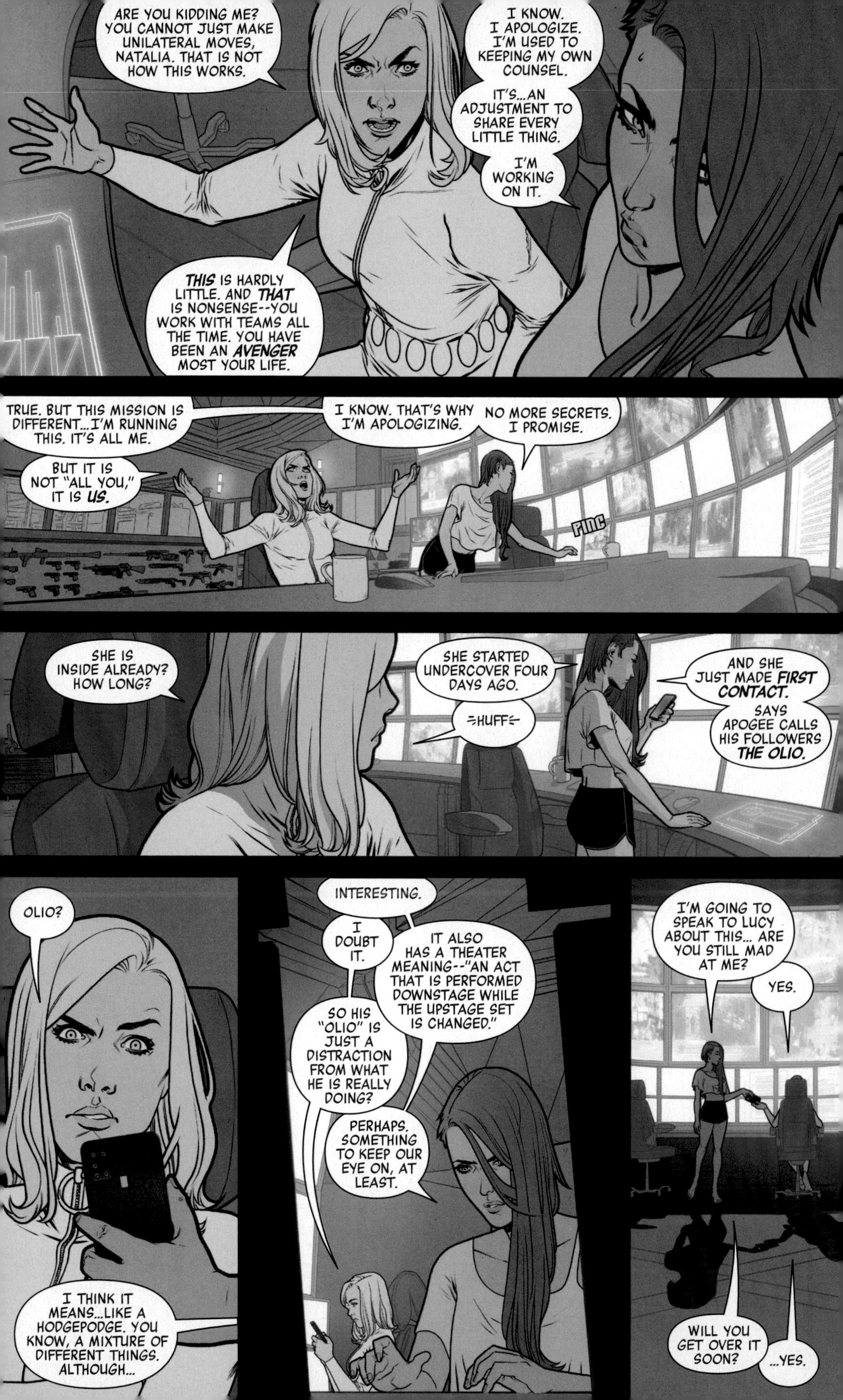
ARE YOU KIDDING ME? YOU CANNOT JUST MAKE UNILATERAL MOVES, NATALIA. THAT IS NOT HOW THIS WORKS.
I KNOW. I APOLOGIZE. I'M USED TO KEEPING MY OWN COUNSEL.
IT'S...AN ADJUSTMENT TO SHARE EVERY LITTLE THING.
I'M WORKING ON IT.
THIS IS HARDLY LITTLE. AND THAT IS NONSENSE--YOU WORK WITH TEAMS ALL THE TIME. YOU HAVE BEEN AN AVENGER MOST YOUR LIFE.
TRUE. BUT THIS MISSION IS DIFFERENT...I'M RUNNING THIS. IT'S ALL ME.
BUT IT IS NOT "ALL YOU," IT IS US.
I KNOW. THAT'S WHY I'M APOLOGIZING.
NO MORE SECRETS. I PROMISE.
PING
SHE IS INSIDE ALREADY? HOW LONG?
SHE STARTED UNDERCOVER FOUR DAYS AGO.
HUFF
AND SHE JUST MADE FIRST CONTACT.
SAYS APOGEE CALLS HIS FOLLOWERS THE OLIO.
OLIO?
I THINK IT MEANS...LIKE A HODGEPODGE. YOU KNOW, A MIXTURE OF DIFFERENT THINGS. ALTHOUGH...
INTERESTING.
I DOUBT IT.
IT ALSO HAS A THEATER MEANING--"AN ACT THAT IS PERFORMED DOWNSTAGE WHILE THE UPSTAGE SET IS CHANGED."
SO HIS "OLIO" IS JUST A DISTRACTION FROM WHAT HE IS REALLY DOING?
PERHAPS. SOMETHING TO KEEP OUR EYE ON, AT LEAST.
I'M GOING TO SPEAK TO LUCY ABOUT THIS... ARE YOU STILL MAD AT ME?
YES.
WILL YOU GET OVER IT SOON?
...YES.

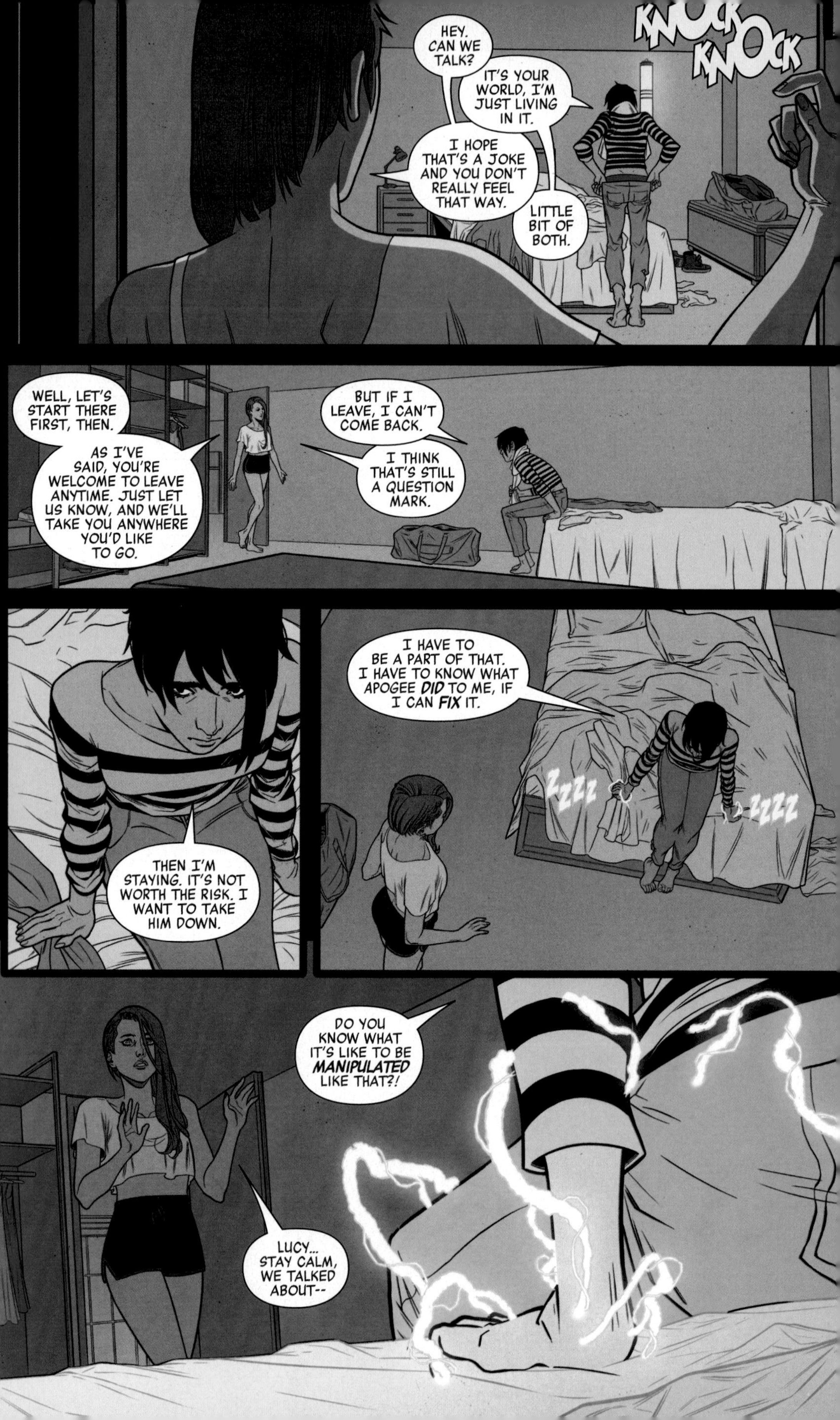
KNOCK KNOCK
HEY. CAN WE TALK?
IT'S YOUR WORLD, I'M JUST LIVING IN IT.
I HOPE THAT'S A JOKE AND YOU DON'T REALLY FEEL THAT WAY.
LITTLE BIT OF BOTH.
WELL, LET'S START THERE FIRST, THEN.
AS I'VE SAID, YOU'RE WELCOME TO LEAVE ANYTIME. JUST LET US KNOW, AND WE'LL TAKE YOU ANYWHERE YOU'D LIKE TO GO.
BUT IF I LEAVE, I CAN'T COME BACK.
I THINK THAT'S STILL A QUESTION MARK.
THEN I'M STAYING. IT'S NOT WORTH THE RISK. I WANT TO TAKE HIM DOWN.
I HAVE TO BE A PART OF THAT. I HAVE TO KNOW WHAT APOGEE *DID* TO ME, IF I CAN *FIX* IT.
ZZZZ
ZZZZ
DO YOU KNOW WHAT IT'S LIKE TO BE *MANIPULATED* LIKE THAT?!
LUCY... STAY CALM, WE TALKED ABOUT--

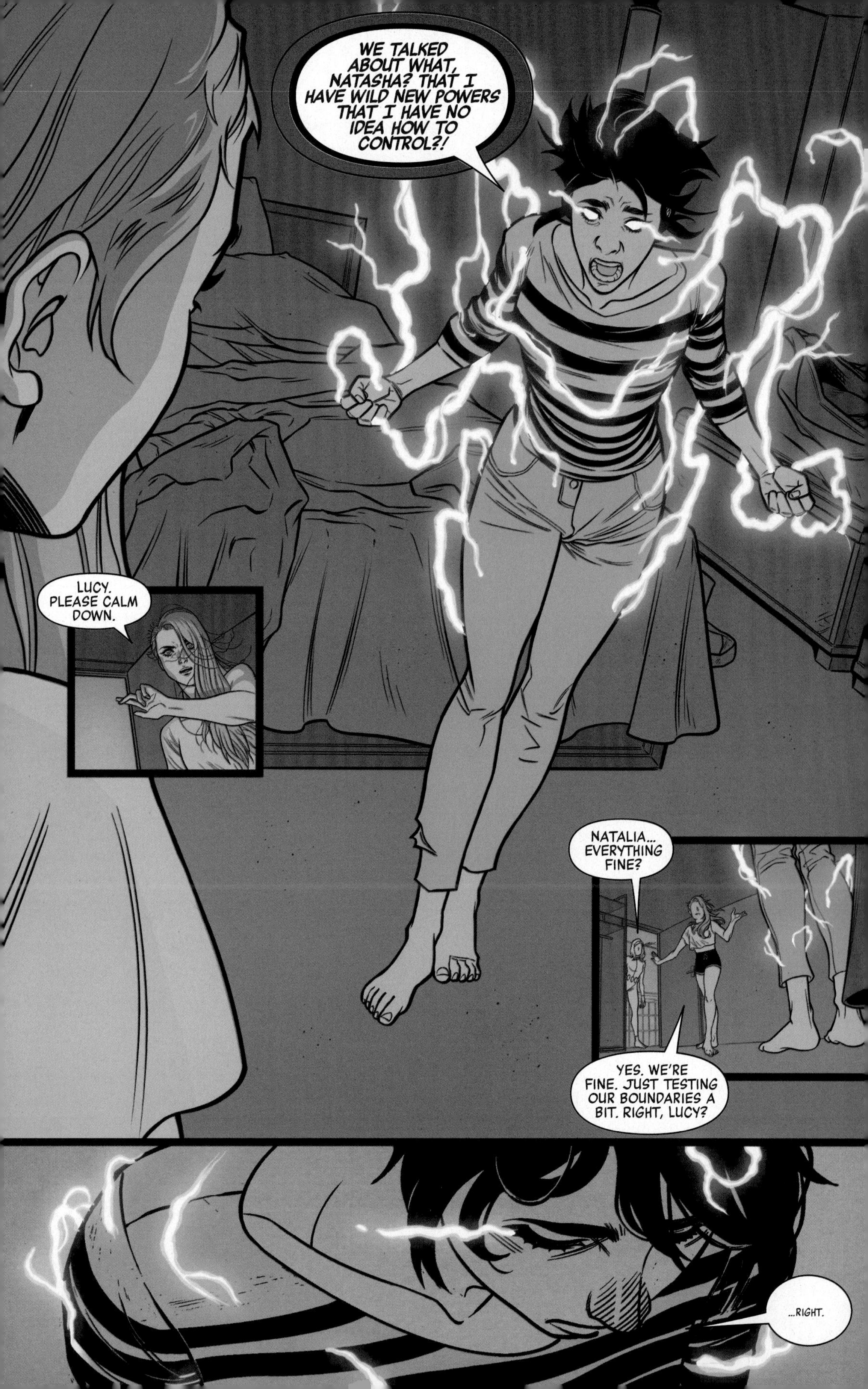
WE TALKED ABOUT WHAT, NATASHA? THAT I HAVE WILD NEW POWERS THAT I HAVE NO IDEA HOW TO CONTROL?!
LUCY. PLEASE CALM DOWN.
NATALIA... EVERYTHING FINE?
YES. WE'RE FINE. JUST TESTING OUR BOUNDARIES A BIT. RIGHT, LUCY?
...RIGHT.

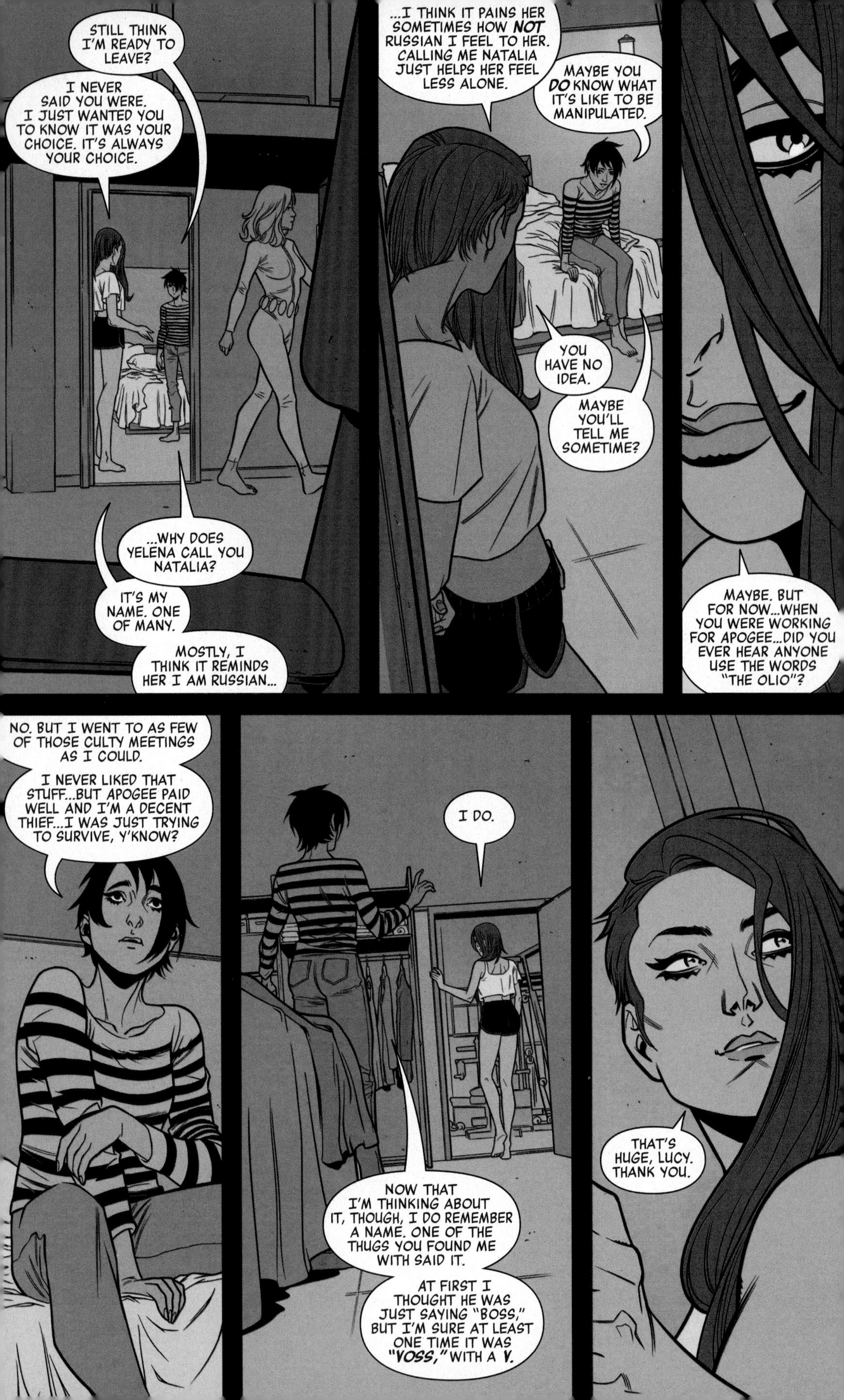
STILL THINK I'M READY TO LEAVE?
I NEVER SAID YOU WERE. I JUST WANTED YOU TO KNOW IT WAS YOUR CHOICE. IT'S ALWAYS YOUR CHOICE.
...WHY DOES YELENA CALL YOU NATALIA?
IT'S MY NAME. ONE OF MANY.
MOSTLY, I THINK IT REMINDS HER I AM RUSSIAN...
...I THINK IT PAINS HER SOMETIMES HOW NOT RUSSIAN I FEEL TO HER. CALLING ME NATALIA JUST HELPS HER FEEL LESS ALONE.
MAYBE YOU DO KNOW WHAT IT'S LIKE TO BE MANIPULATED.
YOU HAVE NO IDEA.
MAYBE YOU'LL TELL ME SOMETIME?
MAYBE. BUT FOR NOW...WHEN YOU WERE WORKING FOR APOGEE...DID YOU EVER HEAR ANYONE USE THE WORDS "THE OLIO"?
NO. BUT I WENT TO AS FEW OF THOSE CULTY MEETINGS AS I COULD.
I NEVER LIKED THAT STUFF...BUT APOGEE PAID WELL AND I'M A DECENT THIEF...I WAS JUST TRYING TO SURVIVE, Y'KNOW?
I DO.
NOW THAT I'M THINKING ABOUT IT, THOUGH, I DO REMEMBER A NAME. ONE OF THE THUGS YOU FOUND ME WITH SAID IT.
AT FIRST I THOUGHT HE WAS JUST SAYING "BOSS," BUT I'M SURE AT LEAST ONE TIME IT WAS "VOSS," WITH A V.
THAT'S HUGE, LUCY. THANK YOU.

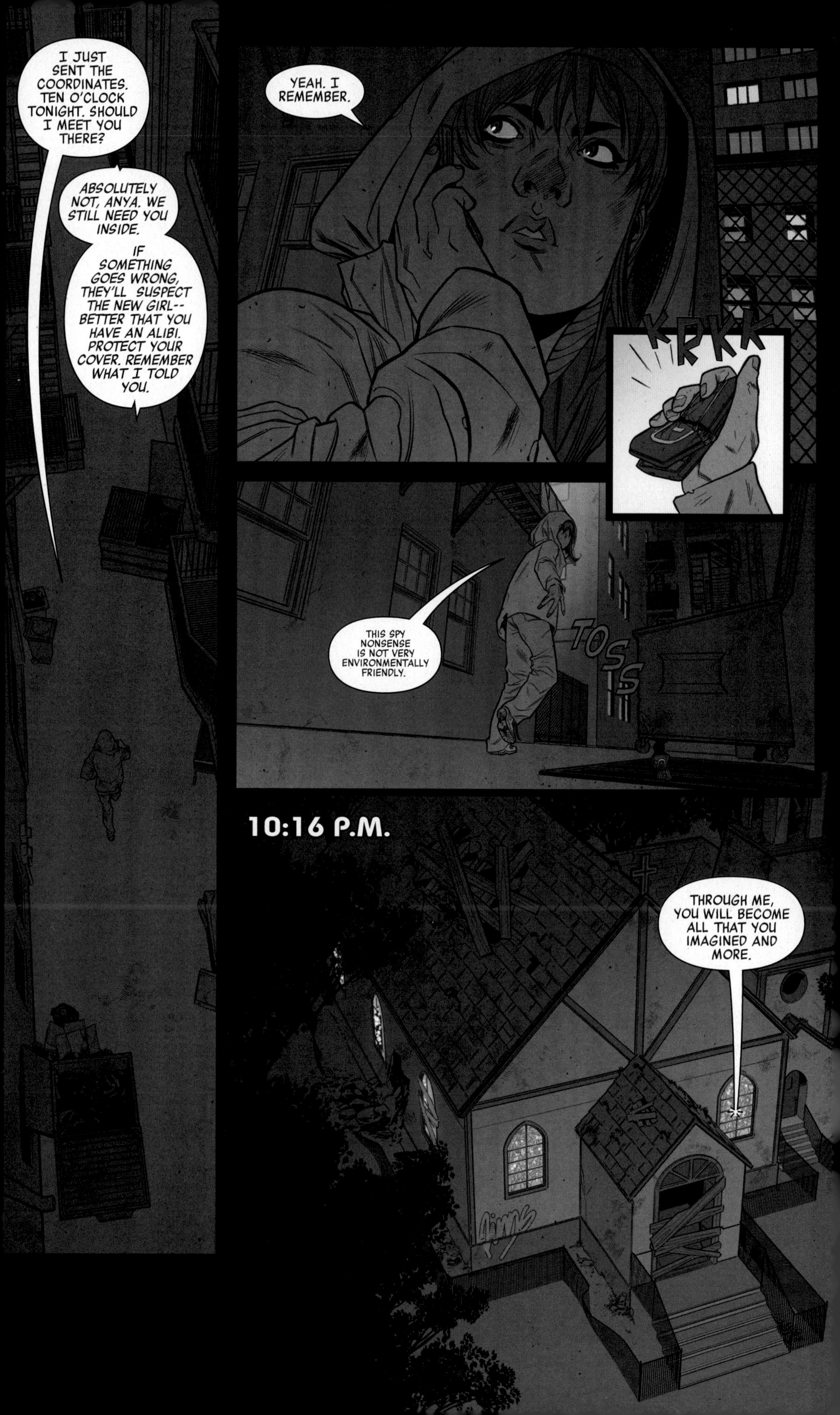

I JUST SENT THE COORDINATES. TEN O'CLOCK TONIGHT. SHOULD I MEET YOU THERE?
ABSOLUTELY NOT, ANYA. WE STILL NEED YOU INSIDE.
IF SOMETHING GOES WRONG, THEY'LL SUSPECT THE NEW GIRL-- BETTER THAT YOU HAVE AN ALIBI. PROTECT YOUR COVER. REMEMBER WHAT I TOLD YOU.
YEAH. I REMEMBER.
KRKK
THIS SPY NONSENSE IS NOT VERY ENVIRONMENTALLY FRIENDLY.
TOSS
10:16 P.M.
THROUGH ME, YOU WILL BECOME ALL THAT YOU IMAGINED AND MORE.

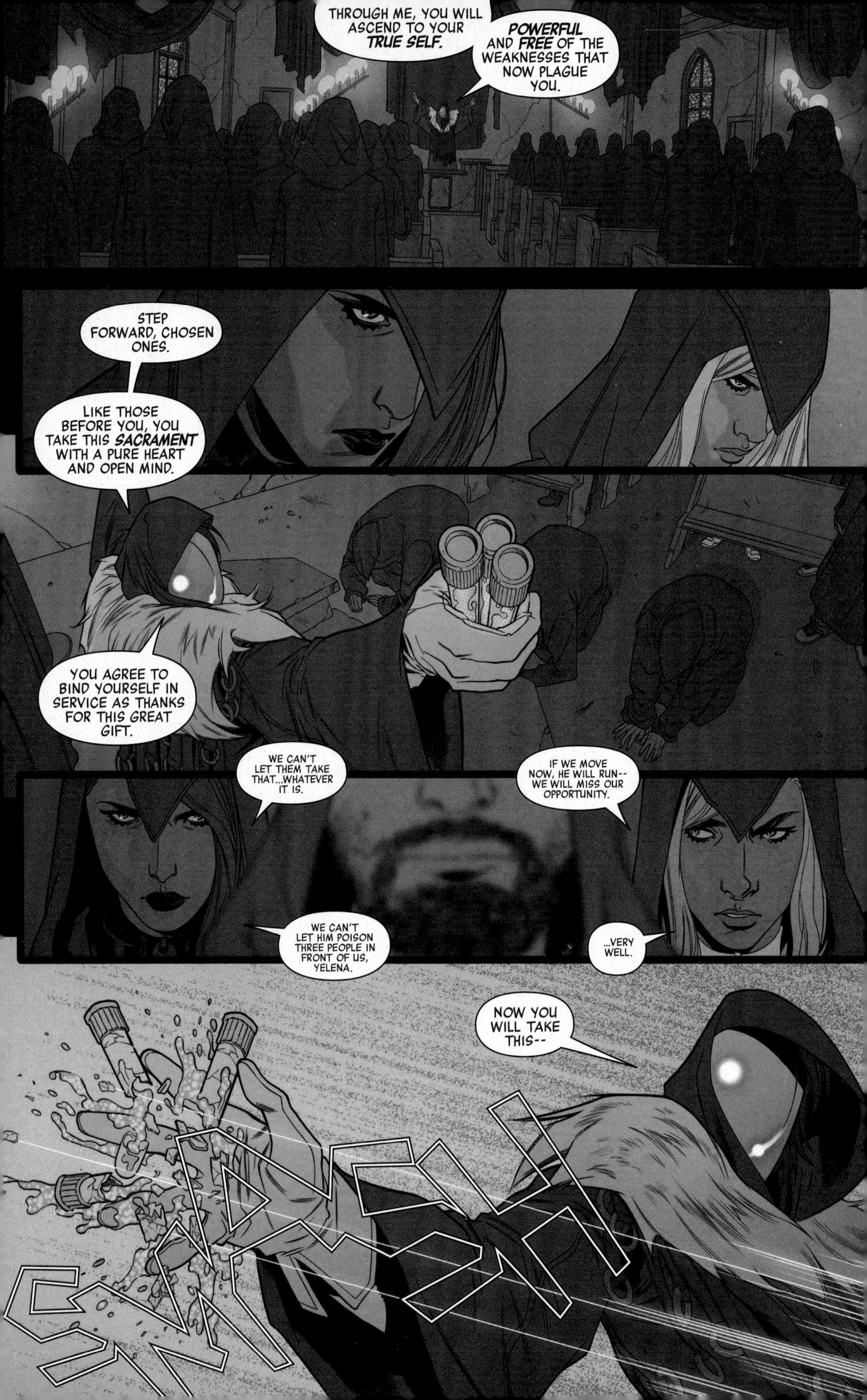
THROUGH ME, YOU WILL ASCEND TO YOUR TRUE SELF.
POWERFUL AND FREE OF THE WEAKNESSES THAT NOW PLAGUE YOU.
STEP FORWARD, CHOSEN ONES.
LIKE THOSE BEFORE YOU, YOU TAKE THIS SACRAMENT WITH A PURE HEART AND OPEN MIND.
YOU AGREE TO BIND YOURSELF IN SERVICE AS THANKS FOR THIS GREAT GIFT.
WE CAN'T LET THEM TAKE THAT...WHATEVER IT IS.
IF WE MOVE NOW, HE WILL RUN--WE WILL MISS OUR OPPORTUNITY.
WE CAN'T LET HIM POISON THREE PEOPLE IN FRONT OF US, YELENA.
...VERY WELL.
NOW YOU WILL TAKE THIS--
SWASH

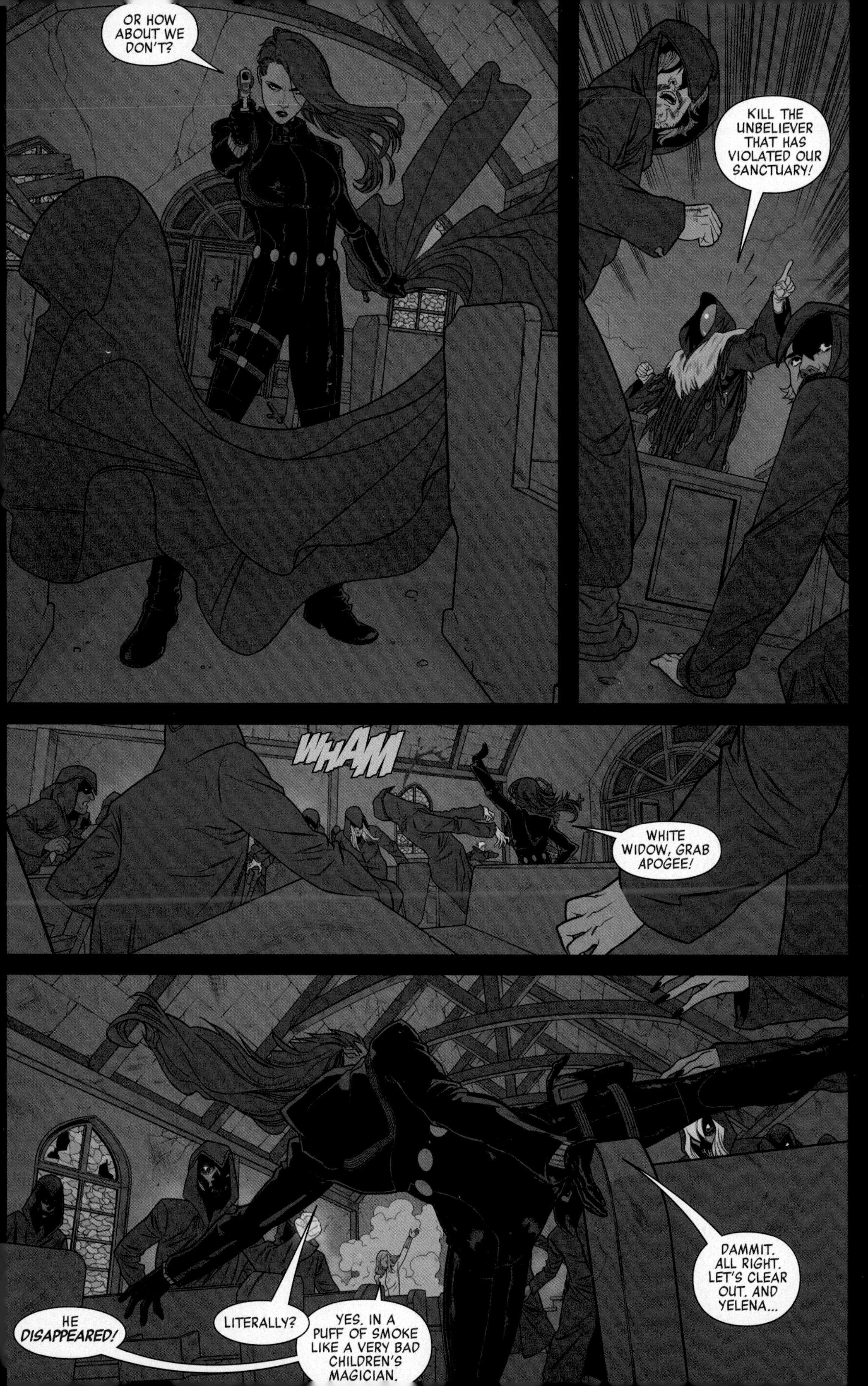
OR HOW ABOUT WE DON'T?
KILL THE UNBELIEVER THAT HAS VIOLATED OUR SANCTUARY!
WHAM
WHITE WIDOW, GRAB APOGEE!
DAMMIT. ALL RIGHT. LET'S CLEAR OUT. AND YELENA...
HE *DISAPPEARED!*
LITERALLY?
YES. IN A PUFF OF SMOKE LIKE A VERY BAD CHILDREN'S MAGICIAN.

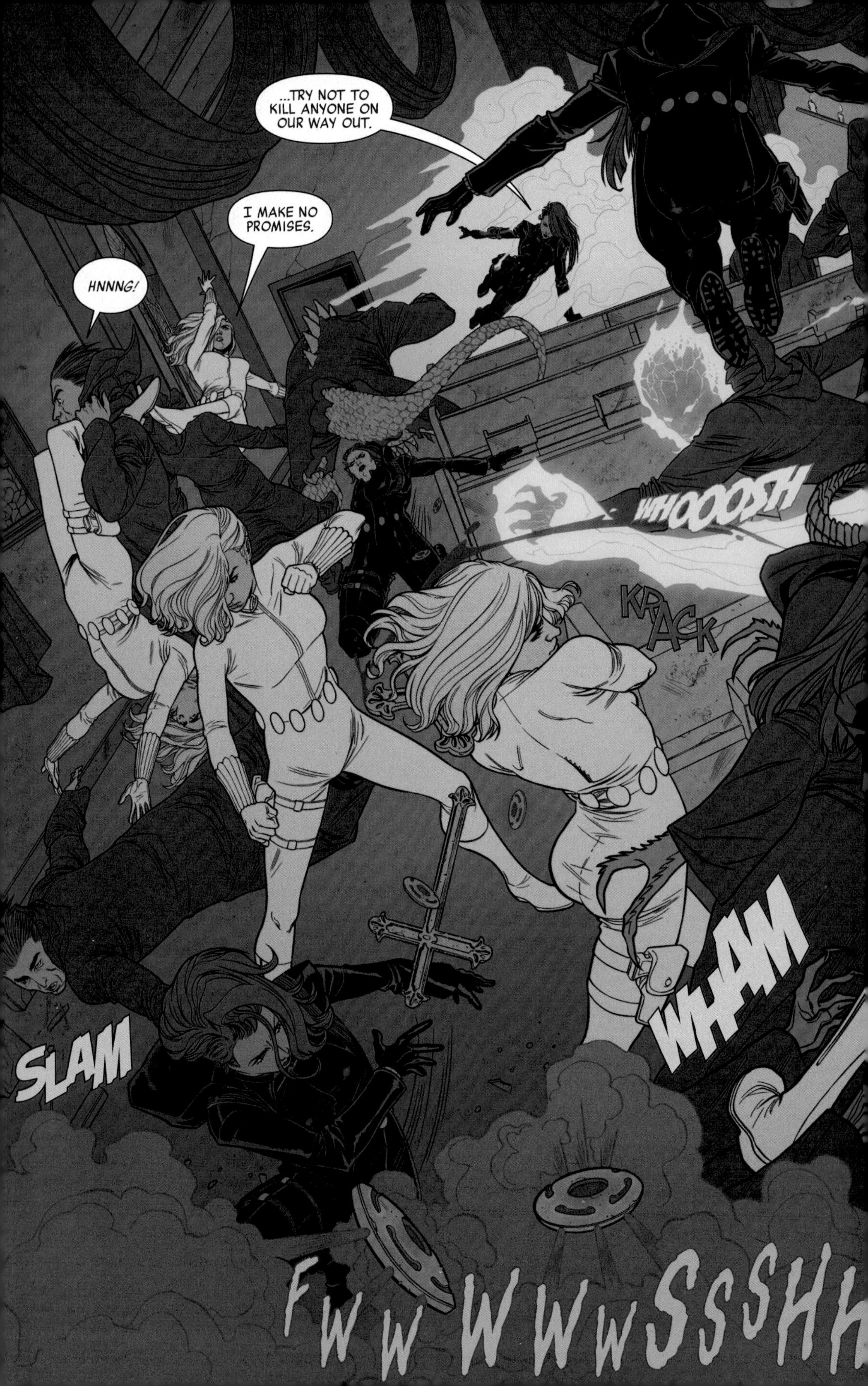
...TRY NOT TO KILL ANYONE ON OUR WAY OUT.
I MAKE NO PROMISES.
HNNNG!
WHOOOOSH
KRACK
WHAM
SLAM
FWWWWWSSSHH

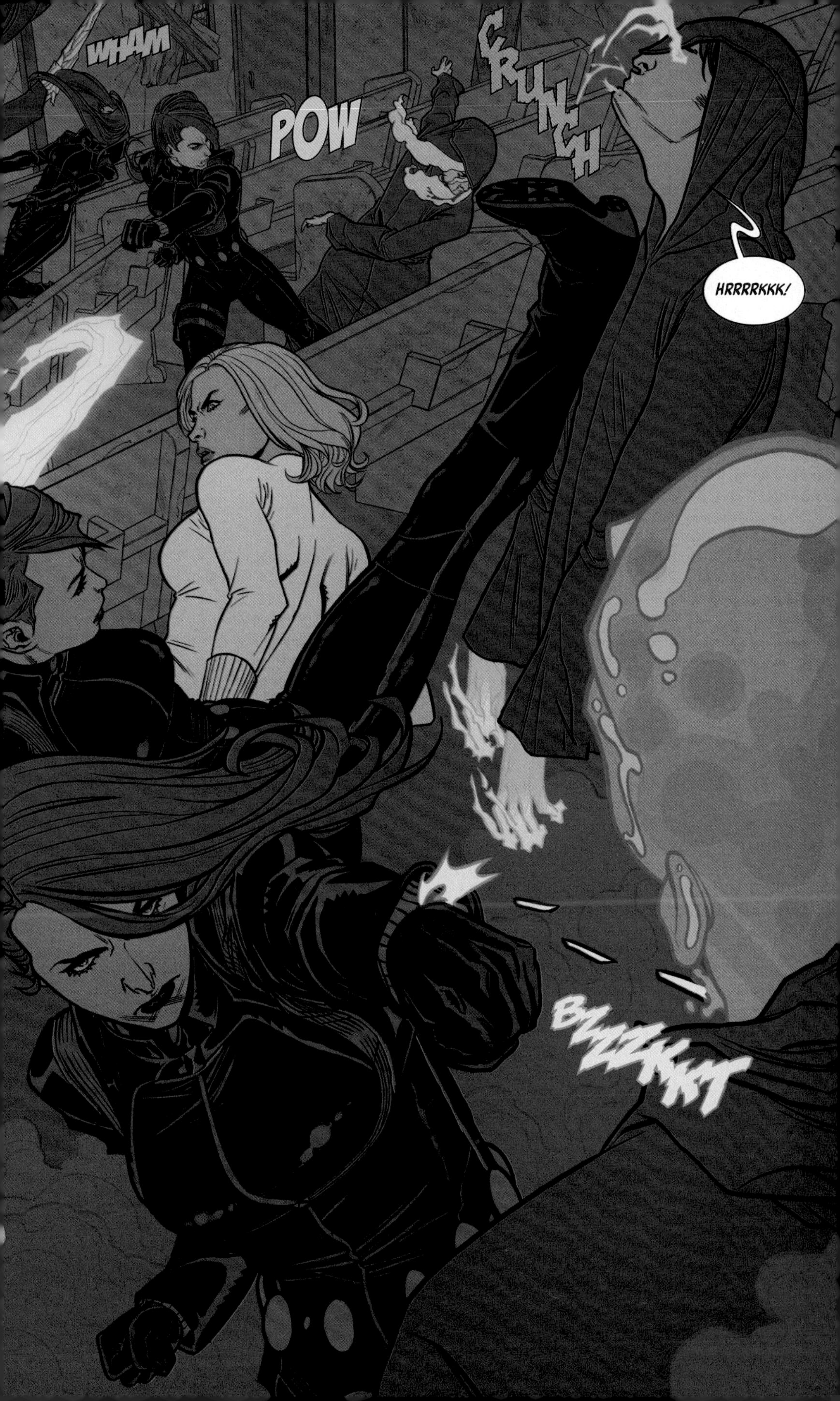
WHAM
POW
CRUNCH
HRRRRKKK!
BZZZKKT

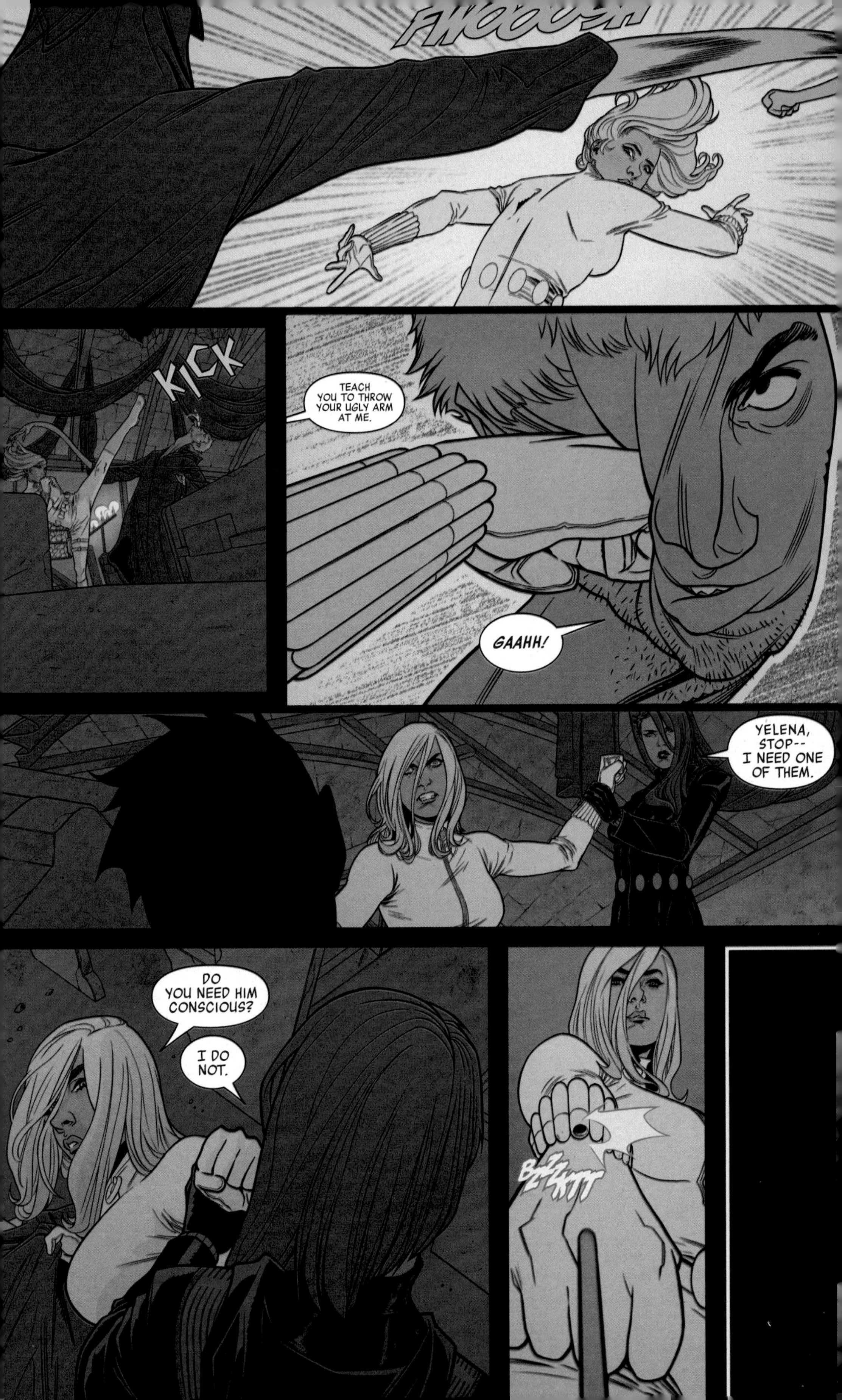
FWOOOSH
KICK
TEACH YOU TO THROW YOUR UGLY ARM AT ME.
GAAHH!
YELENA, STOP-- I NEED ONE OF THEM.
DO YOU NEED HIM CONSCIOUS?
I DO NOT.
BZZZKTT

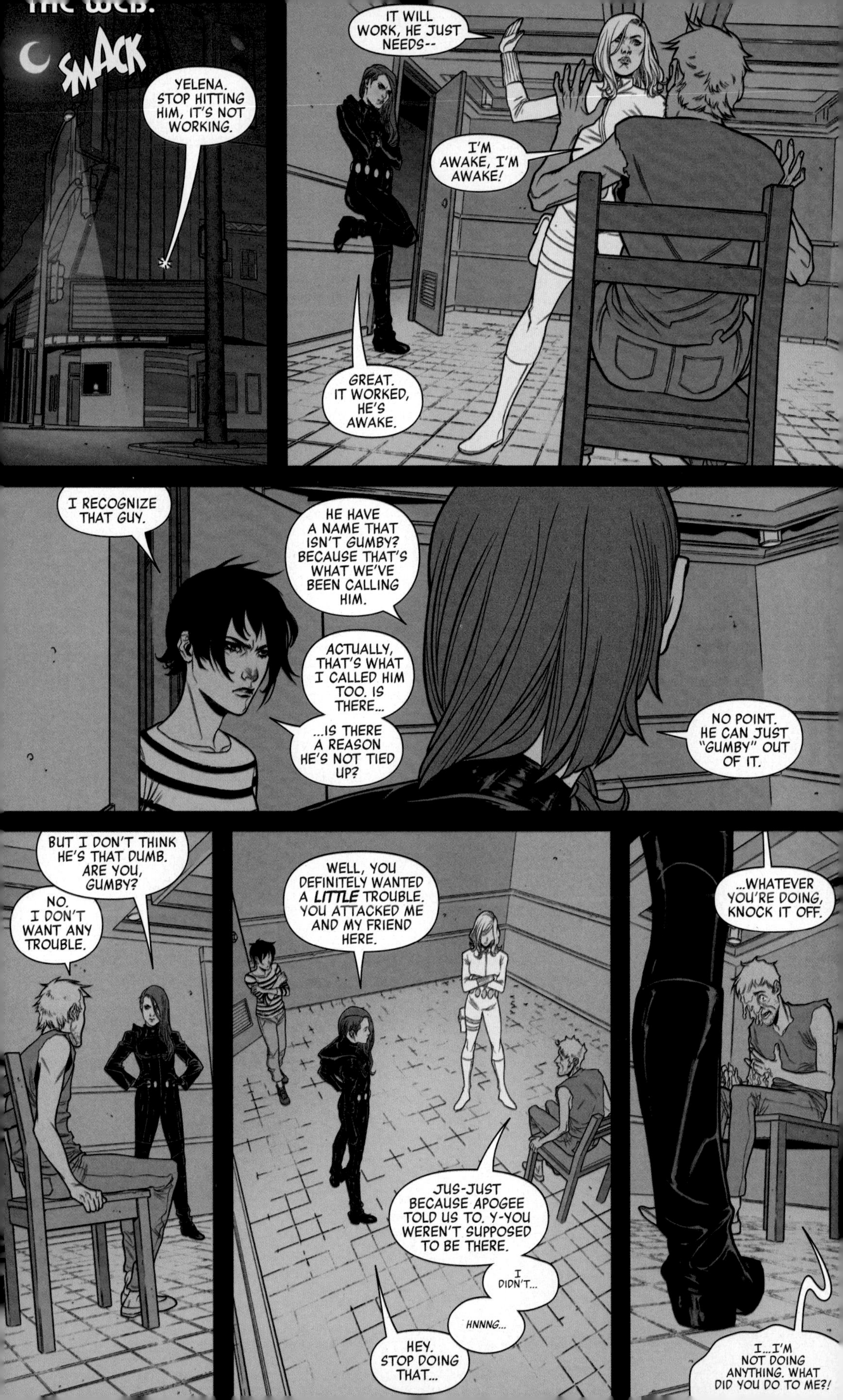
SMACK
YELENA. STOP HITTING HIM, IT'S NOT WORKING.
IT WILL WORK, HE JUST NEEDS--
I'M AWAKE, I'M AWAKE!
GREAT. IT WORKED, HE'S AWAKE.
I RECOGNIZE THAT GUY.
HE HAVE A NAME THAT ISN'T GUMBY? BECAUSE THAT'S WHAT WE'VE BEEN CALLING HIM.
ACTUALLY, THAT'S WHAT I CALLED HIM TOO. IS THERE...
...IS THERE A REASON HE'S NOT TIED UP?
NO POINT. HE CAN JUST "GUMBY" OUT OF IT.
BUT I DON'T THINK HE'S THAT DUMB. ARE YOU, GUMBY?
NO. I DON'T WANT ANY TROUBLE.
WELL, YOU DEFINITELY WANTED A LITTLE TROUBLE. YOU ATTACKED ME AND MY FRIEND HERE.
JUS-JUST BECAUSE APOGEE TOLD US TO. Y-YOU WEREN'T SUPPOSED TO BE THERE.
I DIDN'T...
HNNNG...
HEY. STOP DOING THAT...
...WHATEVER YOU'RE DOING, KNOCK IT OFF.
I...I'M NOT DOING ANYTHING. WHAT DID YOU DO TO ME?!

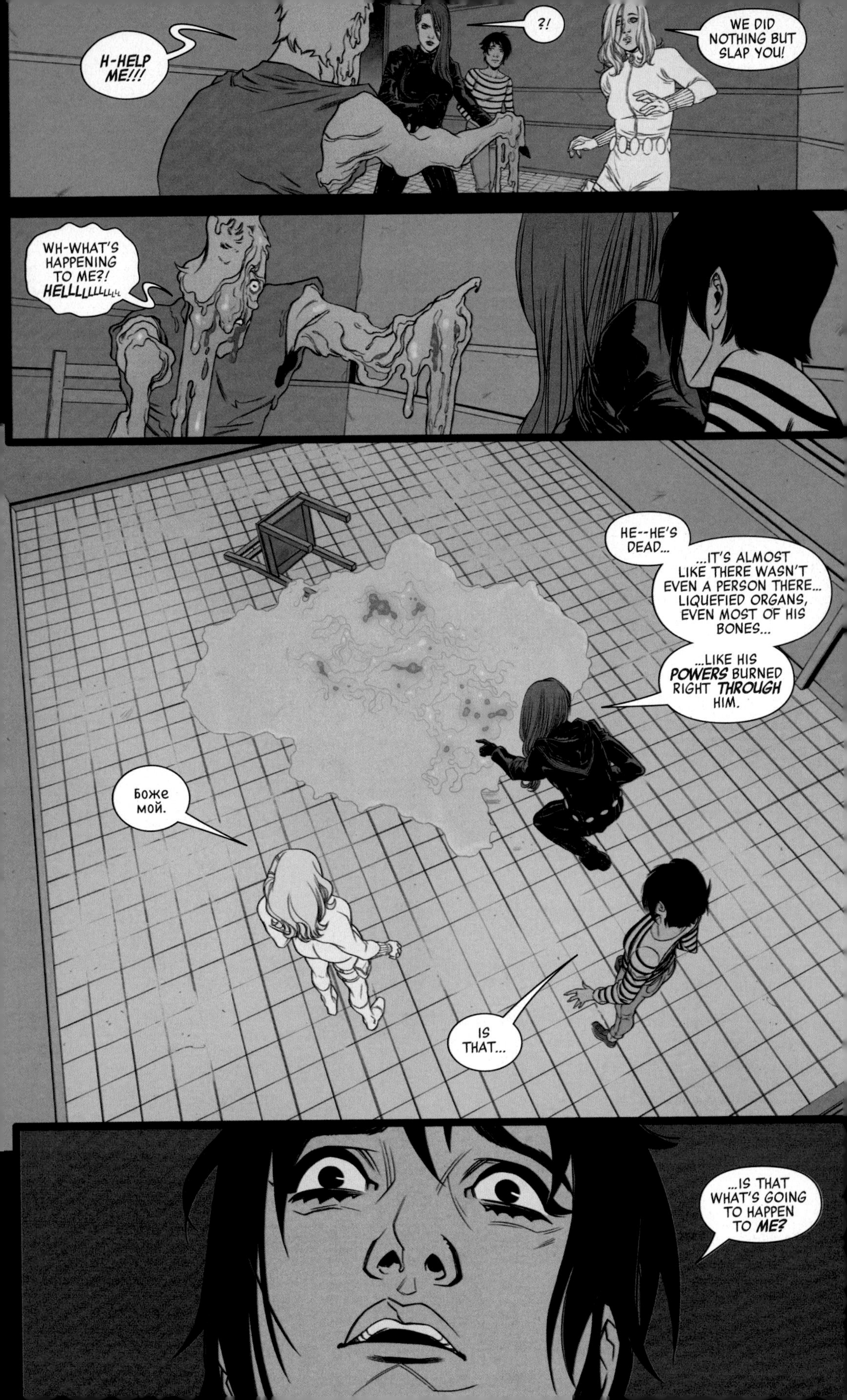
H-HELP ME!!!
?!
WE DID NOTHING BUT SLAP YOU!
WH-WHAT'S HAPPENING TO ME?! HELLLLLLLL
HE--HE'S DEAD...
...IT'S ALMOST LIKE THERE WASN'T EVEN A PERSON THERE... LIQUEFIED ORGANS, EVEN MOST OF HIS BONES...
...LIKE HIS POWERS BURNED RIGHT THROUGH HIM.
Боже мой.
IS THAT...
...IS THAT WHAT'S GOING TO HAPPEN TO ME?

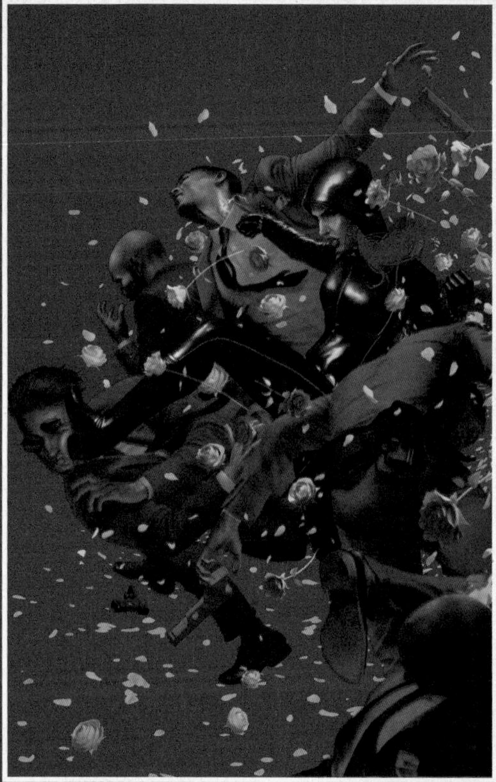

#6 VARIANT BY RAHZZAH

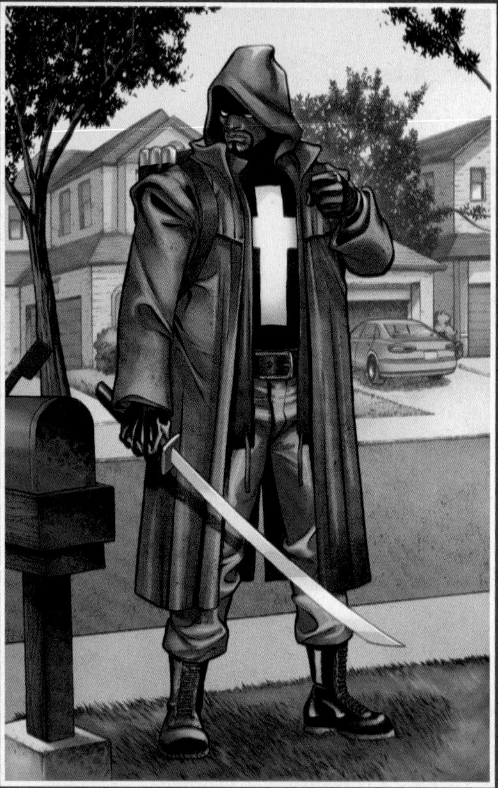

#6 HEROES REBORN VARIANT BY CARLOS PACHECO
RAFAEL FONTERIZ & RACHELLE ROSENBERG

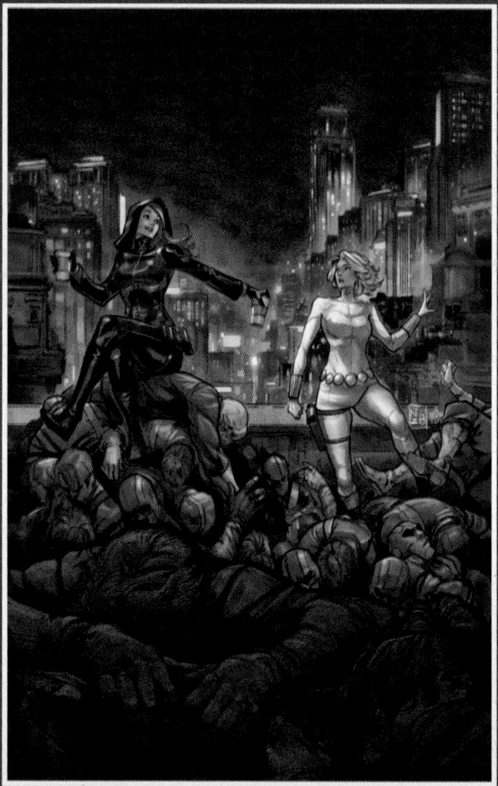

#7 VARIANT BY
NABETSE ZITRO & JESUS ABURTOV

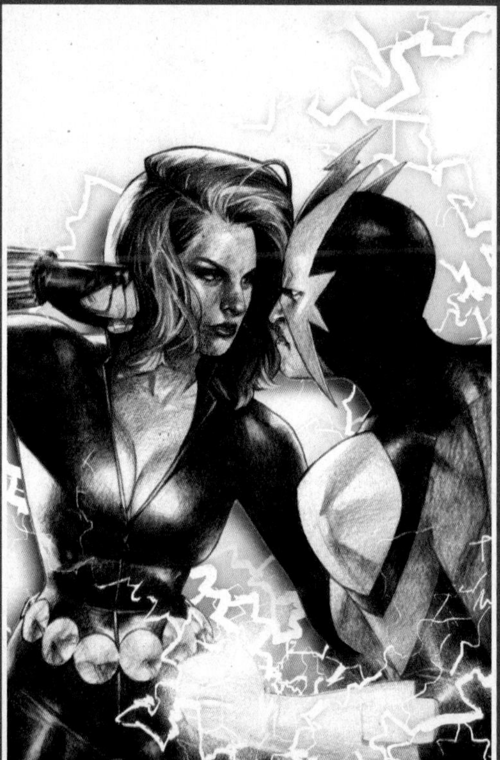

#8 SPIDER-MAN VILLAINS VARIANT BY DAVI GO

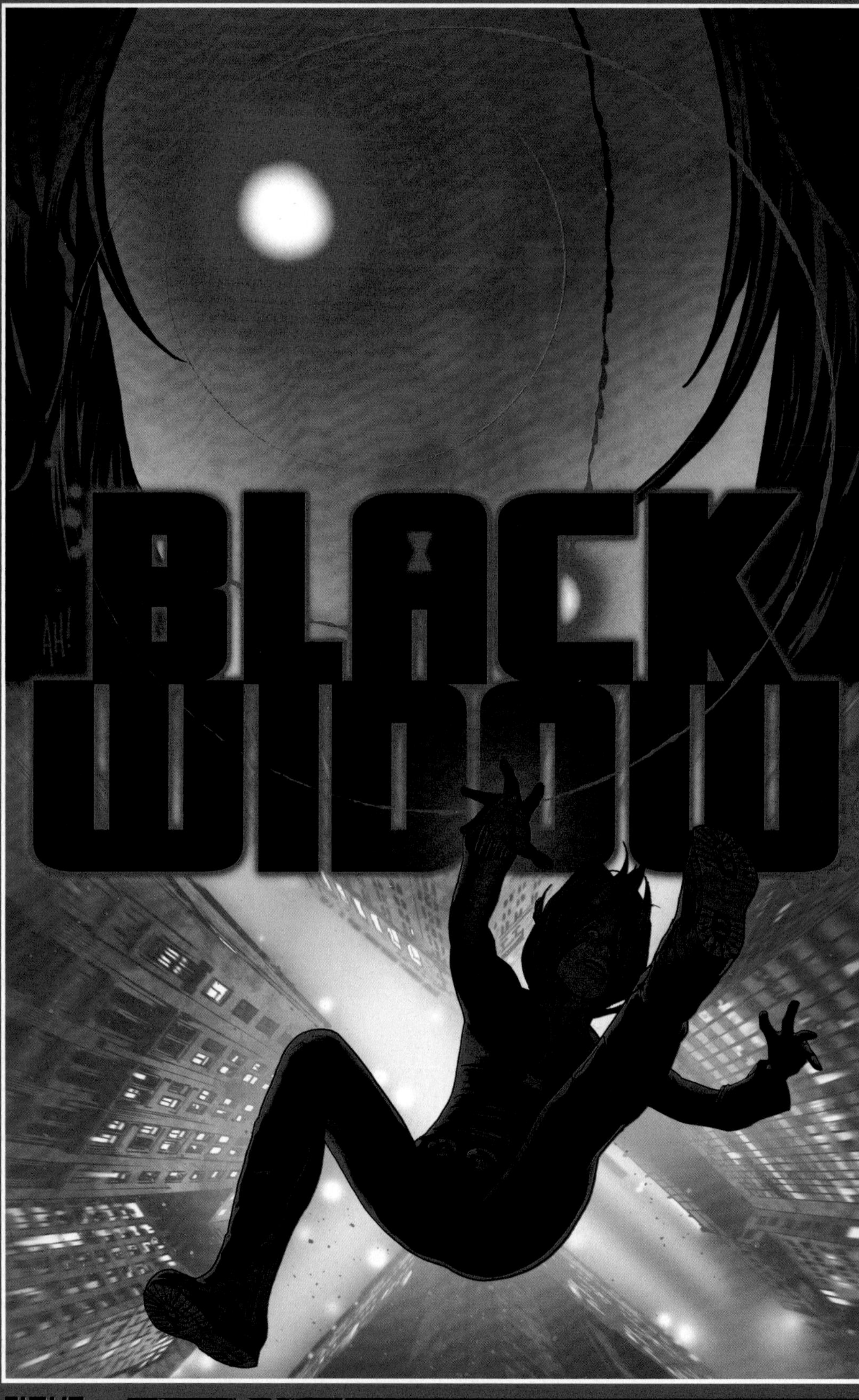
BLACK
WIDOW
AH!

EIGHT

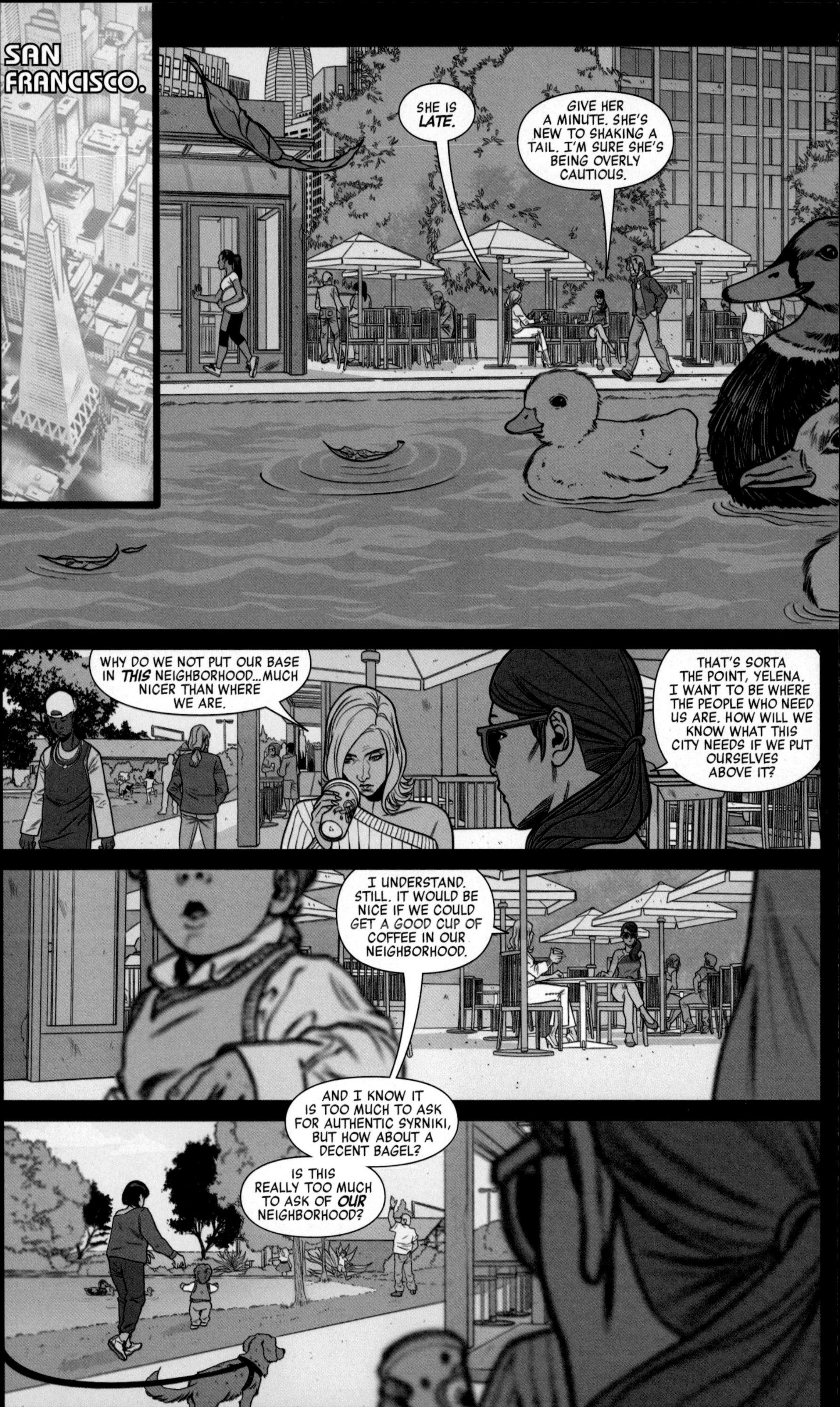
SAN FRANCISCO.
SHE IS *LATE.*
GIVE HER A MINUTE. SHE'S NEW TO SHAKING A TAIL. I'M SURE SHE'S BEING OVERLY CAUTIOUS.
WHY DO WE NOT PUT OUR BASE IN *THIS* NEIGHBORHOOD...MUCH NICER THAN WHERE WE ARE.
THAT'S SORTA THE POINT, YELENA. I WANT TO BE WHERE THE PEOPLE WHO NEED US ARE. HOW WILL WE KNOW WHAT THIS CITY NEEDS IF WE PUT OURSELVES ABOVE IT?
I UNDERSTAND. STILL. IT WOULD BE NICE IF WE COULD GET A GOOD CUP OF COFFEE IN OUR NEIGHBORHOOD.
AND I KNOW IT IS TOO MUCH TO ASK FOR AUTHENTIC SYRNIKI, BUT HOW ABOUT A DECENT BAGEL?
IS THIS REALLY TOO MUCH TO ASK OF *OUR* NEIGHBORHOOD?

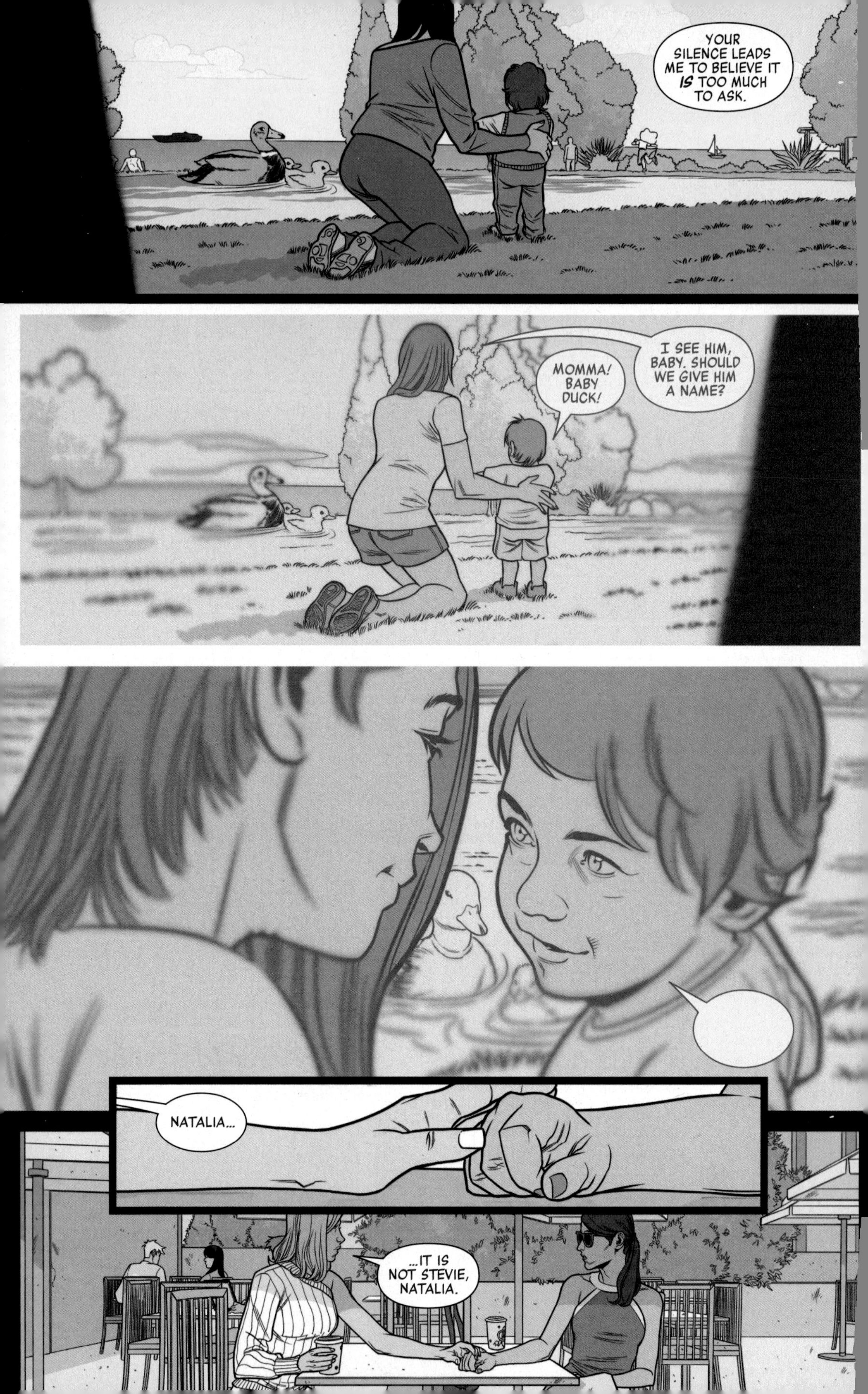
YOUR SILENCE LEADS ME TO BELIEVE IT IS TOO MUCH TO ASK.
MOMMA! BABY DUCK!
I SEE HIM, BABY. SHOULD WE GIVE HIM A NAME?
NATALIA...
...IT IS NOT STEVIE, NATALIA.

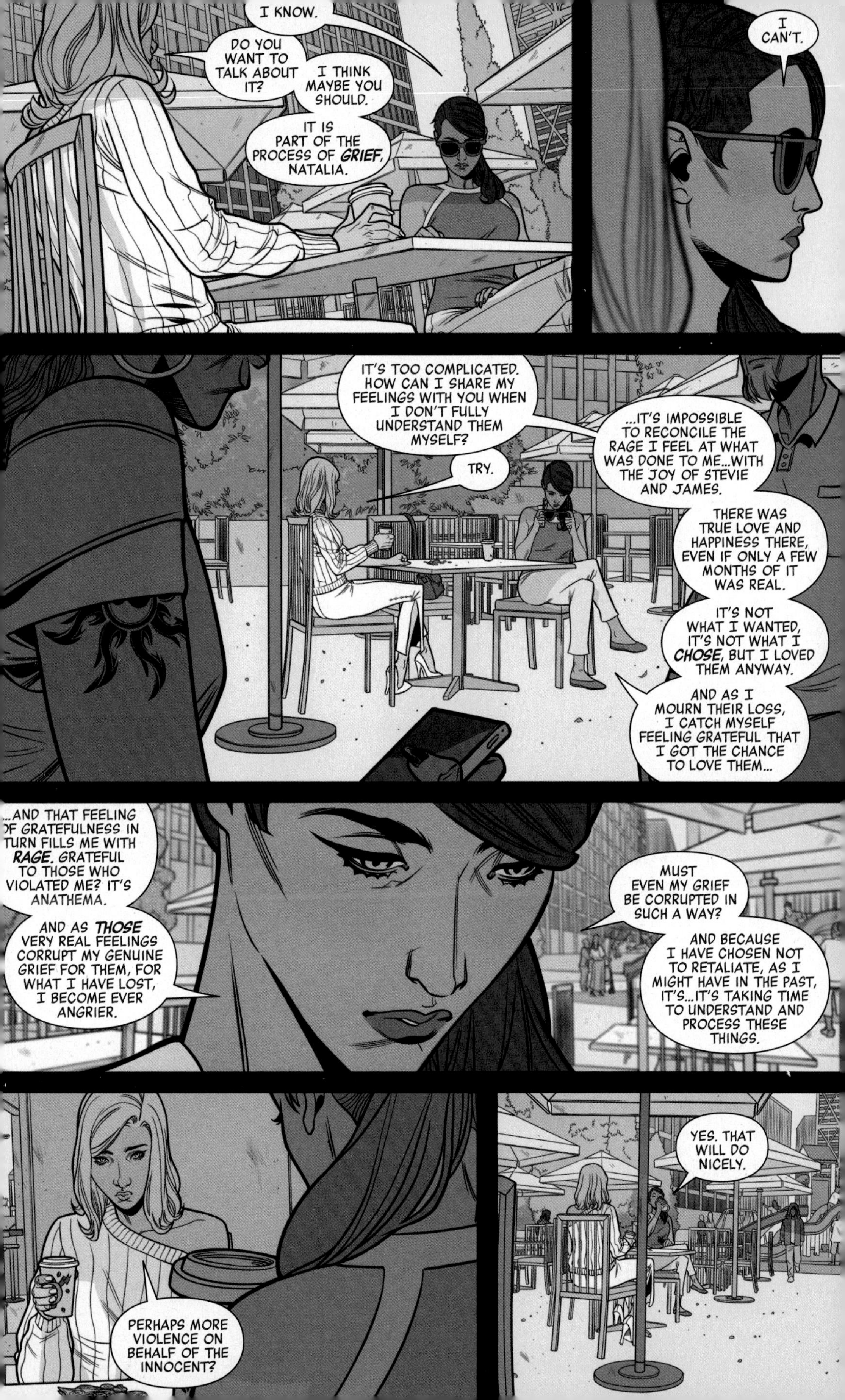
I KNOW.
DO YOU WANT TO TALK ABOUT IT?
I THINK MAYBE YOU SHOULD.
IT IS PART OF THE PROCESS OF GRIEF, NATALIA.
I CAN'T.
IT'S TOO COMPLICATED. HOW CAN I SHARE MY FEELINGS WITH YOU WHEN I DON'T FULLY UNDERSTAND THEM MYSELF?
TRY.
...IT'S IMPOSSIBLE TO RECONCILE THE RAGE I FEEL AT WHAT WAS DONE TO ME...WITH THE JOY OF STEVIE AND JAMES.
THERE WAS TRUE LOVE AND HAPPINESS THERE, EVEN IF ONLY A FEW MONTHS OF IT WAS REAL.
IT'S NOT WHAT I WANTED, IT'S NOT WHAT I CHOSE, BUT I LOVED THEM ANYWAY.
AND AS I MOURN THEIR LOSS, I CATCH MYSELF FEELING GRATEFUL THAT I GOT THE CHANCE TO LOVE THEM...
...AND THAT FEELING OF GRATEFULNESS IN TURN FILLS ME WITH RAGE. GRATEFUL TO THOSE WHO VIOLATED ME? IT'S ANATHEMA.
AND AS THOSE VERY REAL FEELINGS CORRUPT MY GENUINE GRIEF FOR THEM, FOR WHAT I HAVE LOST, I BECOME EVER ANGRIER.
MUST EVEN MY GRIEF BE CORRUPTED IN SUCH A WAY?
AND BECAUSE I HAVE CHOSEN NOT TO RETALIATE, AS I MIGHT HAVE IN THE PAST, IT'S...IT'S TAKING TIME TO UNDERSTAND AND PROCESS THESE THINGS.
PERHAPS MORE VIOLENCE ON BEHALF OF THE INNOCENT?
YES. THAT WILL DO NICELY.

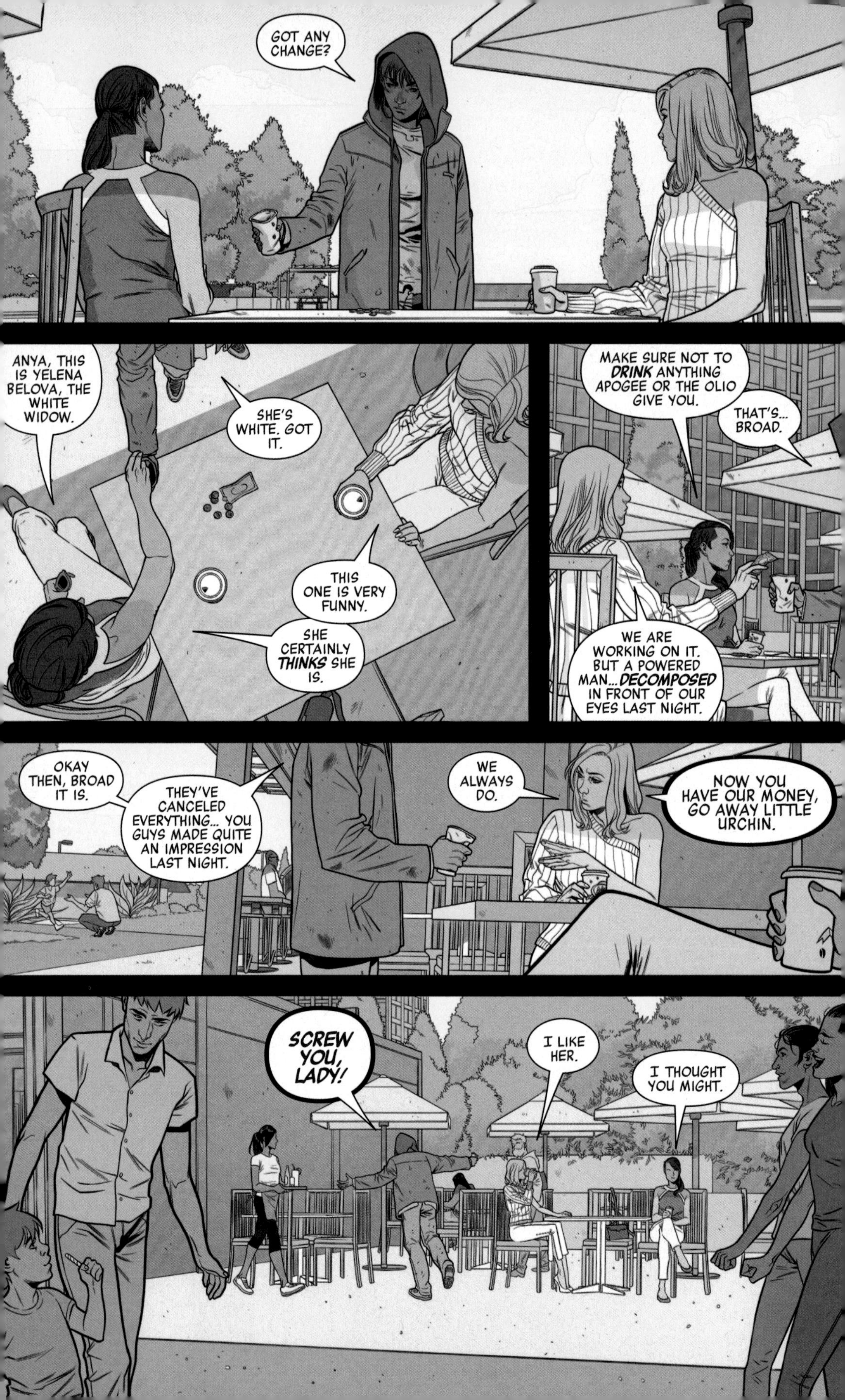
GOT ANY CHANGE?
ANYA, THIS IS YELENA BELOVA, THE WHITE WIDOW.
SHE'S WHITE. GOT IT.
THIS ONE IS VERY FUNNY.
SHE CERTAINLY THINKS SHE IS.
MAKE SURE NOT TO DRINK ANYTHING APOGEE OR THE OLIO GIVE YOU.
THAT'S... BROAD.
WE ARE WORKING ON IT. BUT A POWERED MAN... DECOMPOSED IN FRONT OF OUR EYES LAST NIGHT.
OKAY THEN, BROAD IT IS.
THEY'VE CANCELED EVERYTHING... YOU GUYS MADE QUITE AN IMPRESSION LAST NIGHT.
WE ALWAYS DO.
NOW YOU HAVE OUR MONEY, GO AWAY LITTLE URCHIN.
SCREW YOU, LADY!
I LIKE HER.
I THOUGHT YOU MIGHT.

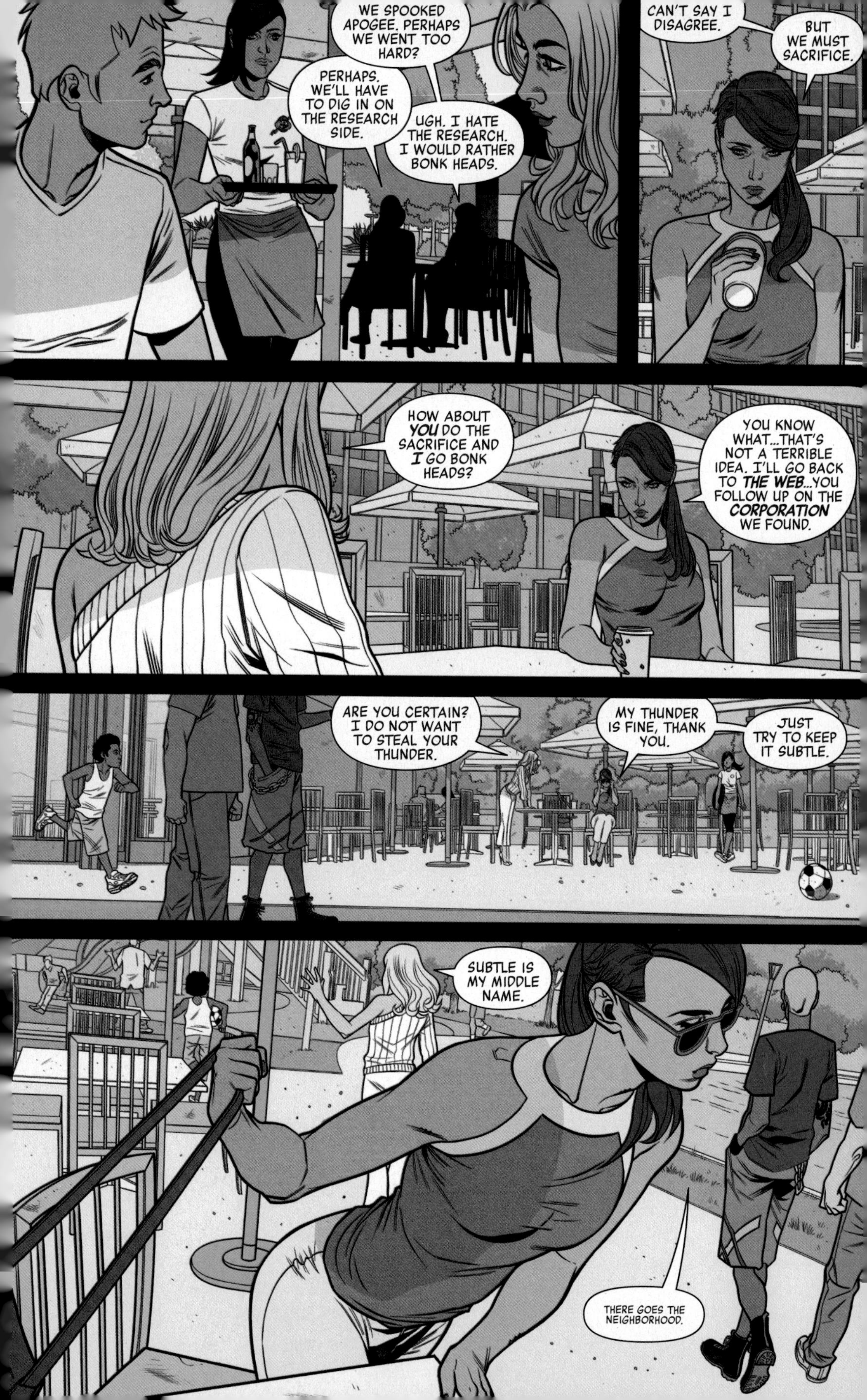
WE SPOOKED APOGEE. PERHAPS WE WENT TOO HARD?
PERHAPS. WE'LL HAVE TO DIG IN ON THE RESEARCH SIDE.
UGH. I HATE THE RESEARCH. I WOULD RATHER BONK HEADS.
CAN'T SAY I DISAGREE.
BUT WE MUST SACRIFICE.
HOW ABOUT YOU DO THE SACRIFICE AND I GO BONK HEADS?
YOU KNOW WHAT...THAT'S NOT A TERRIBLE IDEA. I'LL GO BACK TO THE WEB...YOU FOLLOW UP ON THE CORPORATION WE FOUND.
ARE YOU CERTAIN? I DO NOT WANT TO STEAL YOUR THUNDER.
MY THUNDER IS FINE, THANK YOU.
JUST TRY TO KEEP IT SUBTLE.
SUBTLE IS MY MIDDLE NAME.
THERE GOES THE NEIGHBORHOOD.

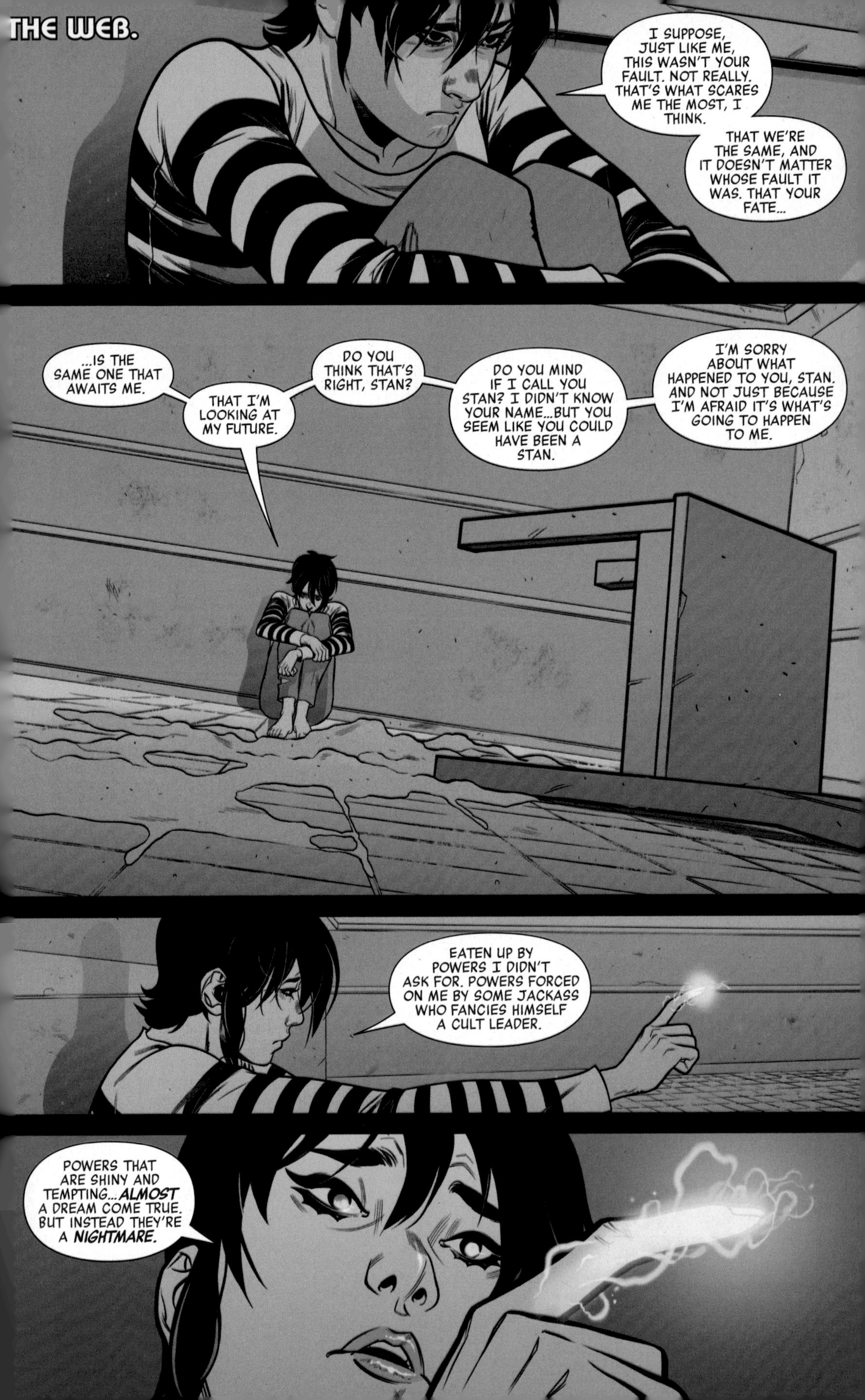
THE WEB.
I SUPPOSE, JUST LIKE ME, THIS WASN'T YOUR FAULT. NOT REALLY. THAT'S WHAT SCARES ME THE MOST, I THINK.
THAT WE'RE THE SAME, AND IT DOESN'T MATTER WHOSE FAULT IT WAS. THAT YOUR FATE...
...IS THE SAME ONE THAT AWAITS ME.
THAT I'M LOOKING AT MY FUTURE.
DO YOU THINK THAT'S RIGHT, STAN?
DO YOU MIND IF I CALL YOU STAN? I DIDN'T KNOW YOUR NAME...BUT YOU SEEM LIKE YOU COULD HAVE BEEN A STAN.
I'M SORRY ABOUT WHAT HAPPENED TO YOU, STAN. AND NOT JUST BECAUSE I'M AFRAID IT'S WHAT'S GOING TO HAPPEN TO ME.
EATEN UP BY POWERS I DIDN'T ASK FOR. POWERS FORCED ON ME BY SOME JACKASS WHO FANCIES HIMSELF A CULT LEADER.
POWERS THAT ARE SHINY AND TEMPTING...**ALMOST** A DREAM COME TRUE. BUT INSTEAD THEY'RE A **NIGHTMARE.**

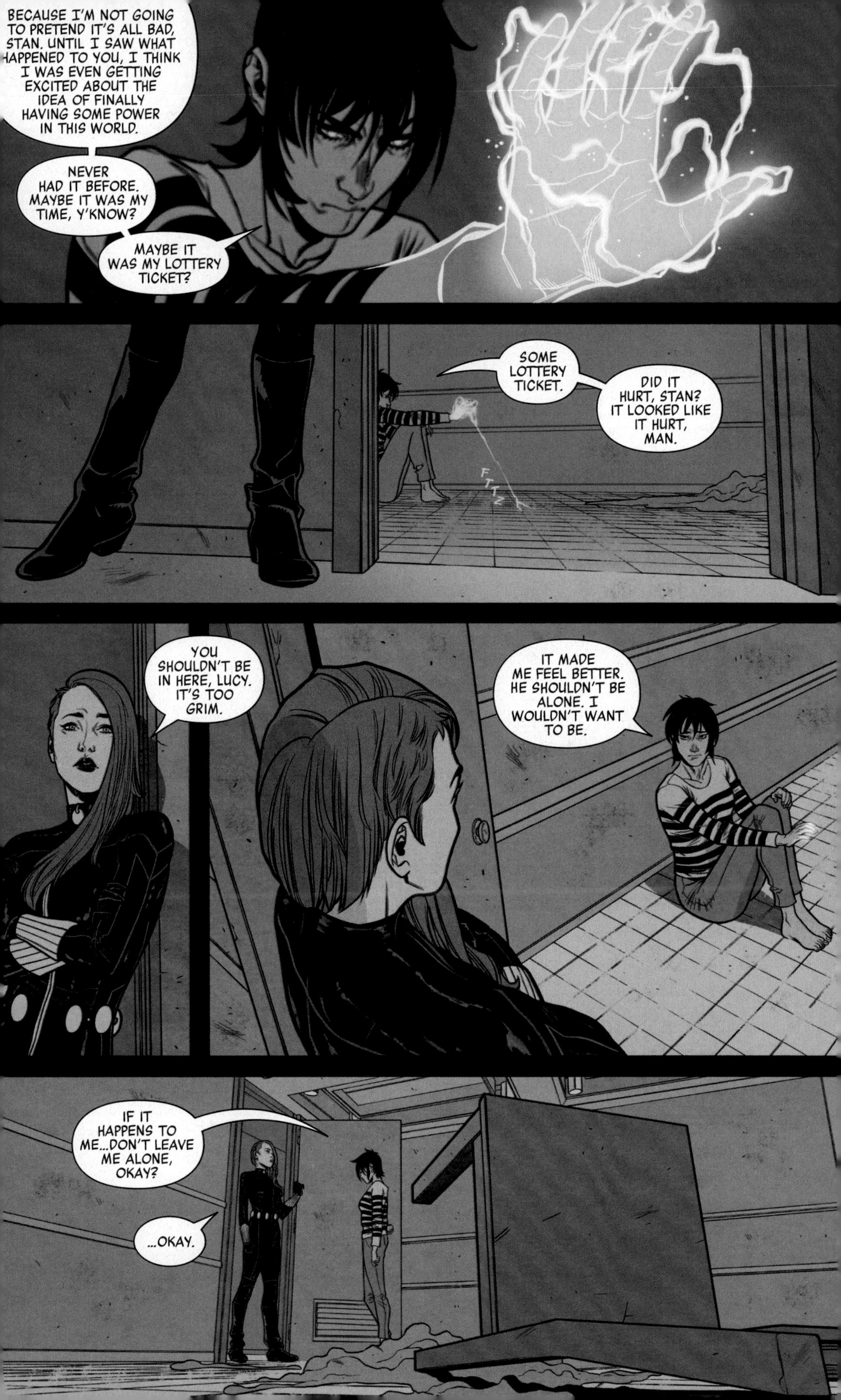
BECAUSE I'M NOT GOING TO PRETEND IT'S ALL BAD, STAN. UNTIL I SAW WHAT HAPPENED TO YOU, I THINK I WAS EVEN GETTING EXCITED ABOUT THE IDEA OF FINALLY HAVING SOME POWER IN THIS WORLD.
NEVER HAD IT BEFORE. MAYBE IT WAS MY TIME, Y'KNOW?
MAYBE IT WAS MY LOTTERY TICKET?
SOME LOTTERY TICKET.
DID IT HURT, STAN? IT LOOKED LIKE IT HURT, MAN.
FTTZ
YOU SHOULDN'T BE IN HERE, LUCY. IT'S TOO GRIM.
IT MADE ME FEEL BETTER. HE SHOULDN'T BE ALONE. I WOULDN'T WANT TO BE.
IF IT HAPPENS TO ME...DON'T LEAVE ME ALONE, OKAY?
...OKAY.

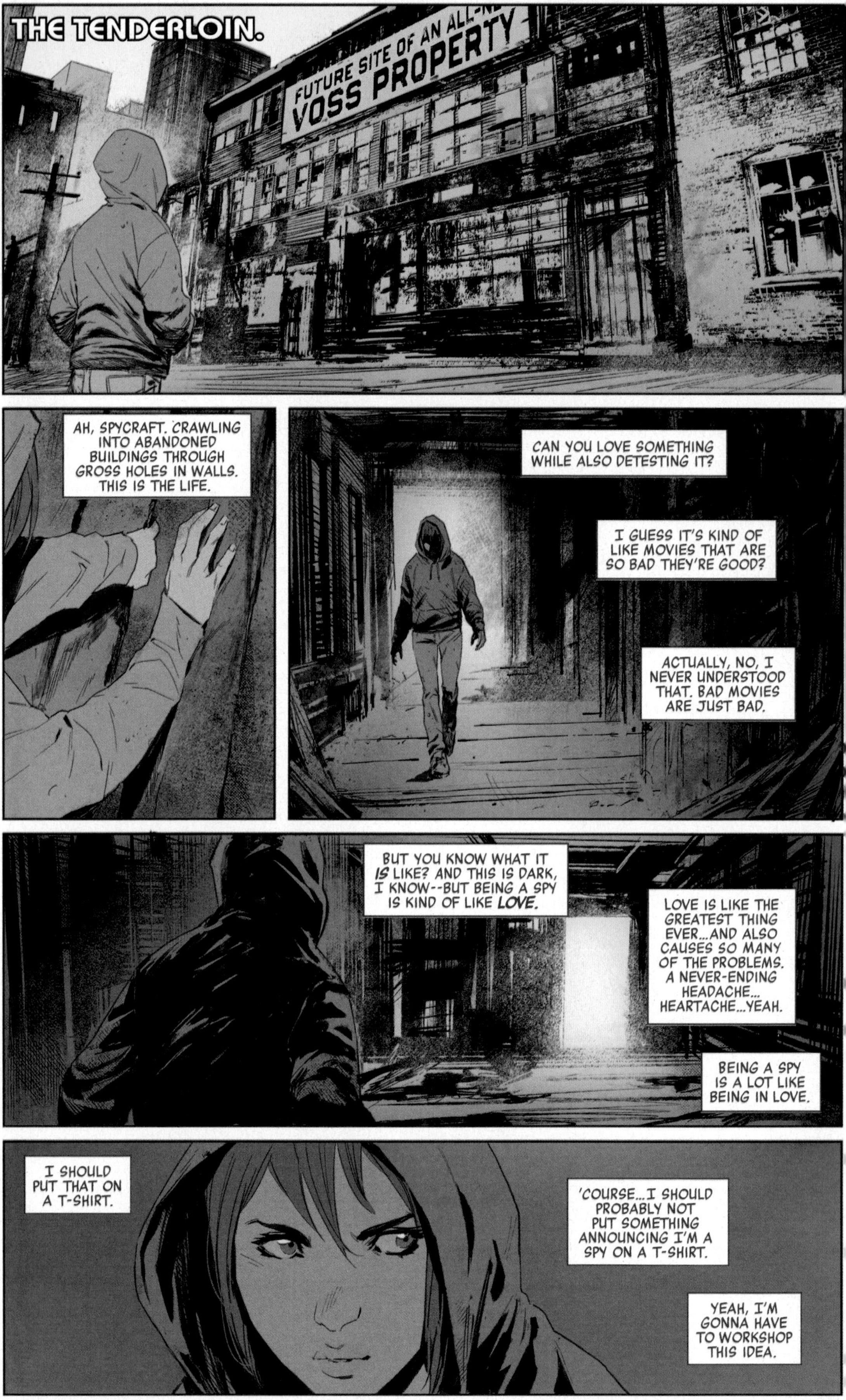
THE TENDERLOIN.
FUTURE SITE OF AN ALL-
VOSS PROPERTY
AH, SPYCRAFT. CRAWLING INTO ABANDONED BUILDINGS THROUGH GROSS HOLES IN WALLS. THIS IS THE LIFE.
CAN YOU LOVE SOMETHING WHILE ALSO DETESTING IT?
I GUESS IT'S KIND OF LIKE MOVIES THAT ARE SO BAD THEY'RE GOOD?
ACTUALLY, NO, I NEVER UNDERSTOOD THAT. BAD MOVIES ARE JUST BAD.
BUT YOU KNOW WHAT IT *IS* LIKE? AND THIS IS DARK, I KNOW--BUT BEING A SPY IS KIND OF LIKE *LOVE.*
LOVE IS LIKE THE GREATEST THING EVER...AND ALSO CAUSES SO MANY OF THE PROBLEMS. A NEVER-ENDING HEADACHE... HEARTACHE...YEAH.
BEING A SPY IS A LOT LIKE BEING IN LOVE.
I SHOULD PUT THAT ON A T-SHIRT.
'COURSE...I SHOULD PROBABLY NOT PUT SOMETHING ANNOUNCING I'M A SPY ON A T-SHIRT.
YEAH, I'M GONNA HAVE TO WORKSHOP THIS IDEA.

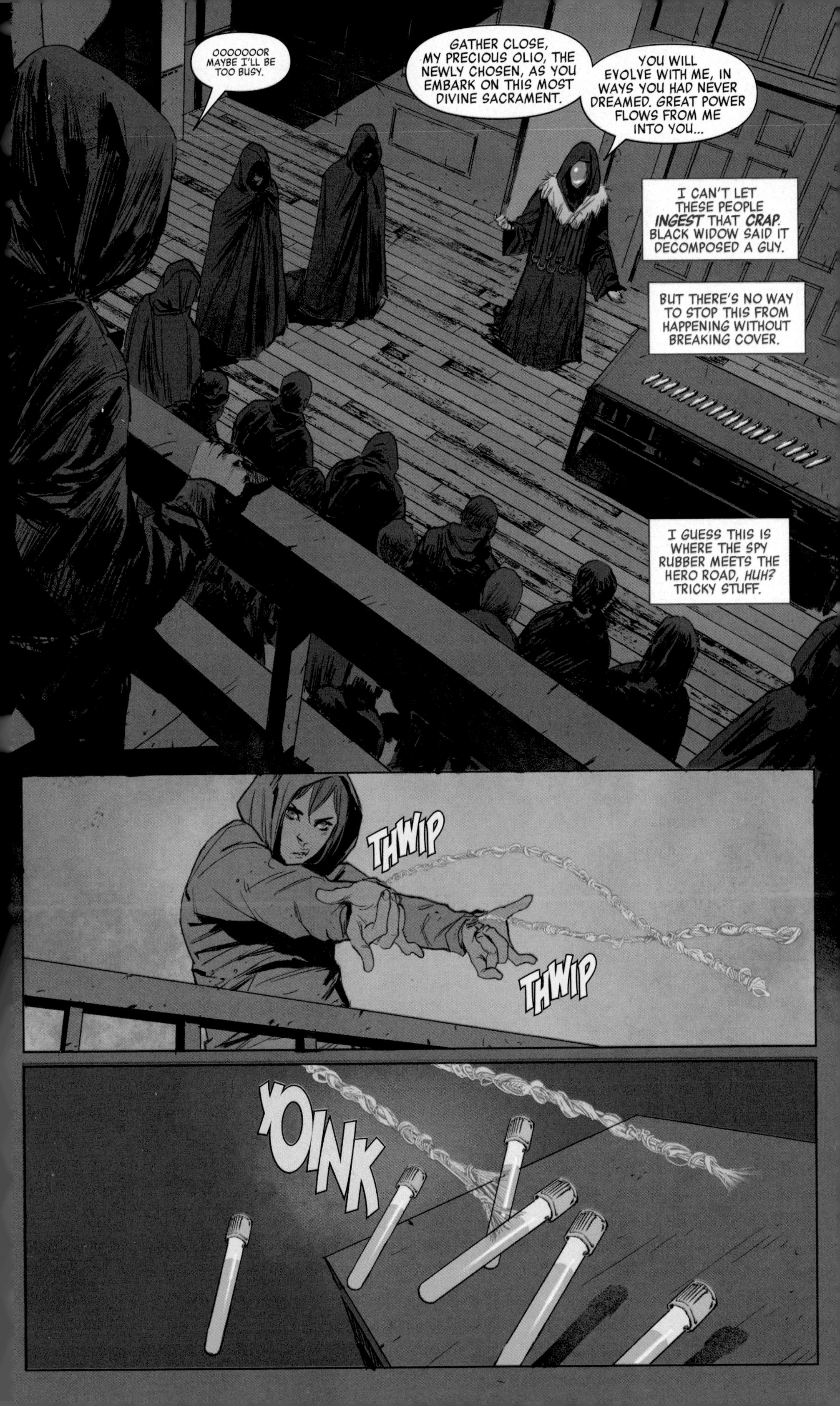

OOOOOOOR MAYBE I'LL BE TOO BUSY.
GATHER CLOSE, MY PRECIOUS OLIO, THE NEWLY CHOSEN, AS YOU EMBARK ON THIS MOST DIVINE SACRAMENT.
YOU WILL EVOLVE WITH ME, IN WAYS YOU HAD NEVER DREAMED. GREAT POWER FLOWS FROM ME INTO YOU...
I CAN'T LET THESE PEOPLE INGEST THAT CRAP. BLACK WIDOW SAID IT DECOMPOSED A GUY.
BUT THERE'S NO WAY TO STOP THIS FROM HAPPENING WITHOUT BREAKING COVER.
I GUESS THIS IS WHERE THE SPY RUBBER MEETS THE HERO ROAD, HUH? TRICKY STUFF.
THWIP
THWIP
YOINK

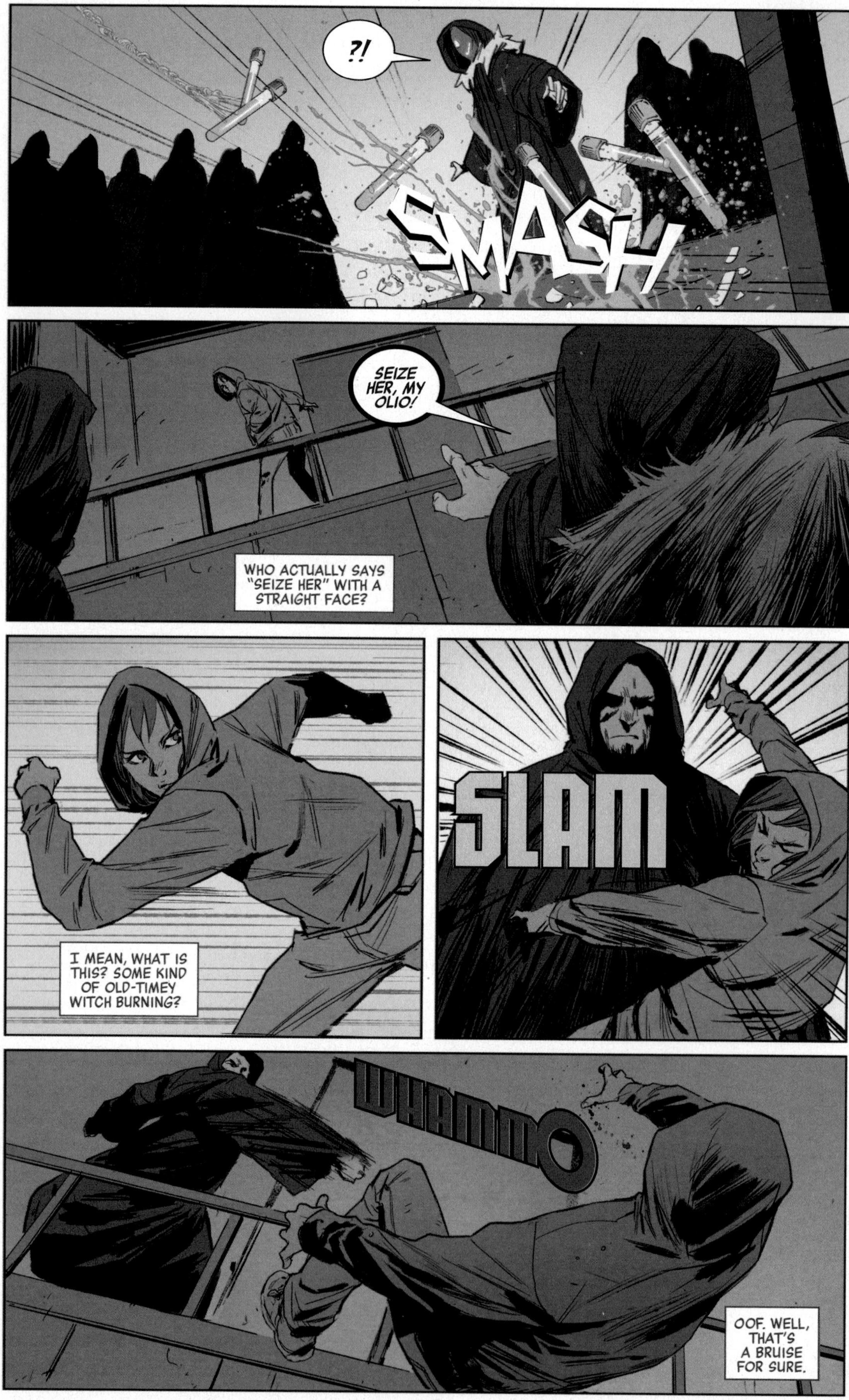
?!
SMASH
SEIZE HER, MY OLIO!
WHO ACTUALLY SAYS "SEIZE HER" WITH A STRAIGHT FACE?
I MEAN, WHAT IS THIS? SOME KIND OF OLD-TIMEY WITCH BURNING?
SLAM
WHAMMO
OOF. WELL, THAT'S A BRUISE FOR SURE.

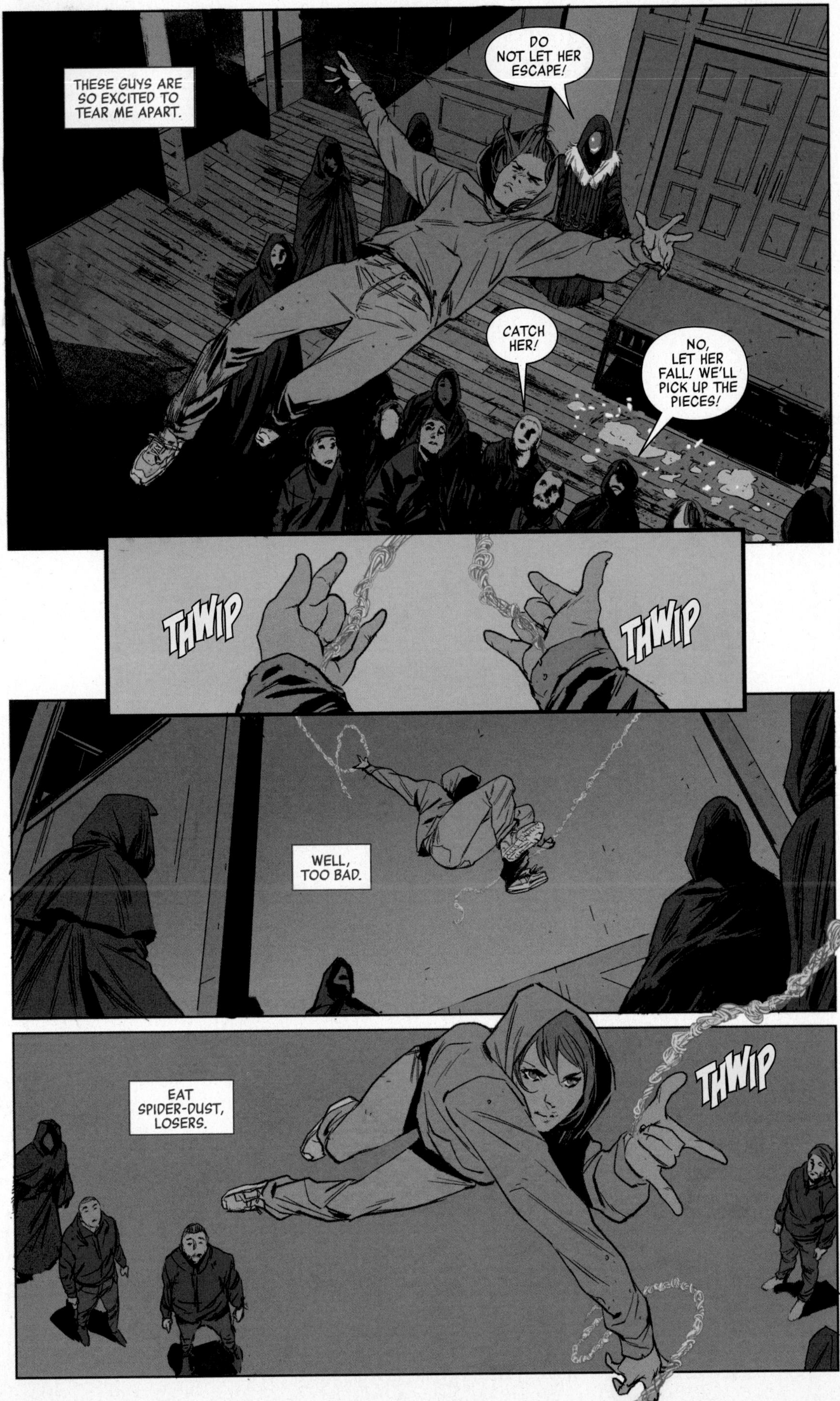
THESE GUYS ARE SO EXCITED TO TEAR ME APART.
DO NOT LET HER ESCAPE!
CATCH HER!
NO, LET HER FALL! WE'LL PICK UP THE PIECES!
THWIP
THWIP
WELL, TOO BAD.
EAT SPIDER-DUST, LOSERS.
THWIP

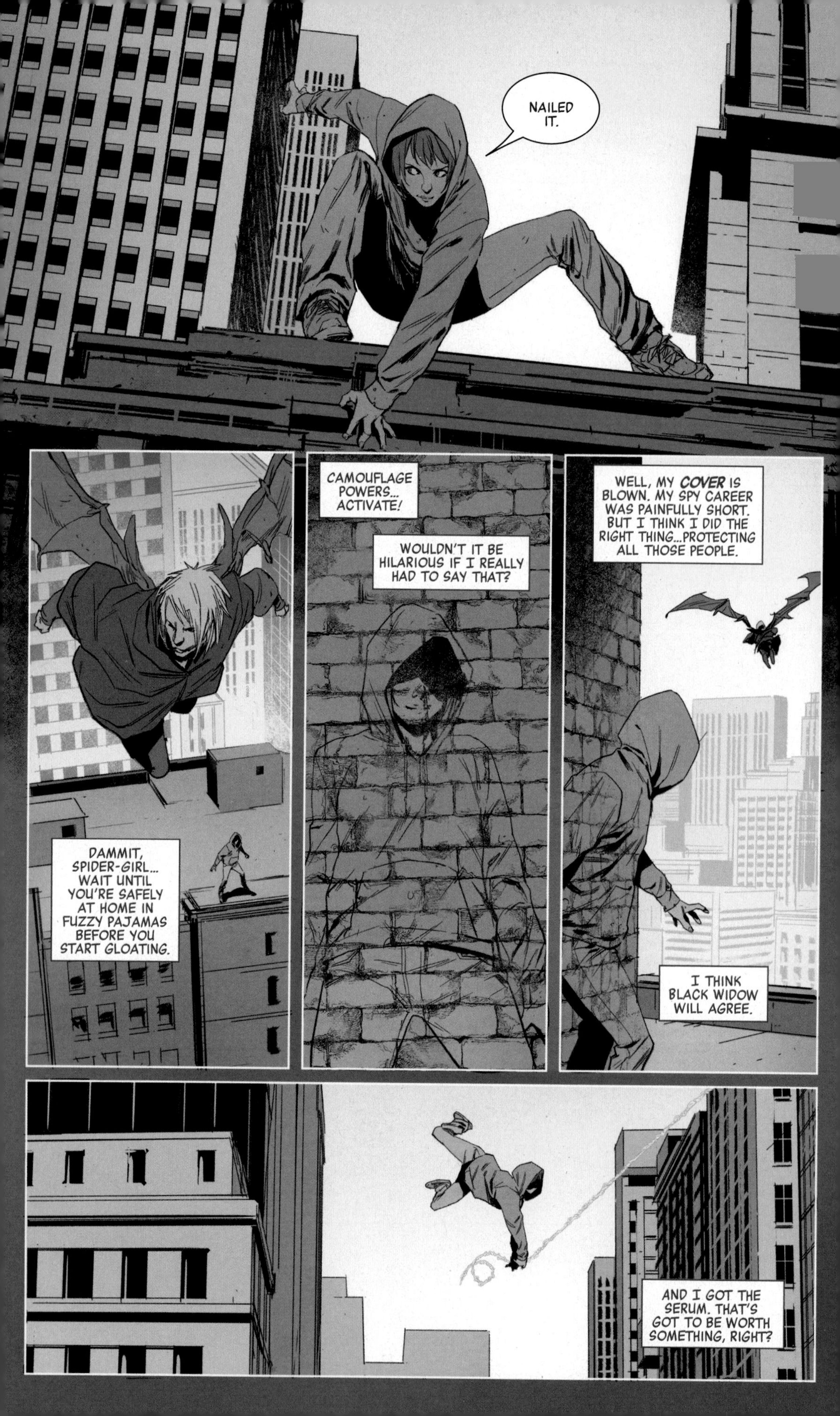
NAILED IT.
CAMOUFLAGE POWERS... ACTIVATE!
WOULDN'T IT BE HILARIOUS IF I REALLY HAD TO SAY THAT?
DAMMIT, SPIDER-GIRL... WAIT UNTIL YOU'RE SAFELY AT HOME IN FUZZY PAJAMAS BEFORE YOU START GLOATING.
WELL, MY COVER IS BLOWN. MY SPY CAREER WAS PAINFULLY SHORT. BUT I THINK I DID THE RIGHT THING...PROTECTING ALL THOSE PEOPLE.
I THINK BLACK WIDOW WILL AGREE.
AND I GOT THE SERUM. THAT'S GOT TO BE WORTH SOMETHING, RIGHT?

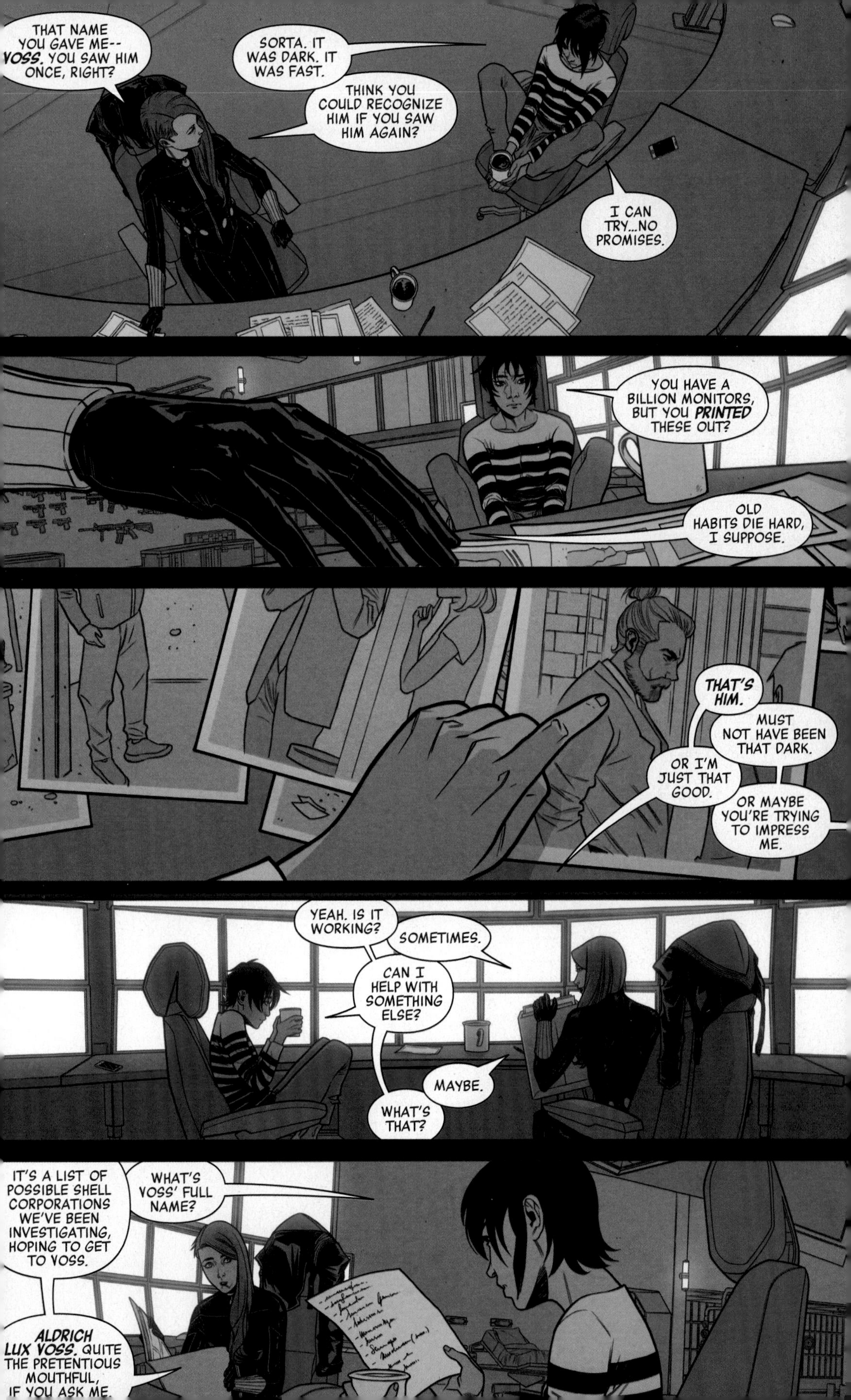
THAT NAME YOU GAVE ME-- VOSS. YOU SAW HIM ONCE, RIGHT?
SORTA. IT WAS DARK. IT WAS FAST.
THINK YOU COULD RECOGNIZE HIM IF YOU SAW HIM AGAIN?
I CAN TRY...NO PROMISES.
YOU HAVE A BILLION MONITORS, BUT YOU PRINTED THESE OUT?
OLD HABITS DIE HARD, I SUPPOSE.
THAT'S HIM.
MUST NOT HAVE BEEN THAT DARK.
OR I'M JUST THAT GOOD.
OR MAYBE YOU'RE TRYING TO IMPRESS ME.
YEAH. IS IT WORKING?
SOMETIMES.
CAN I HELP WITH SOMETHING ELSE?
MAYBE.
WHAT'S THAT?
IT'S A LIST OF POSSIBLE SHELL CORPORATIONS WE'VE BEEN INVESTIGATING, HOPING TO GET TO VOSS.
WHAT'S VOSS' FULL NAME?
ALDRICH LUX VOSS. QUITE THE PRETENTIOUS MOUTHFUL, IF YOU ASK ME.

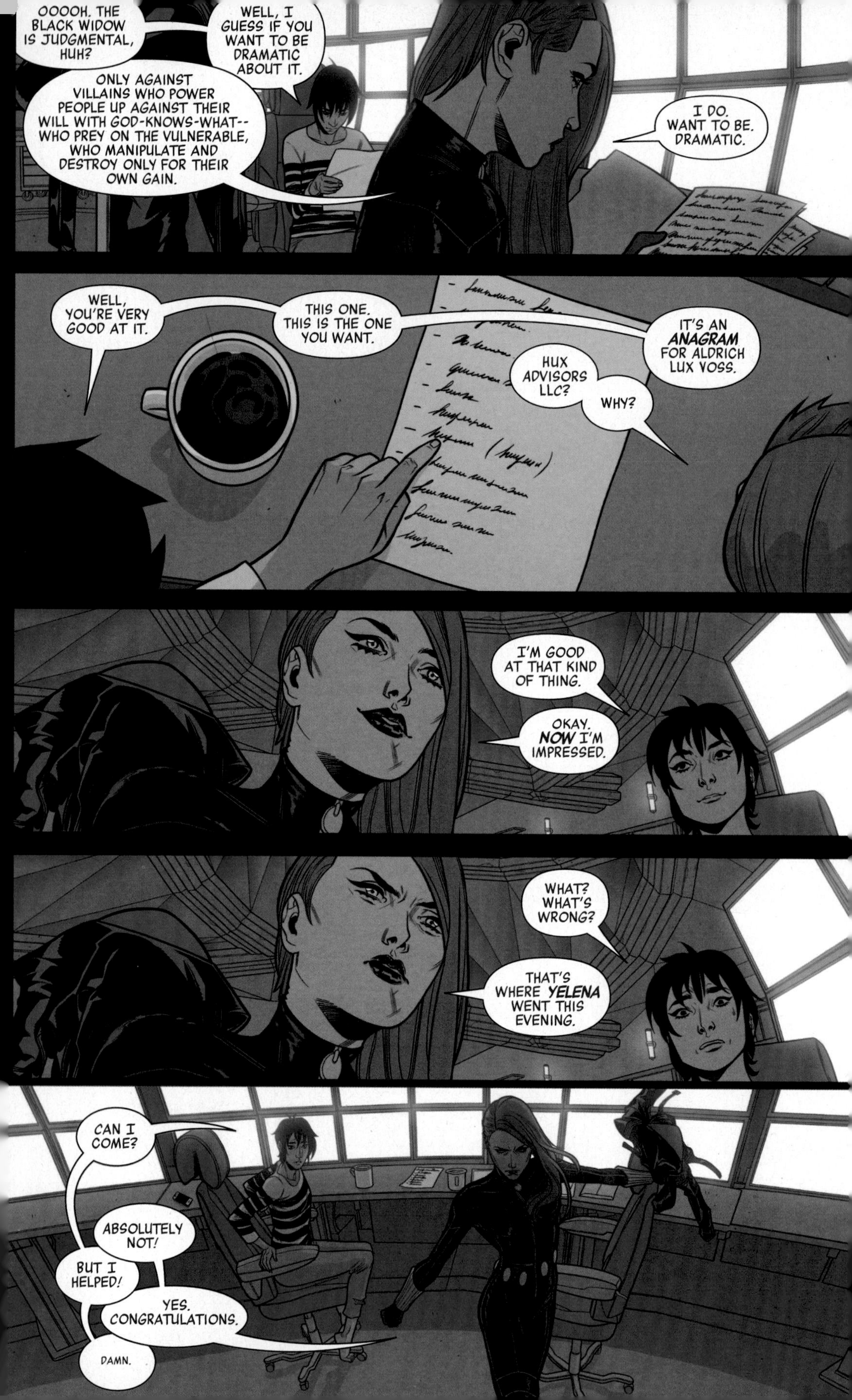
OOOOH. THE BLACK WIDOW IS JUDGMENTAL, HUH?
WELL, I GUESS IF YOU WANT TO BE DRAMATIC ABOUT IT.
ONLY AGAINST VILLAINS WHO POWER PEOPLE UP AGAINST THEIR WILL WITH GOD-KNOWS-WHAT-- WHO PREY ON THE VULNERABLE, WHO MANIPULATE AND DESTROY ONLY FOR THEIR OWN GAIN.
I DO. WANT TO BE. DRAMATIC.
WELL, YOU'RE VERY GOOD AT IT.
THIS ONE. THIS IS THE ONE YOU WANT.
HUX ADVISORS LLC?
WHY?
IT'S AN ANAGRAM FOR ALDRICH LUX VOSS.
I'M GOOD AT THAT KIND OF THING.
OKAY. NOW I'M IMPRESSED.
WHAT? WHAT'S WRONG?
THAT'S WHERE YELENA WENT THIS EVENING.
CAN I COME?
ABSOLUTELY NOT!
BUT I HELPED!
YES. CONGRATULATIONS.
DAMN.

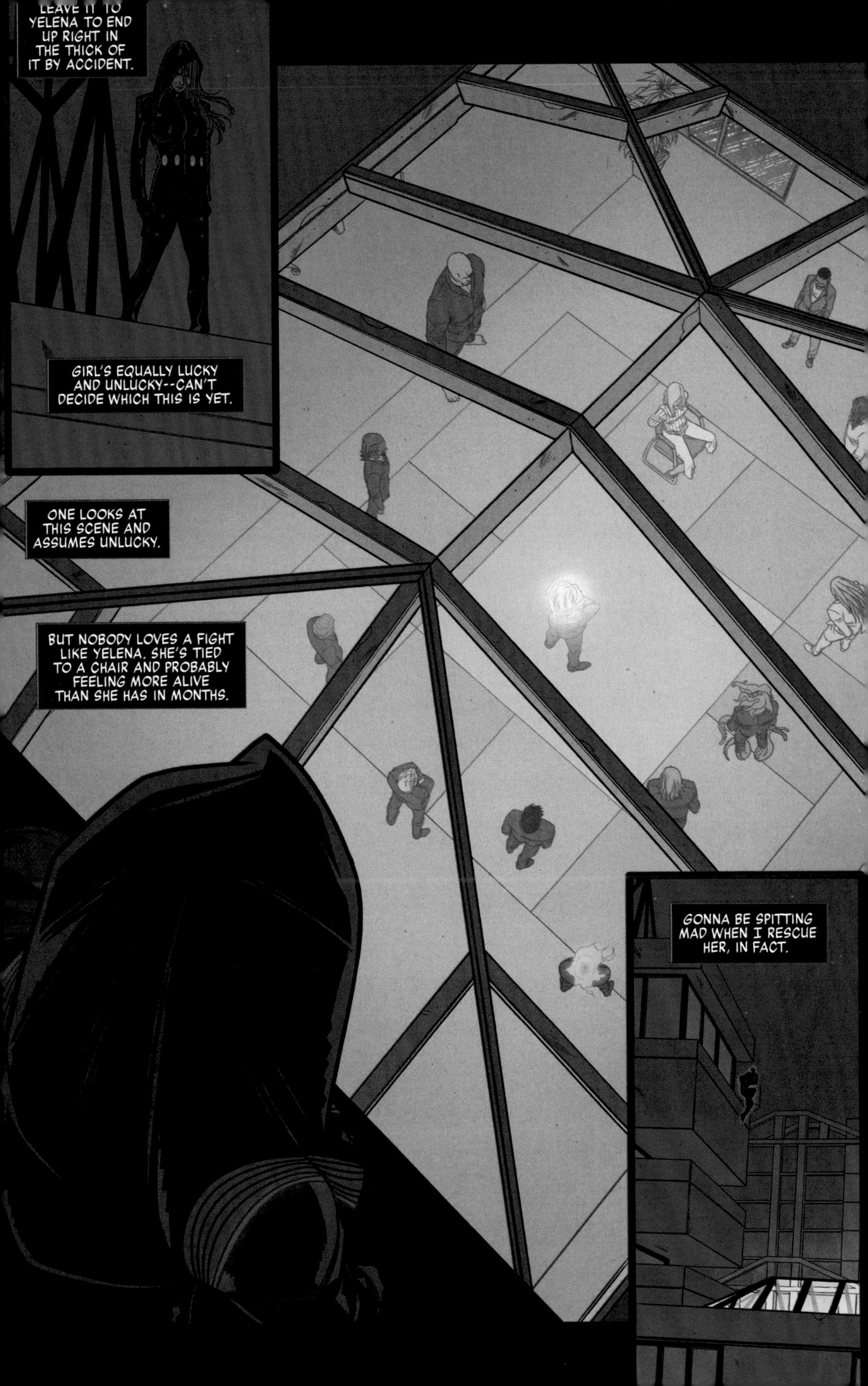
LEAVE IT TO YELENA TO END UP RIGHT IN THE THICK OF IT BY ACCIDENT.
GIRL'S EQUALLY LUCKY AND UNLUCKY--CAN'T DECIDE WHICH THIS IS YET.
ONE LOOKS AT THIS SCENE AND ASSUMES UNLUCKY.
BUT NOBODY LOVES A FIGHT LIKE YELENA. SHE'S TIED TO A CHAIR AND PROBABLY FEELING MORE ALIVE THAN SHE HAS IN MONTHS.
GONNA BE SPITTING MAD WHEN I RESCUE HER, IN FACT.

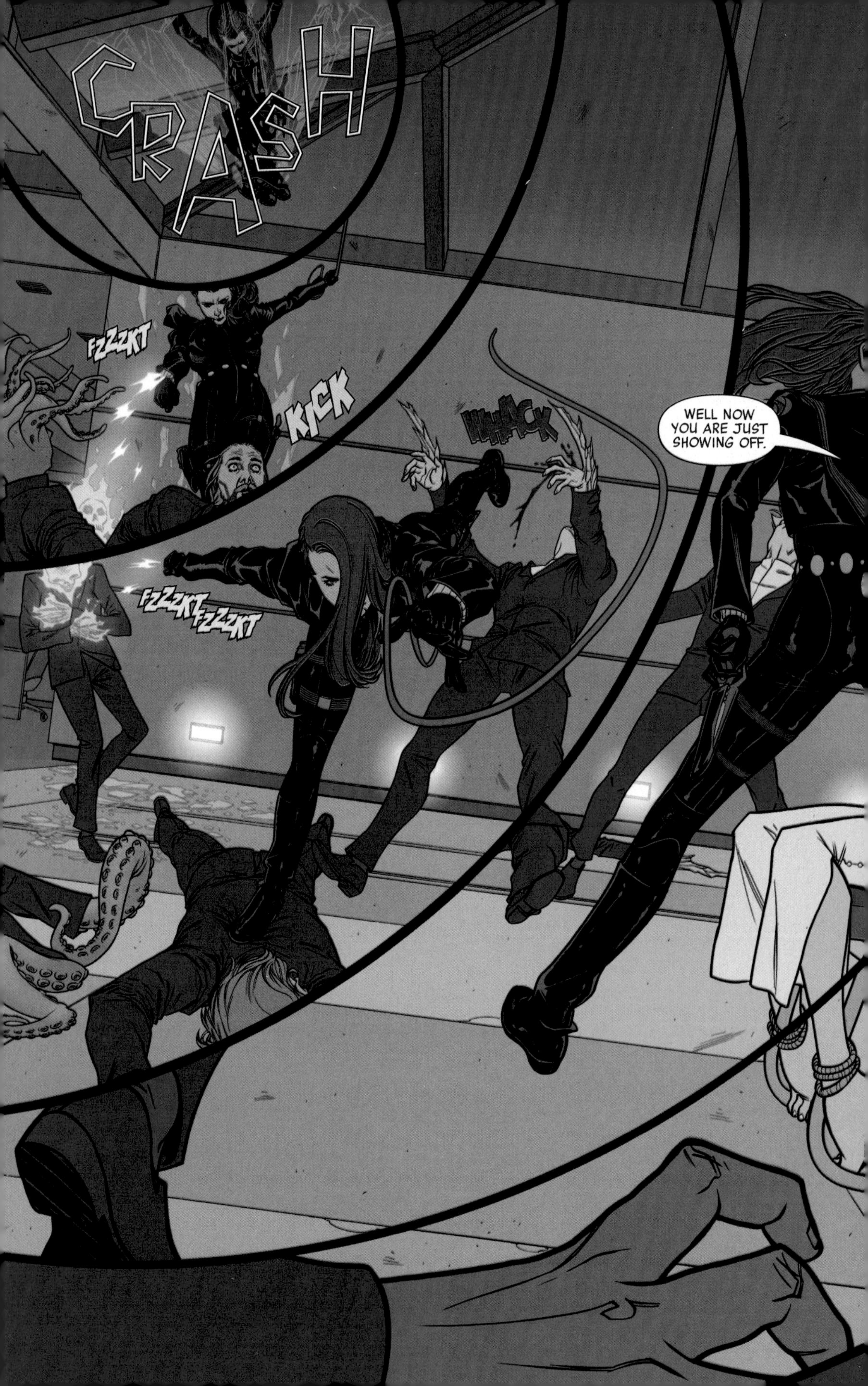
CRASH
FZZZKT
KICK
WHACK
WELL NOW YOU ARE JUST SHOWING OFF.
FZZZKT FZZZKT

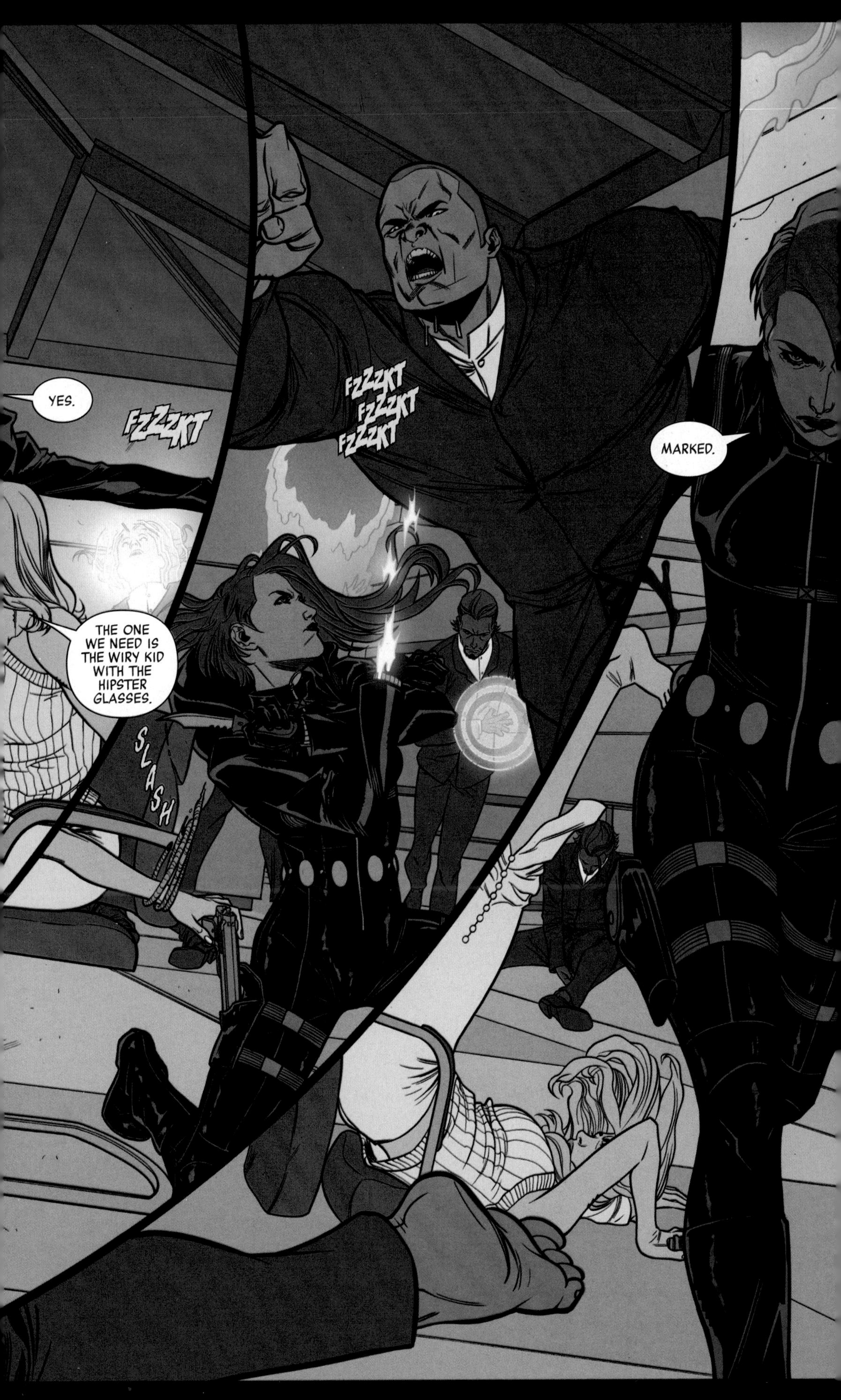
YES.
FZZZKT
FZZZKT
FZZZKT
FZZZKT
MARKED.
THE ONE WE NEED IS THE WIRY KID WITH THE HIPSTER GLASSES.
SLASH

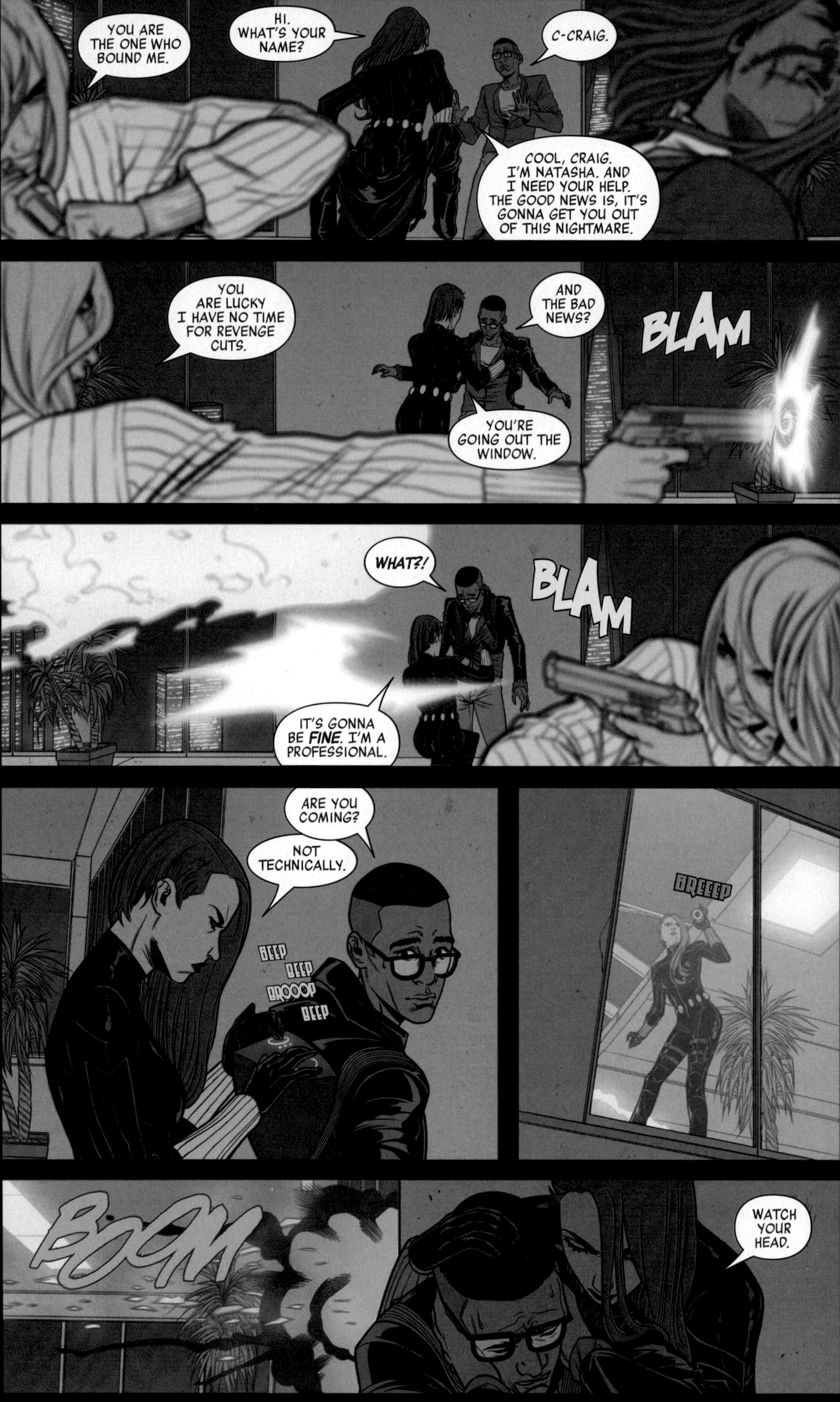
YOU ARE THE ONE WHO BOUND ME.
HI. WHAT'S YOUR NAME?
C-CRAIG.
COOL, CRAIG. I'M NATASHA. AND I NEED YOUR HELP. THE GOOD NEWS IS, IT'S GONNA GET YOU OUT OF THIS NIGHTMARE.
YOU ARE LUCKY I HAVE NO TIME FOR REVENGE CUTS.
AND THE BAD NEWS?
YOU'RE GOING OUT THE WINDOW.
BLAM
WHAT?!
BLAM
IT'S GONNA BE *FINE*. I'M A PROFESSIONAL.
ARE YOU COMING?
NOT TECHNICALLY.
BEEP
BEEP
BROOOP
BEEP
BREEEP
BOOM
WATCH YOUR HEAD.

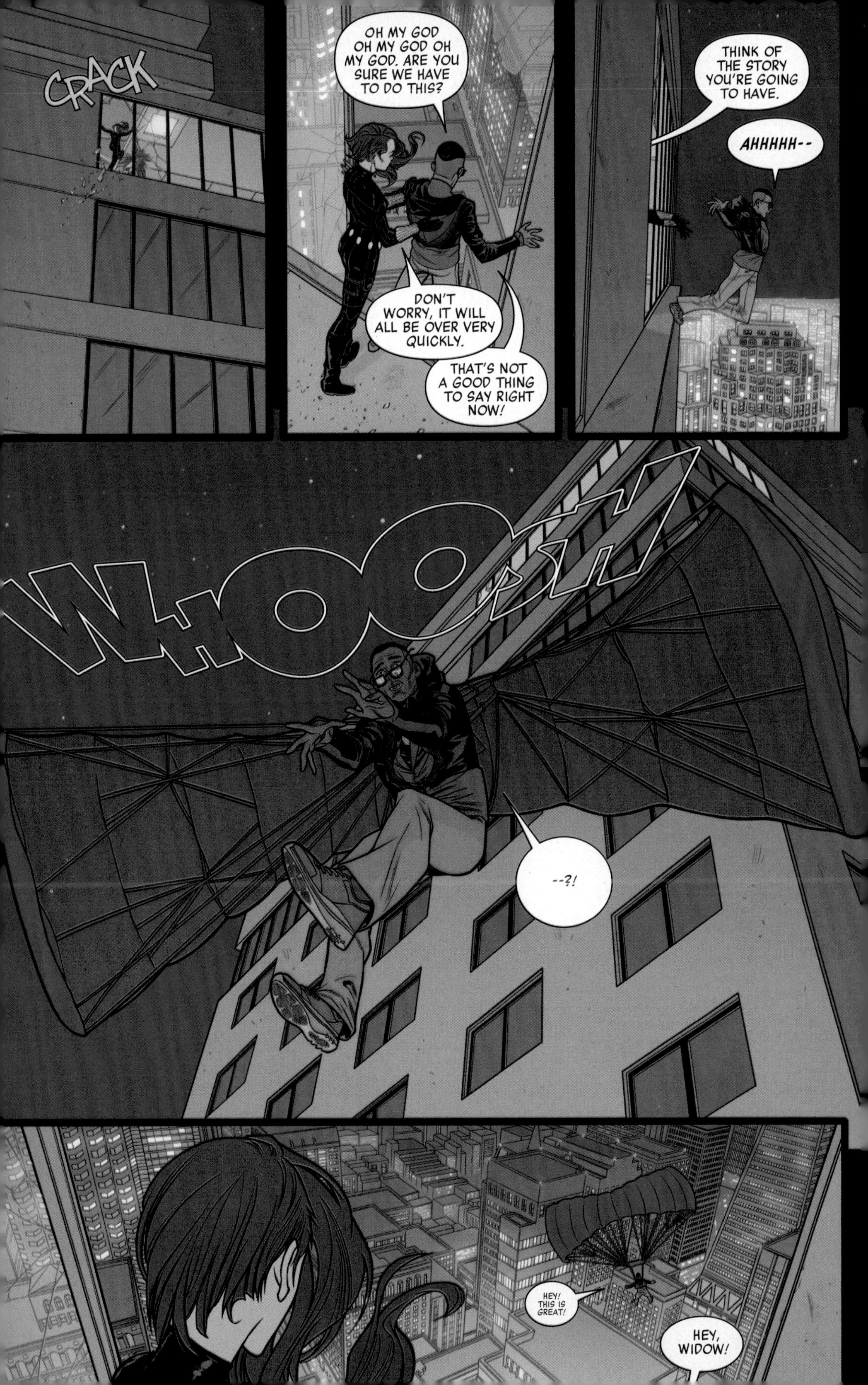
CRACK
OH MY GOD OH MY GOD OH MY GOD. ARE YOU SURE WE HAVE TO DO THIS?
DON'T WORRY, IT WILL ALL BE OVER VERY QUICKLY.
THAT'S NOT A GOOD THING TO SAY RIGHT NOW!
THINK OF THE STORY YOU'RE GOING TO HAVE.
AHHHHH--
WHOOSH
--?!
HEY! THIS IS GREAT!
HEY, WIDOW!

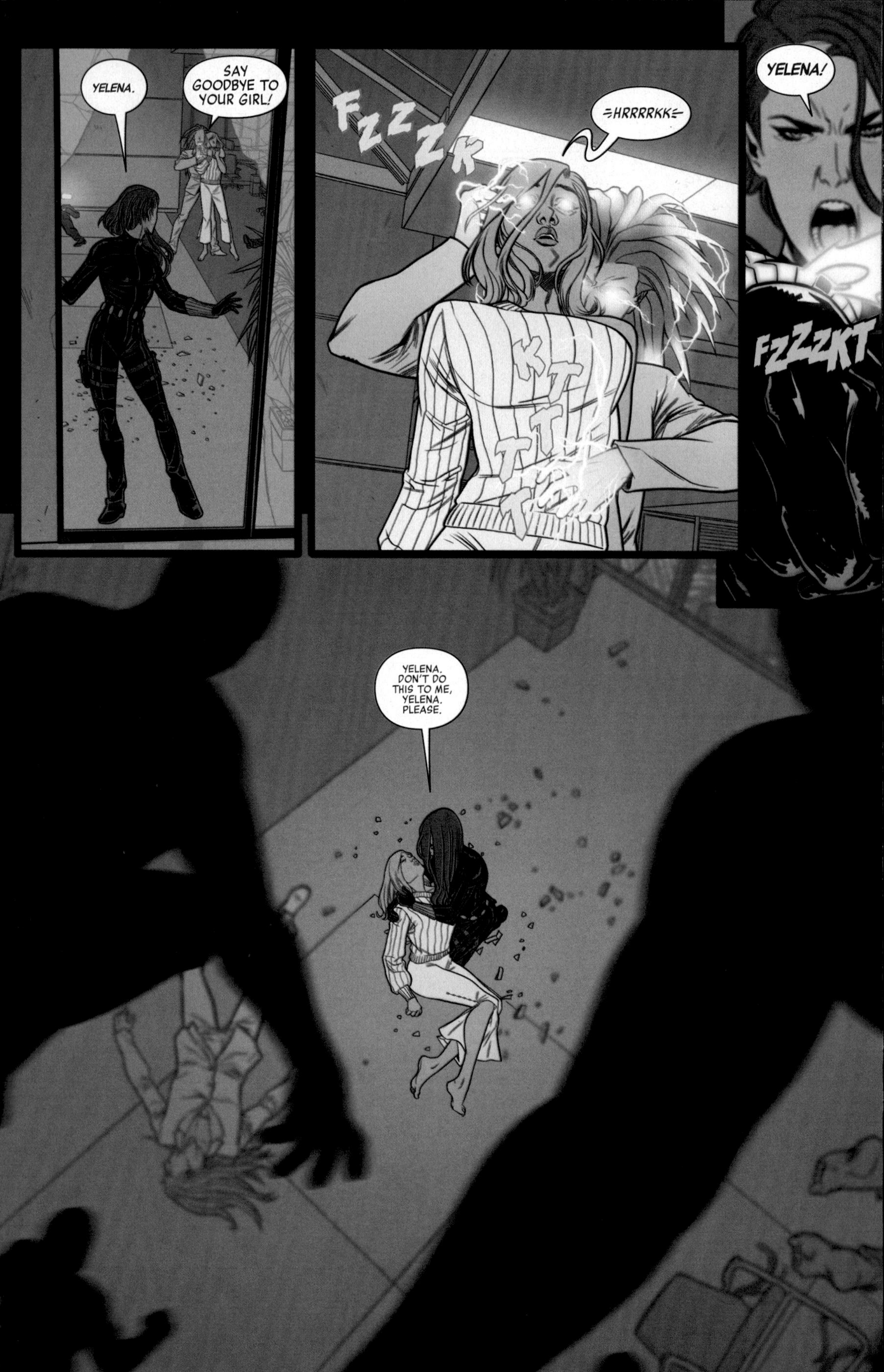
YELENA.
SAY GOODBYE TO YOUR GIRL!
FZZZK
=HRRRRKK=
KTTTTT
YELENA!
FZZZKT
YELENA. DON'T DO THIS TO ME, YELENA. PLEASE.

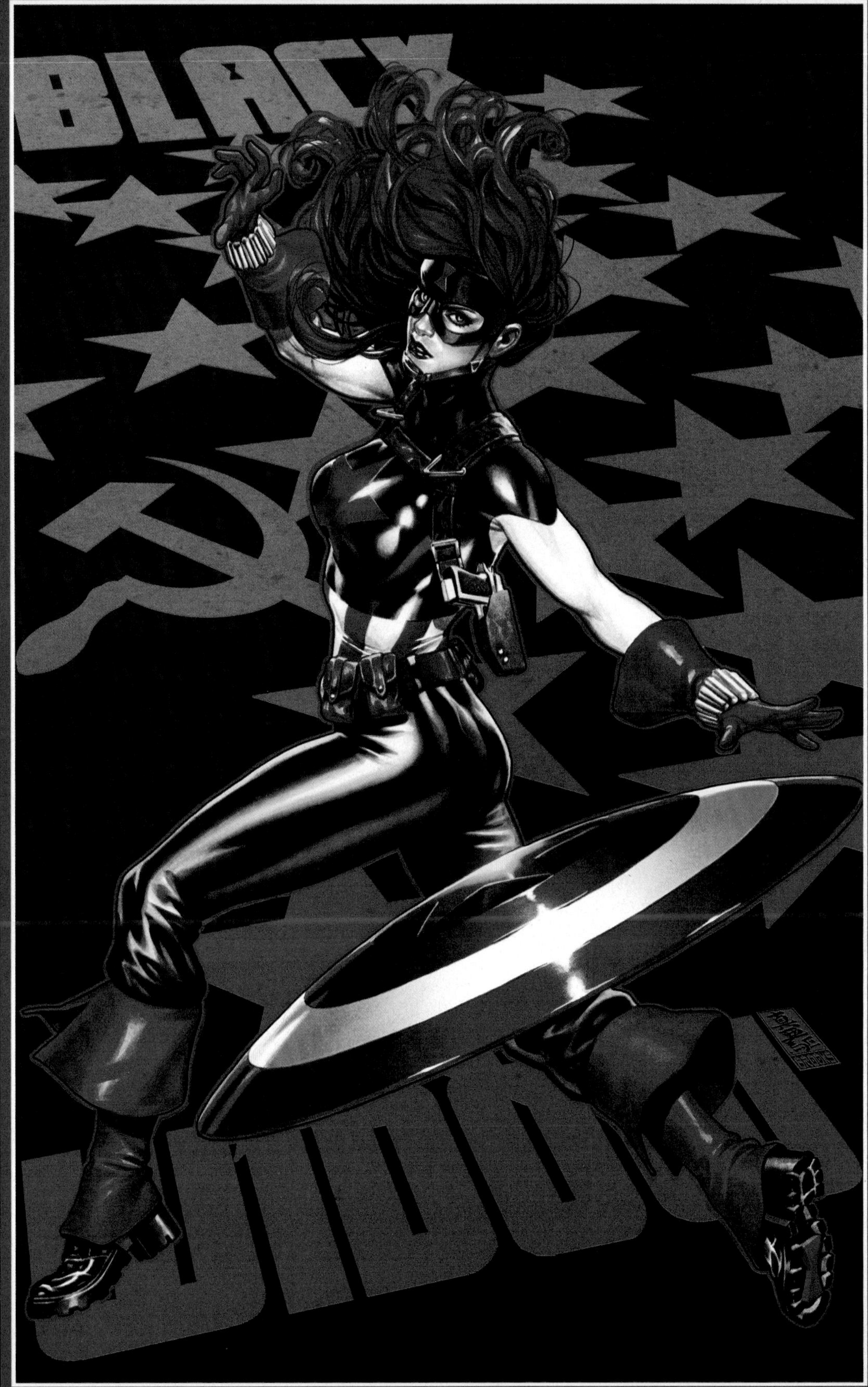

#3 CAPTAIN AMERICA VARIANT BY MARK BROOKS

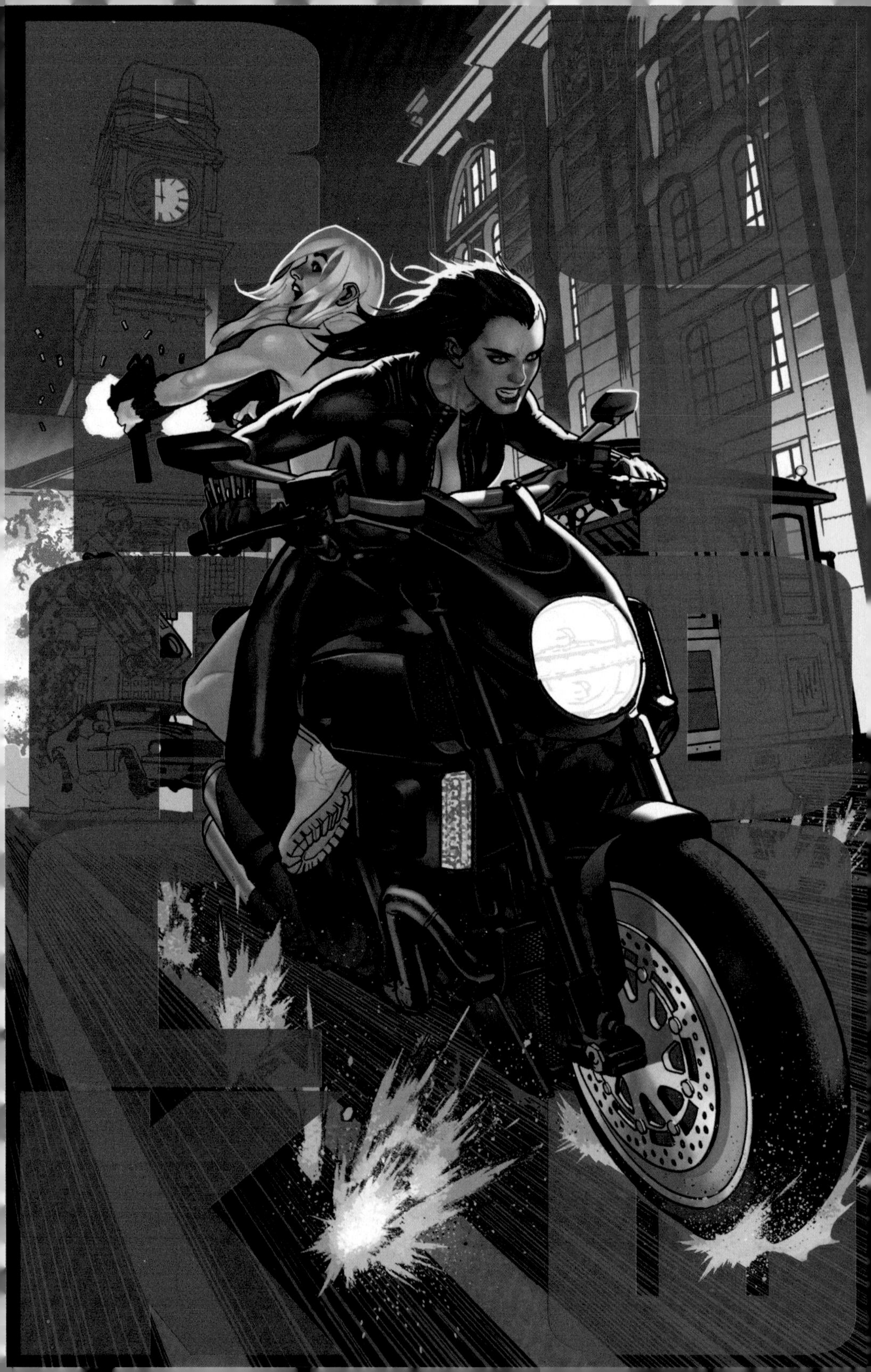

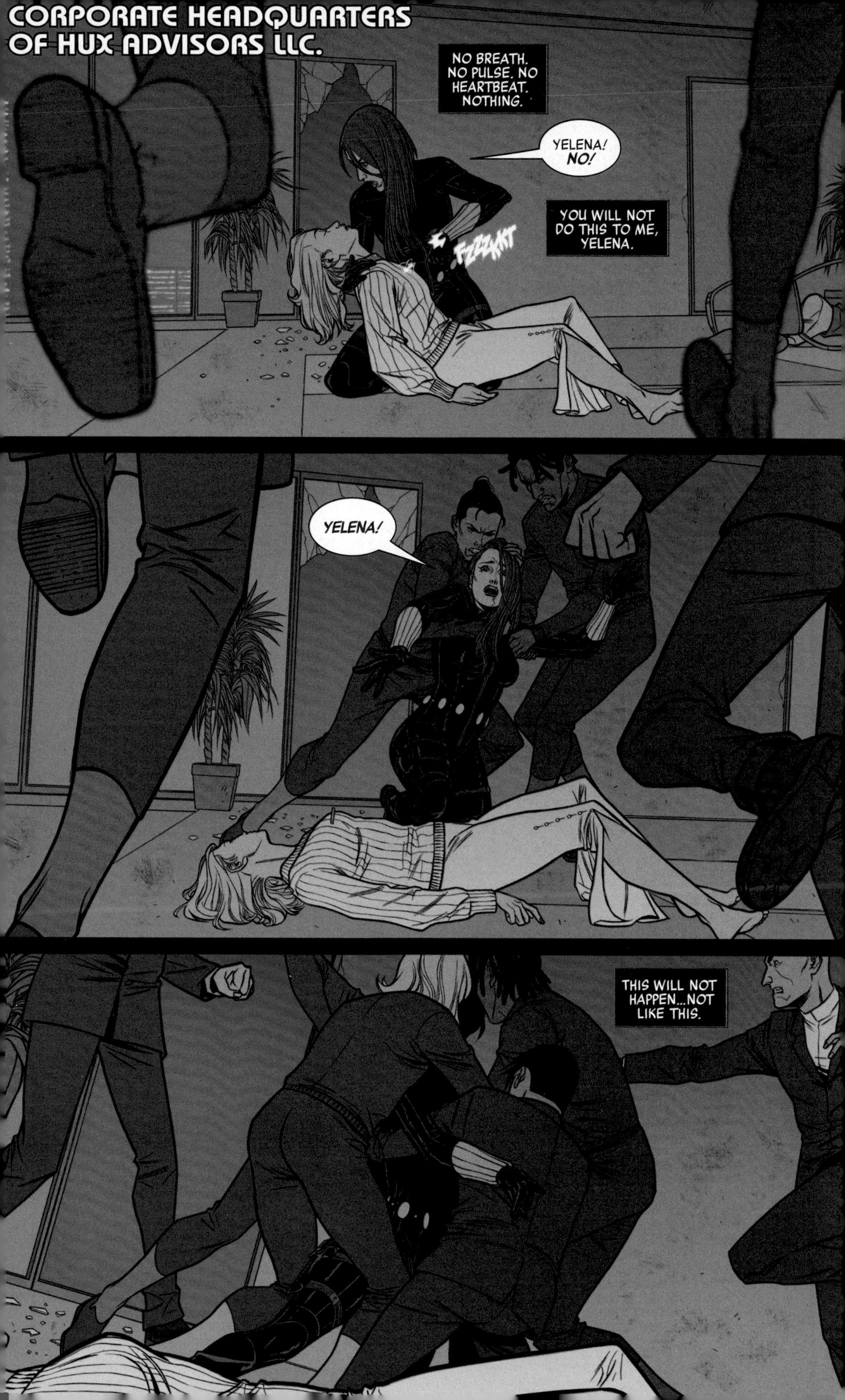
CORPORATE HEADQUARTERS OF HUX ADVISORS LLC.
NO BREATH. NO PULSE. NO HEARTBEAT. NOTHING.
YELENA! NO!
YOU WILL NOT DO THIS TO ME, YELENA.
FZZZZAKT
YELENA!
THIS WILL NOT HAPPEN...NOT LIKE THIS.

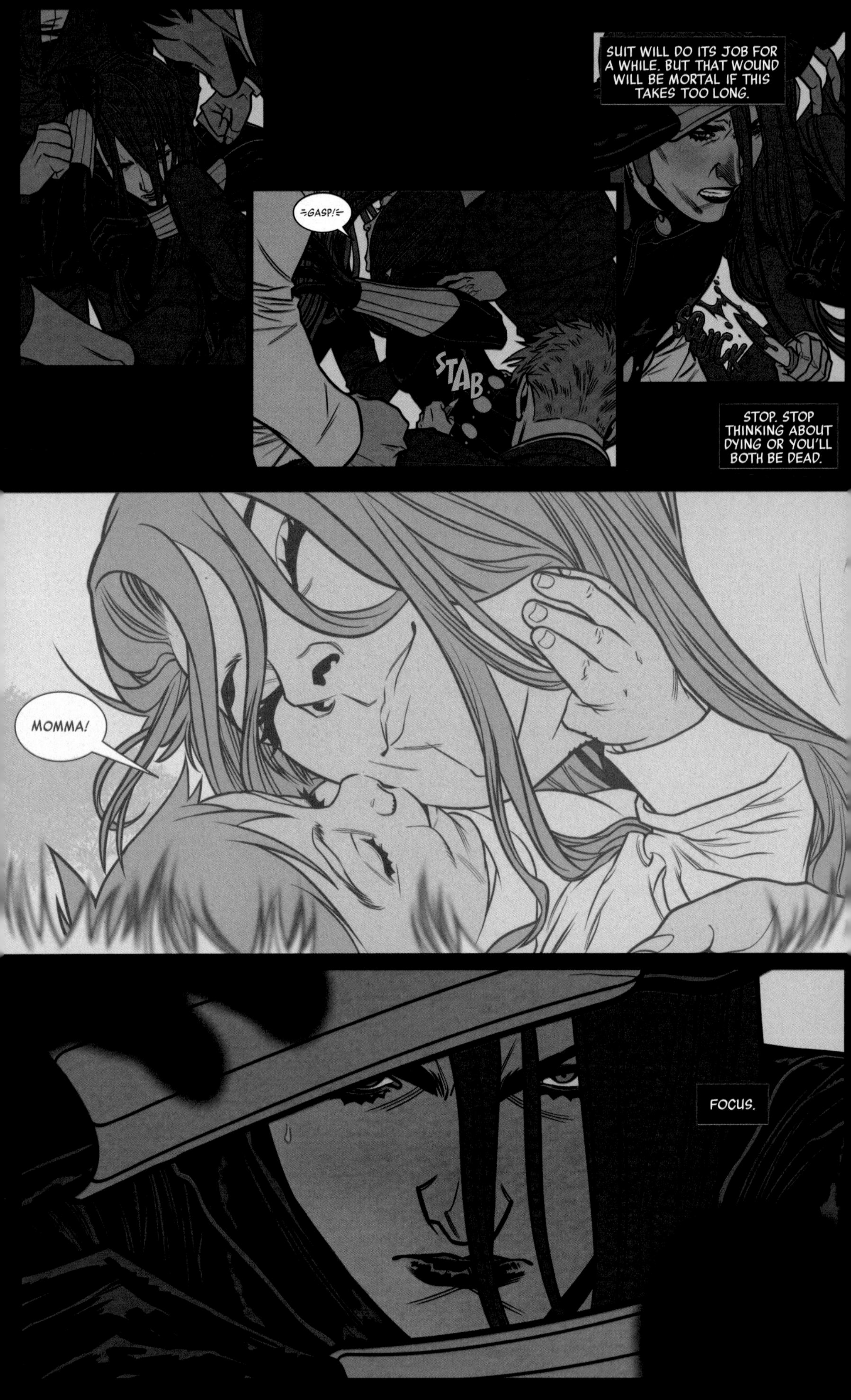

SUIT WILL DO ITS JOB FOR A WHILE. BUT THAT WOUND WILL BE MORTAL IF THIS TAKES TOO LONG.
=GASP!=
STAB
SHUNK!
STOP. STOP THINKING ABOUT DYING OR YOU'LL BOTH BE DEAD.
MOMMA!
FOCUS.

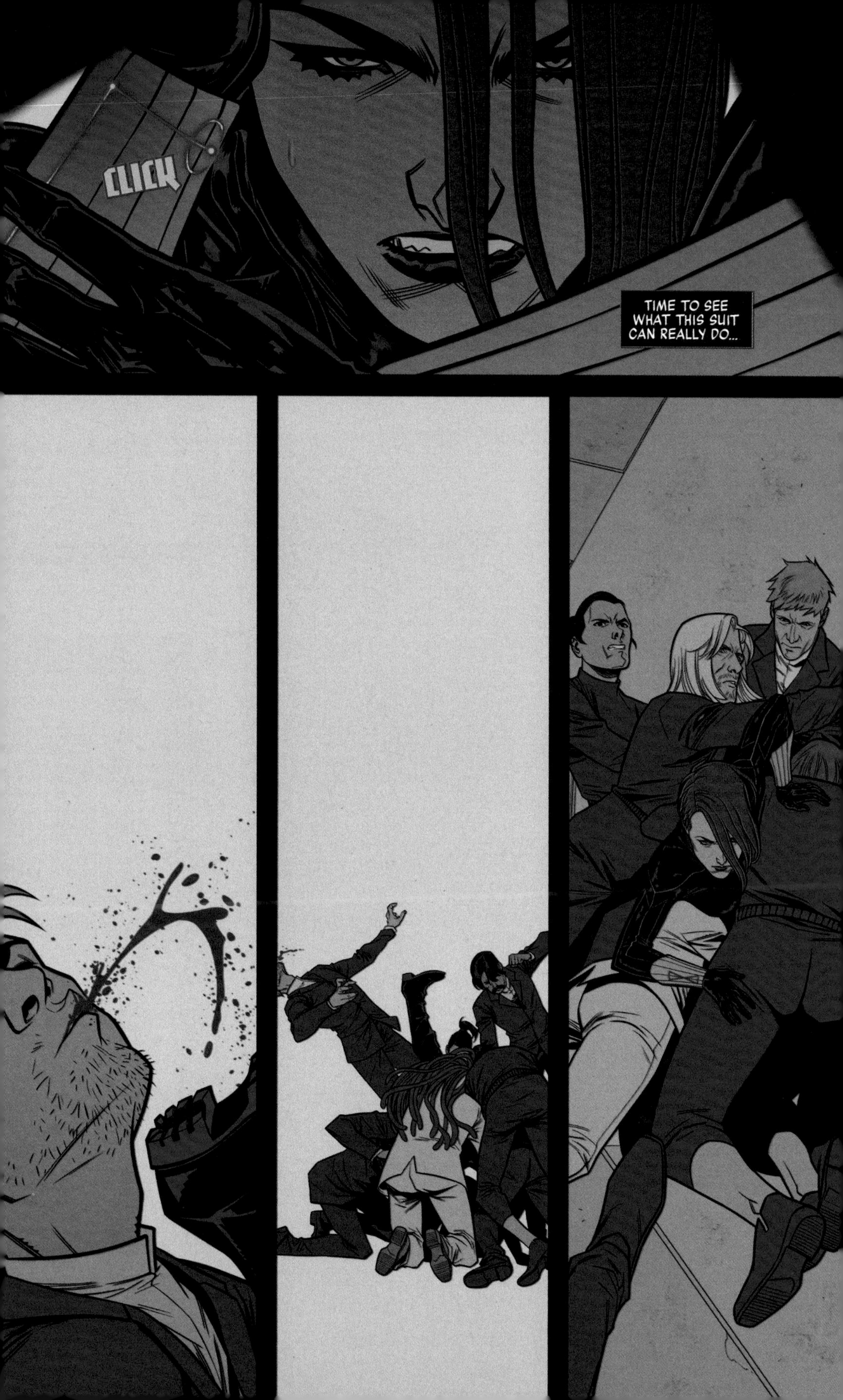
CLICK
TIME TO SEE WHAT THIS SUIT CAN REALLY DO...

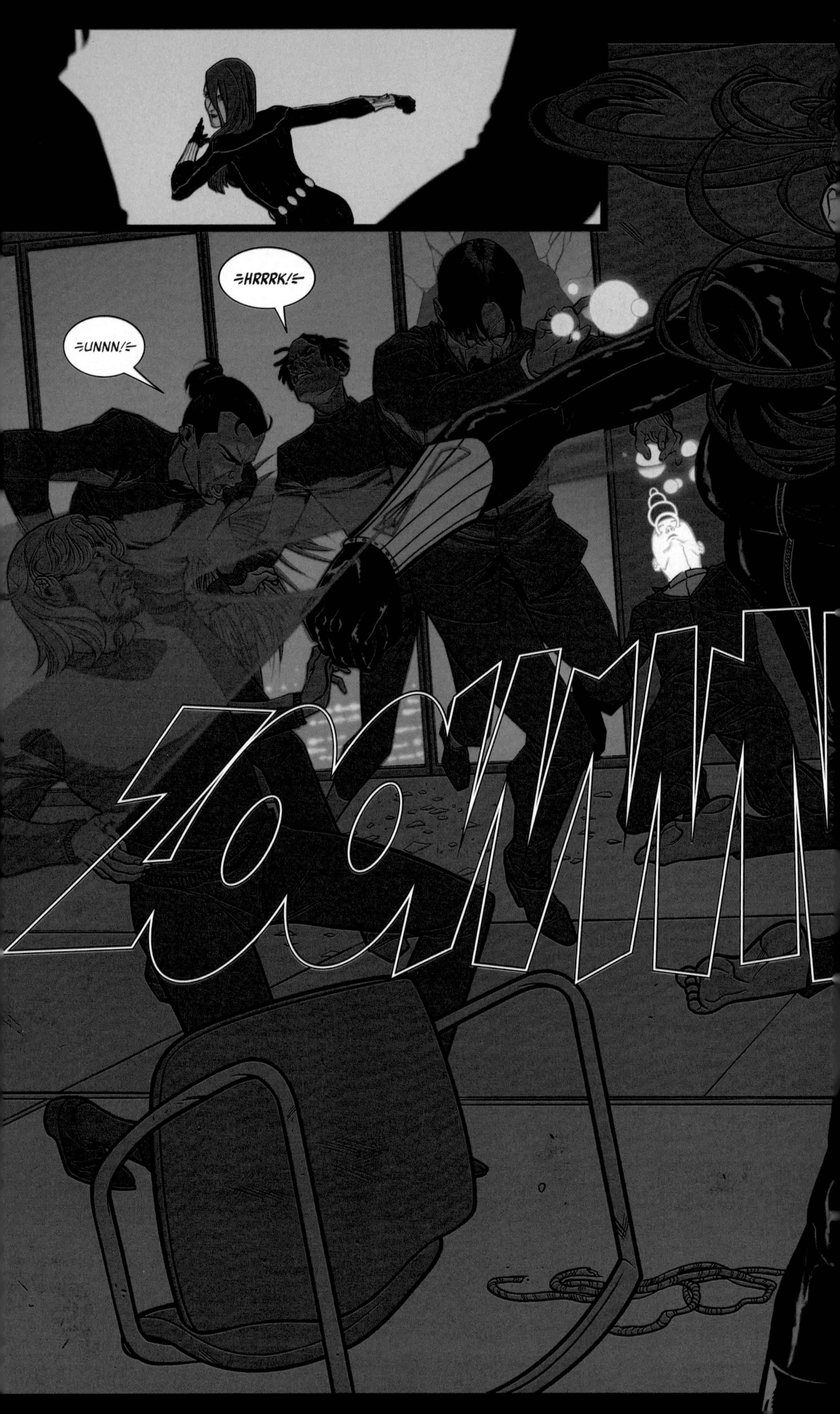

UNNN!
HRRRK!
WOOMMM

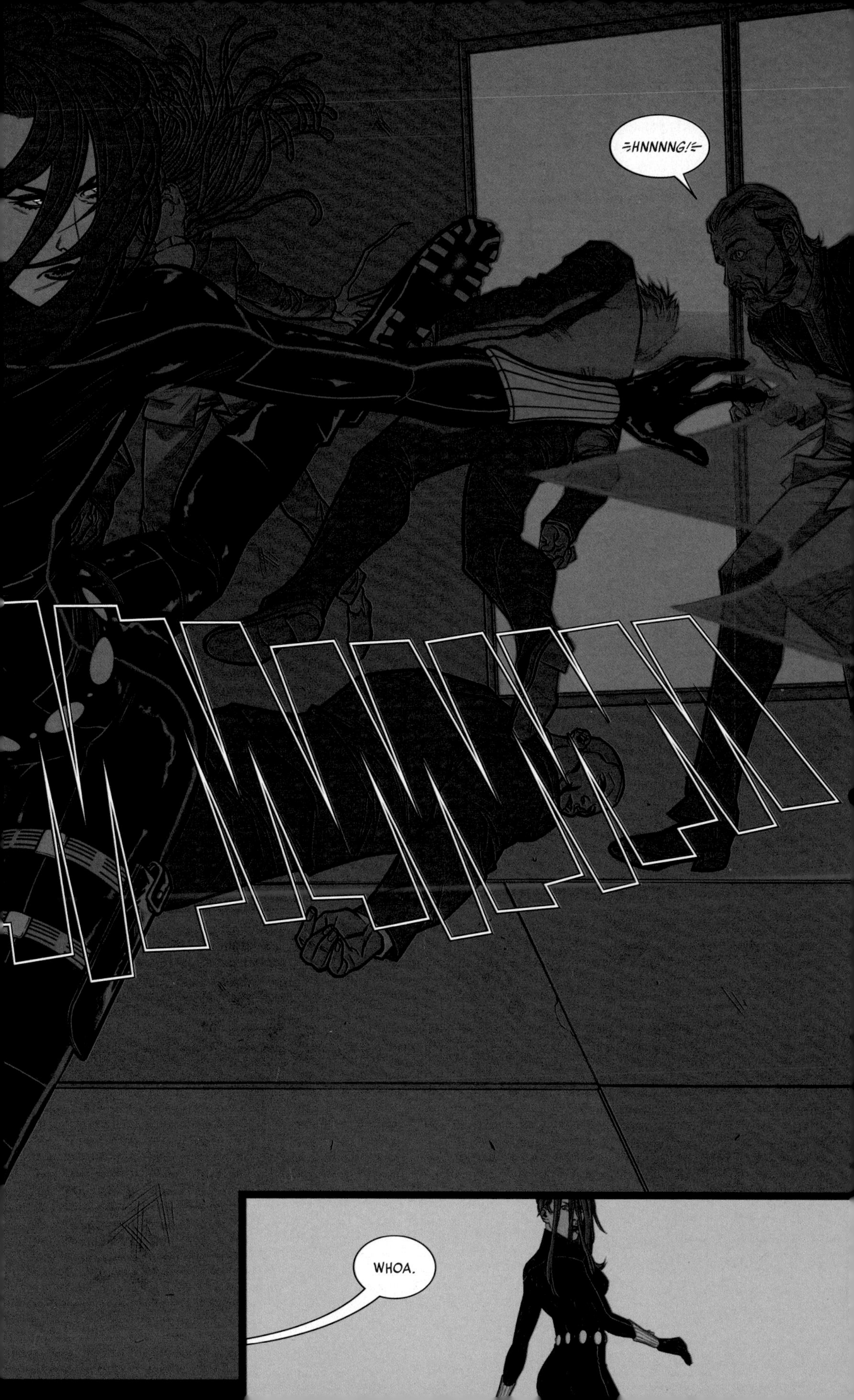
=HNNNNG!=
WHOA.

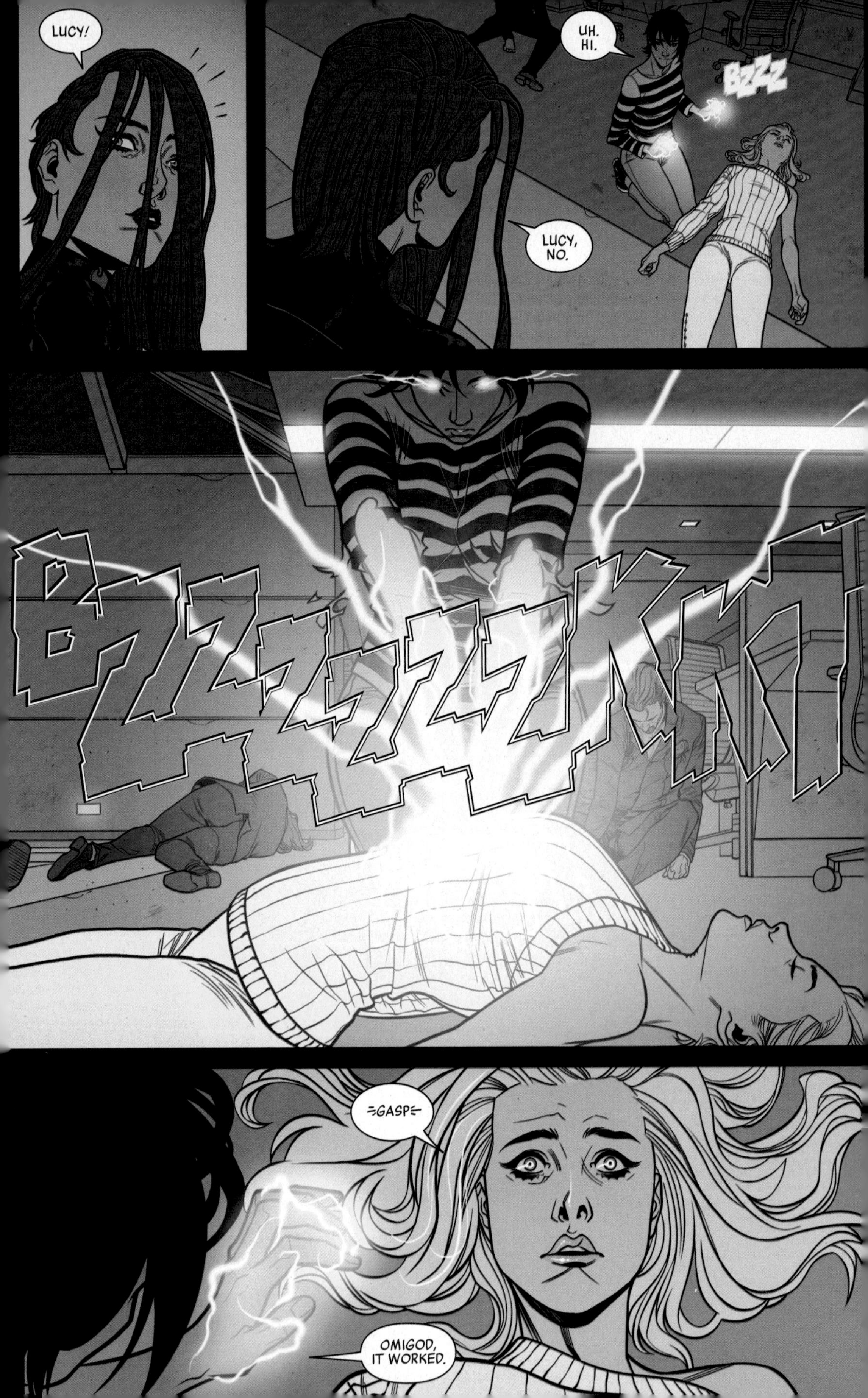
LUCY!
UH. HI.
BZZZ
LUCY, NO.
BZZZZZZZZKKT
=GASP=
OMIGOD, IT WORKED.

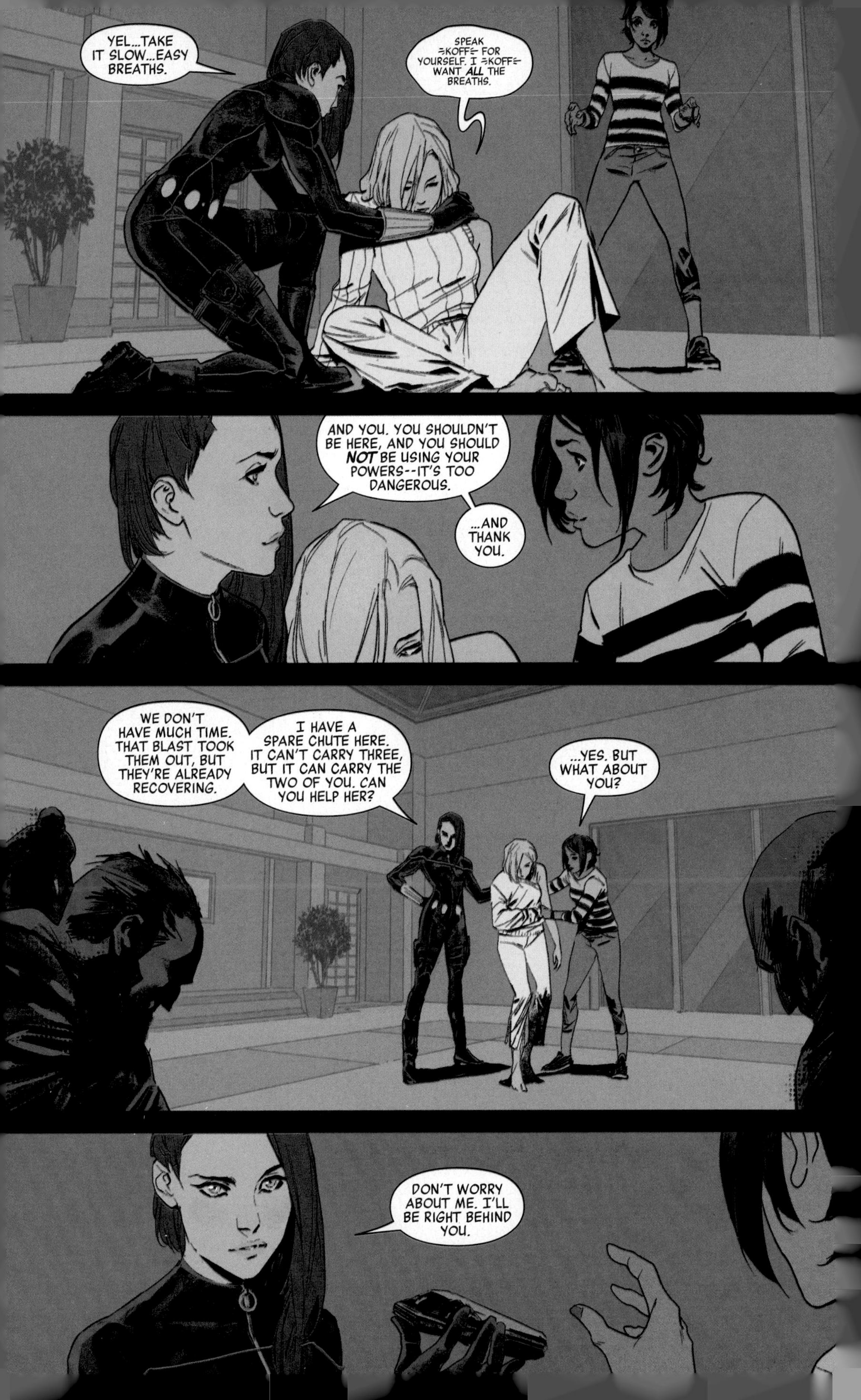
YEL...TAKE IT SLOW...EASY BREATHS.
SPEAK =KOFF= FOR YOURSELF. I =KOFF= WANT ALL THE BREATHS.
AND YOU. YOU SHOULDN'T BE HERE, AND YOU SHOULD NOT BE USING YOUR POWERS--IT'S TOO DANGEROUS.
...AND THANK YOU.
WE DON'T HAVE MUCH TIME. THAT BLAST TOOK THEM OUT, BUT THEY'RE ALREADY RECOVERING.
I HAVE A SPARE CHUTE HERE. IT CAN'T CARRY THREE, BUT IT CAN CARRY THE TWO OF YOU. CAN YOU HELP HER?
...YES. BUT WHAT ABOUT YOU?
DON'T WORRY ABOUT ME. I'LL BE RIGHT BEHIND YOU.

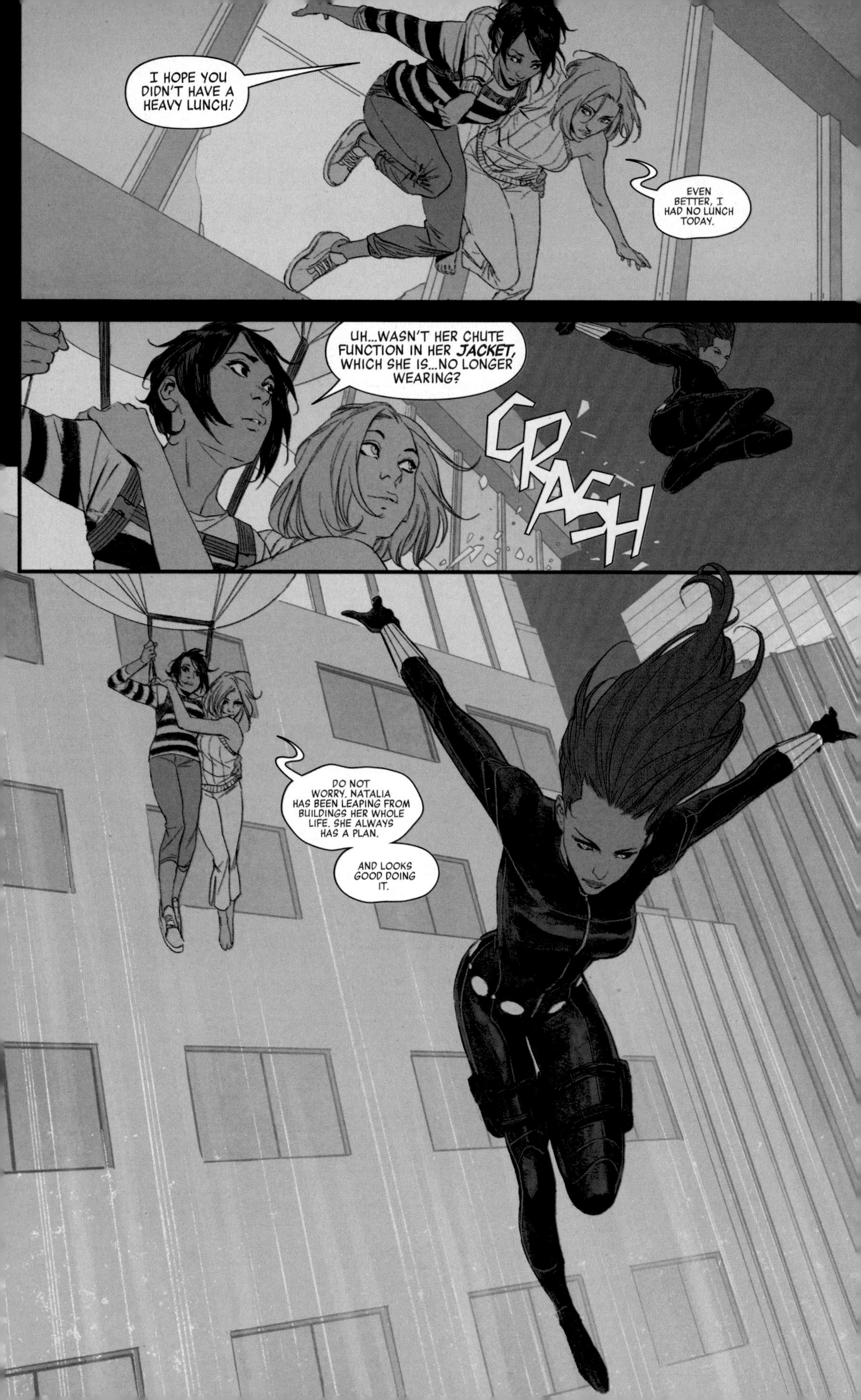
I HOPE YOU DIDN'T HAVE A HEAVY LUNCH!
EVEN BETTER, I HAD NO LUNCH TODAY.
UH...WASN'T HER CHUTE FUNCTION IN HER JACKET, WHICH SHE IS...NO LONGER WEARING?
CRASH
DO NOT WORRY. NATALIA HAS BEEN LEAPING FROM BUILDINGS HER WHOLE LIFE. SHE ALWAYS HAS A PLAN.
AND LOOKS GOOD DOING IT.

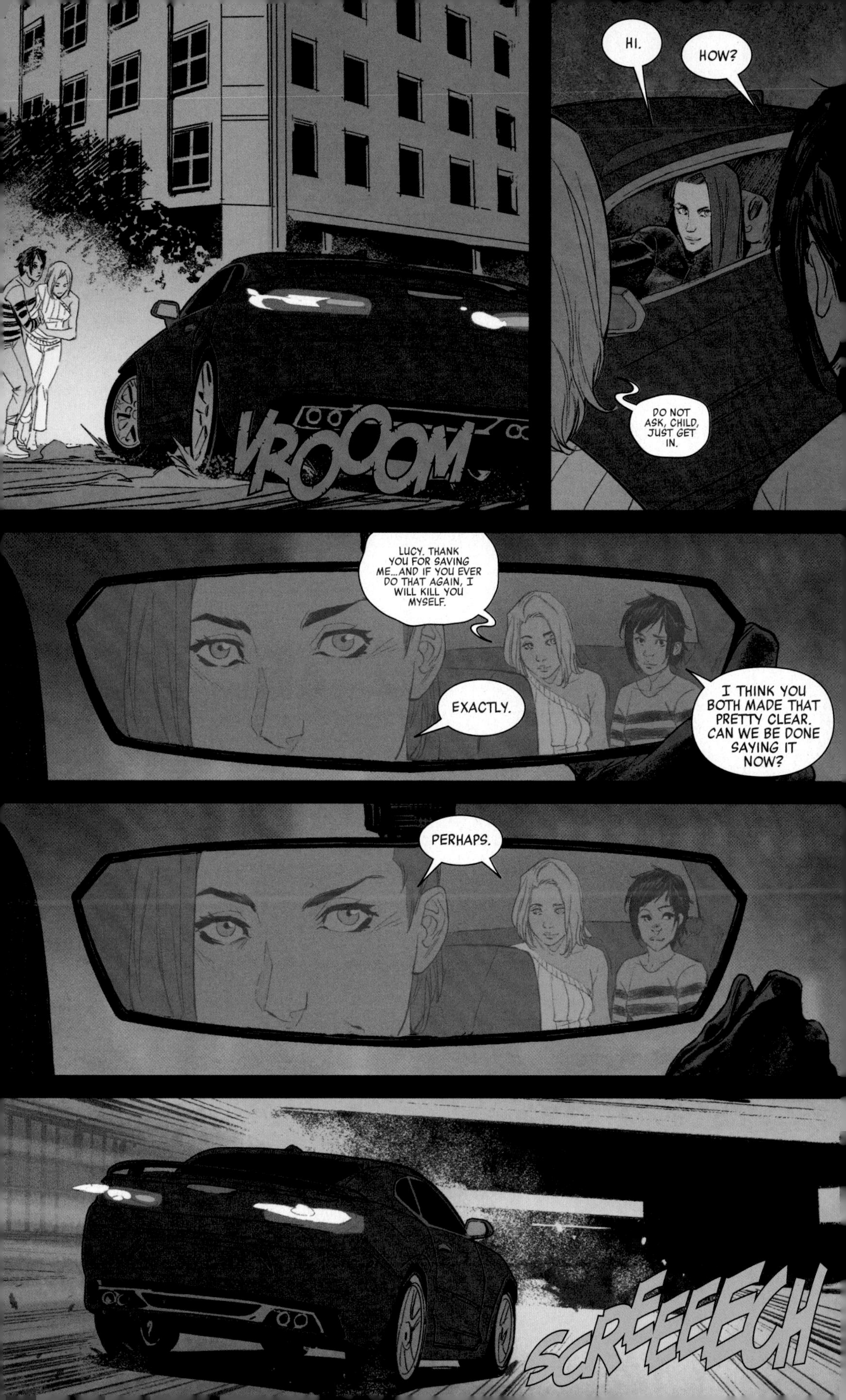
VROOOM
HI.
HOW?
DO NOT ASK, CHILD, JUST GET IN.
LUCY. THANK YOU FOR SAVING ME...AND IF YOU EVER DO THAT AGAIN, I WILL KILL YOU MYSELF.
EXACTLY.
I THINK YOU BOTH MADE THAT PRETTY CLEAR. CAN WE BE DONE SAYING IT NOW?
PERHAPS.
SCREEEECH

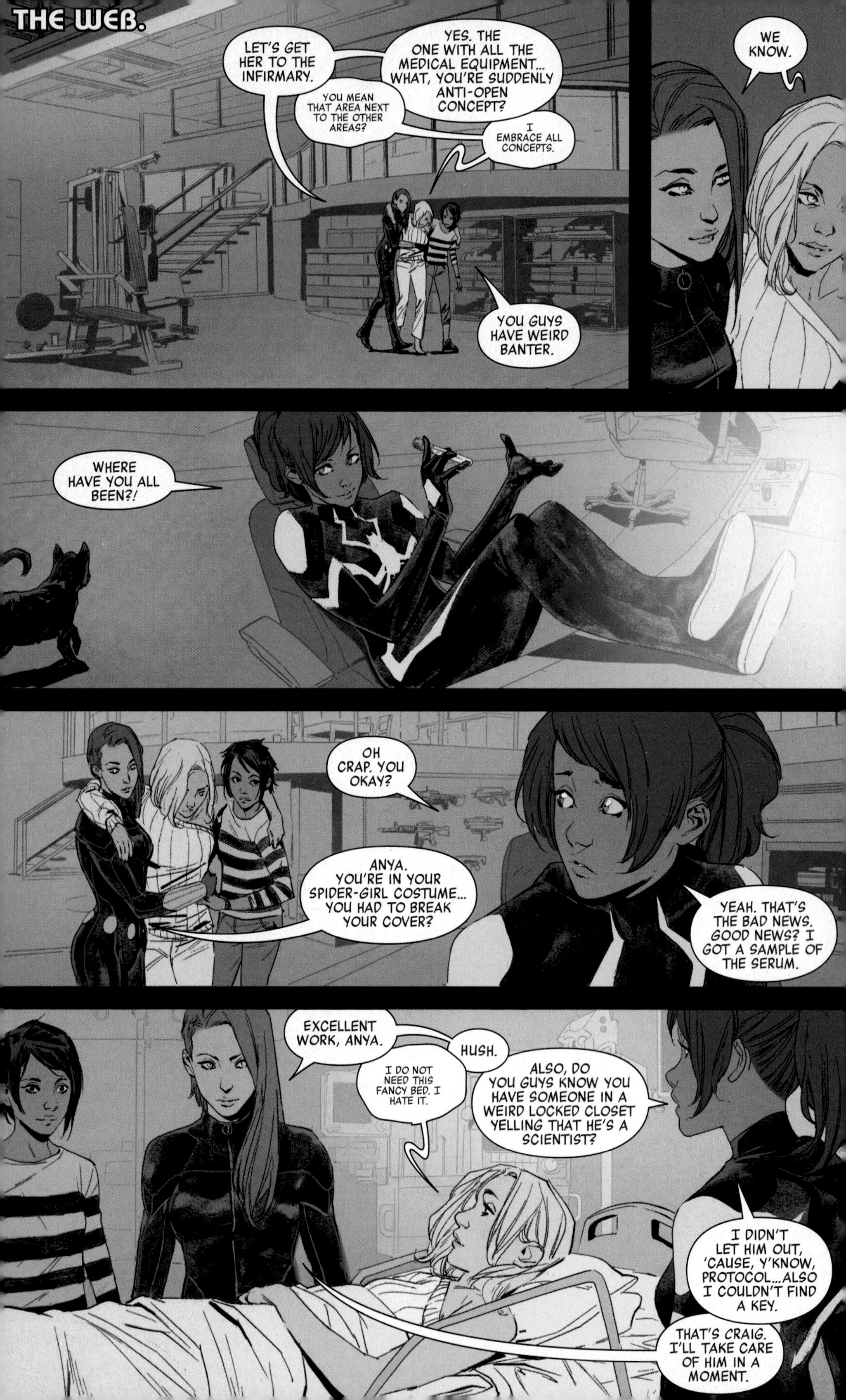
THE WEB.
LET'S GET HER TO THE INFIRMARY.
YES. THE ONE WITH ALL THE MEDICAL EQUIPMENT... WHAT, YOU'RE SUDDENLY ANTI-OPEN CONCEPT?
YOU MEAN THAT AREA NEXT TO THE OTHER AREAS?
I EMBRACE ALL CONCEPTS.
YOU GUYS HAVE WEIRD BANTER.
WE KNOW.
WHERE HAVE YOU ALL BEEN?!
OH CRAP. YOU OKAY?
ANYA. YOU'RE IN YOUR SPIDER-GIRL COSTUME... YOU HAD TO BREAK YOUR COVER?
YEAH. THAT'S THE BAD NEWS. GOOD NEWS? I GOT A SAMPLE OF THE SERUM.
EXCELLENT WORK, ANYA.
HUSH.
I DO NOT NEED THIS FANCY BED. I HATE IT.
ALSO, DO YOU GUYS KNOW YOU HAVE SOMEONE IN A WEIRD LOCKED CLOSET YELLING THAT HE'S A SCIENTIST?
I DIDN'T LET HIM OUT, 'CAUSE, Y'KNOW, PROTOCOL...ALSO I COULDN'T FIND A KEY.
THAT'S CRAIG. I'LL TAKE CARE OF HIM IN A MOMENT.

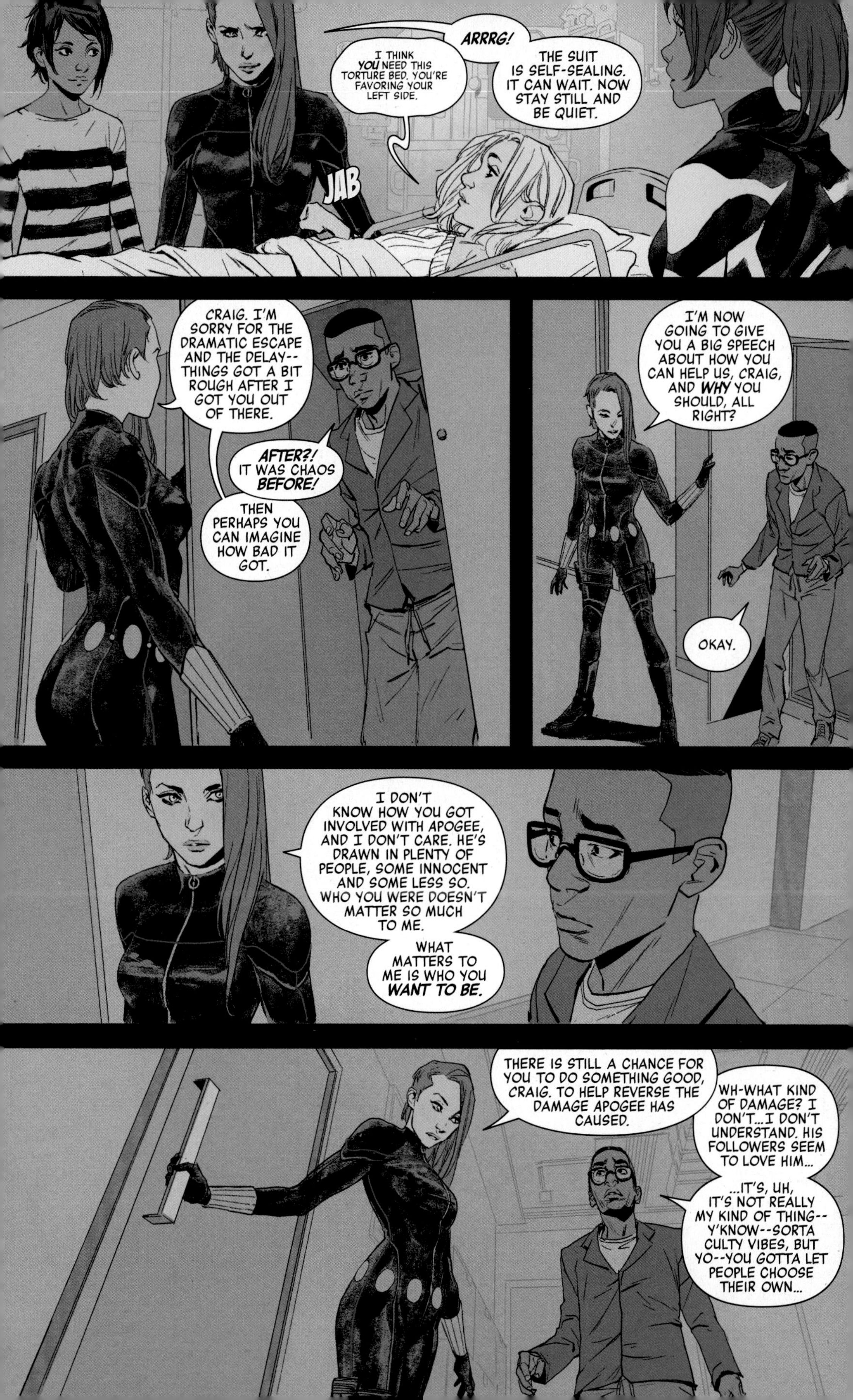

I THINK *YOU* NEED THIS TORTURE BED. YOU'RE FAVORING YOUR LEFT SIDE.
JAB
ARRRG!
THE SUIT IS SELF-SEALING. IT CAN WAIT. NOW STAY STILL AND BE QUIET.
CRAIG. I'M SORRY FOR THE DRAMATIC ESCAPE AND THE DELAY-- THINGS GOT A BIT ROUGH AFTER I GOT YOU OUT OF THERE.
AFTER?! IT WAS CHAOS *BEFORE!*
THEN PERHAPS YOU CAN IMAGINE HOW BAD IT GOT.
I'M NOW GOING TO GIVE YOU A BIG SPEECH ABOUT HOW YOU CAN HELP US, CRAIG, AND *WHY* YOU SHOULD, ALL RIGHT?
OKAY.
I DON'T KNOW HOW YOU GOT INVOLVED WITH APOGEE, AND I DON'T CARE. HE'S DRAWN IN PLENTY OF PEOPLE, SOME INNOCENT AND SOME LESS SO. WHO YOU WERE DOESN'T MATTER SO MUCH TO ME.
WHAT MATTERS TO ME IS WHO YOU *WANT TO BE.*
THERE IS STILL A CHANCE FOR YOU TO DO SOMETHING GOOD, CRAIG. TO HELP REVERSE THE DAMAGE APOGEE HAS CAUSED.
WH-WHAT KIND OF DAMAGE? I DON'T...I DON'T UNDERSTAND. HIS FOLLOWERS SEEM TO LOVE HIM...
...IT'S, UH, IT'S NOT REALLY MY KIND OF THING-- Y'KNOW--SORTA CULTY VIBES, BUT YO--YOU GOTTA LET PEOPLE CHOOSE THEIR OWN...

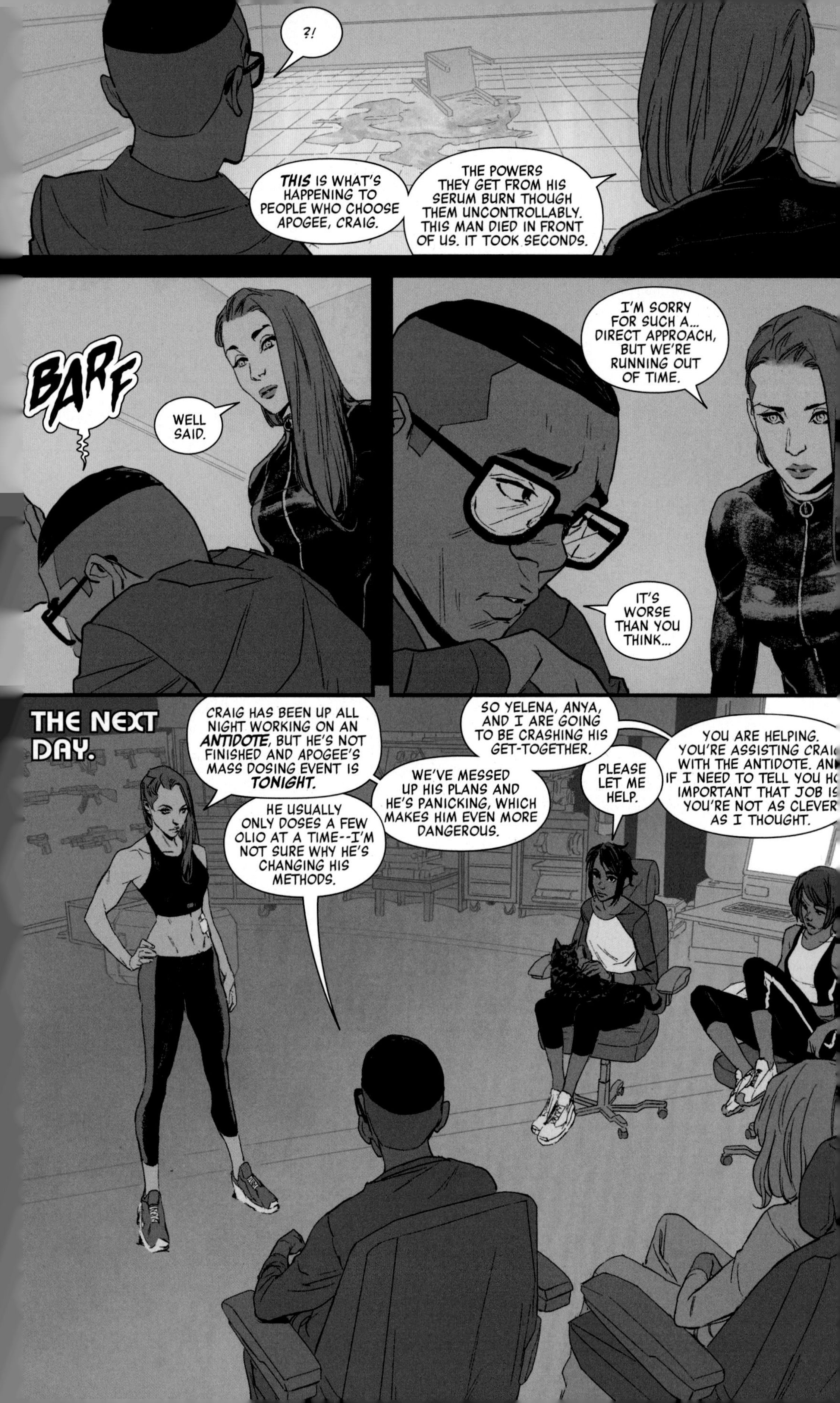
?!
THIS IS WHAT'S HAPPENING TO PEOPLE WHO CHOOSE APOGEE, CRAIG.
THE POWERS THEY GET FROM HIS SERUM BURN THOUGH THEM UNCONTROLLABLY. THIS MAN DIED IN FRONT OF US. IT TOOK SECONDS.
BARF
WELL SAID.
I'M SORRY FOR SUCH A... DIRECT APPROACH, BUT WE'RE RUNNING OUT OF TIME.
IT'S WORSE THAN YOU THINK...
THE NEXT DAY.
CRAIG HAS BEEN UP ALL NIGHT WORKING ON AN ANTIDOTE, BUT HE'S NOT FINISHED AND APOGEE'S MASS DOSING EVENT IS TONIGHT.
HE USUALLY ONLY DOSES A FEW OLIO AT A TIME--I'M NOT SURE WHY HE'S CHANGING HIS METHODS.
WE'VE MESSED UP HIS PLANS AND HE'S PANICKING, WHICH MAKES HIM EVEN MORE DANGEROUS.
SO YELENA, ANYA, AND I ARE GOING TO BE CRASHING HIS GET-TOGETHER.
PLEASE LET ME HELP.
YOU ARE HELPING. YOU'RE ASSISTING CRAI WITH THE ANTIDOTE. AN IF I NEED TO TELL YOU H IMPORTANT THAT JOB I YOU'RE NOT AS CLEVER AS I THOUGHT.

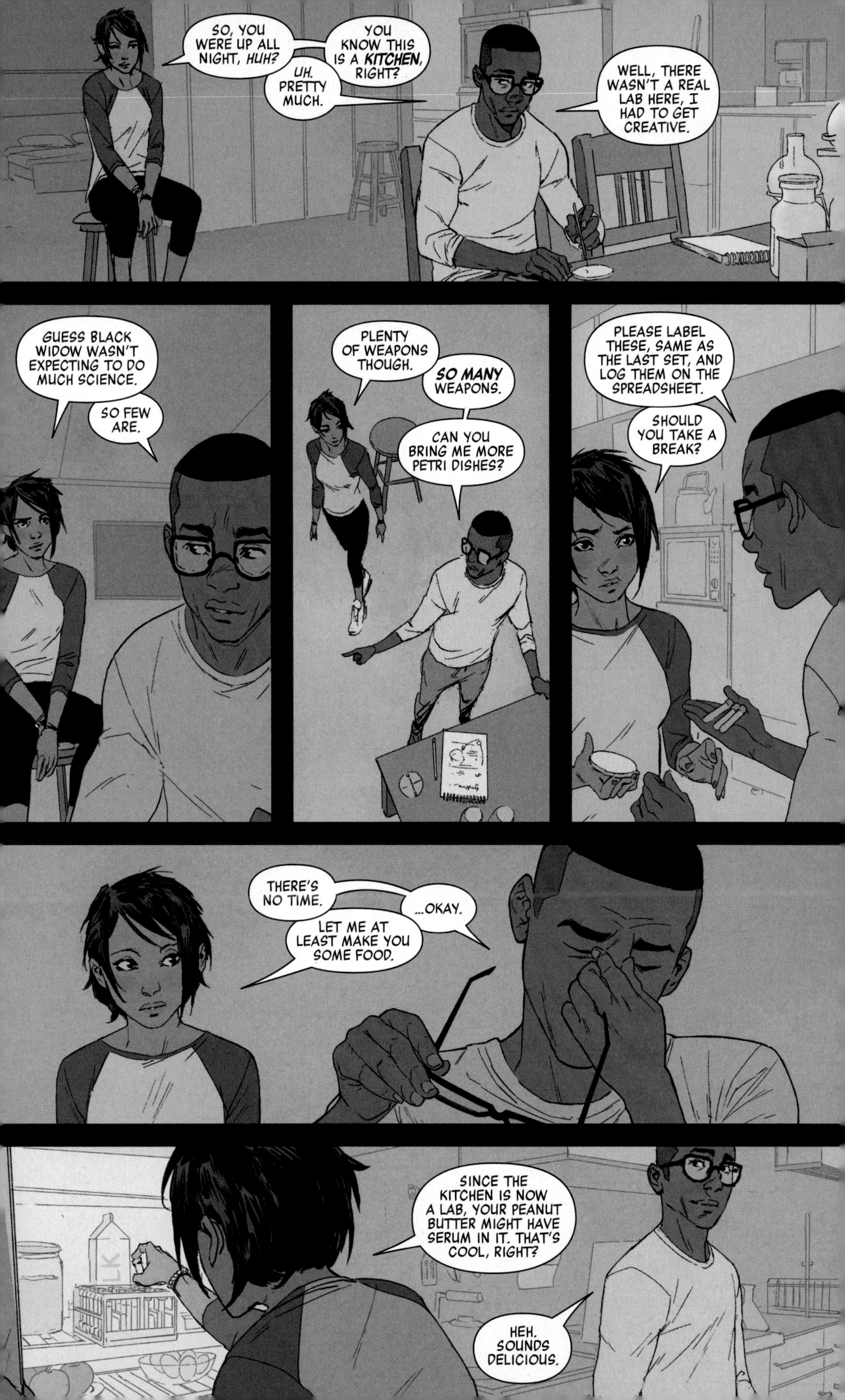
SO, YOU WERE UP ALL NIGHT, *HUH?*
UH. PRETTY MUCH.
YOU KNOW THIS IS A ***KITCHEN***, RIGHT?
WELL, THERE WASN'T A REAL LAB HERE, I HAD TO GET CREATIVE.
GUESS BLACK WIDOW WASN'T EXPECTING TO DO MUCH SCIENCE.
SO FEW ARE.
PLENTY OF WEAPONS THOUGH.
SO MANY WEAPONS.
CAN YOU BRING ME MORE PETRI DISHES?
PLEASE LABEL THESE, SAME AS THE LAST SET, AND LOG THEM ON THE SPREADSHEET.
SHOULD YOU TAKE A BREAK?
THERE'S NO TIME.
...OKAY.
LET ME AT LEAST MAKE YOU SOME FOOD.
SINCE THE KITCHEN IS NOW A LAB, YOUR PEANUT BUTTER MIGHT HAVE SERUM IN IT. THAT'S COOL, RIGHT?
HEH. SOUNDS DELICIOUS.

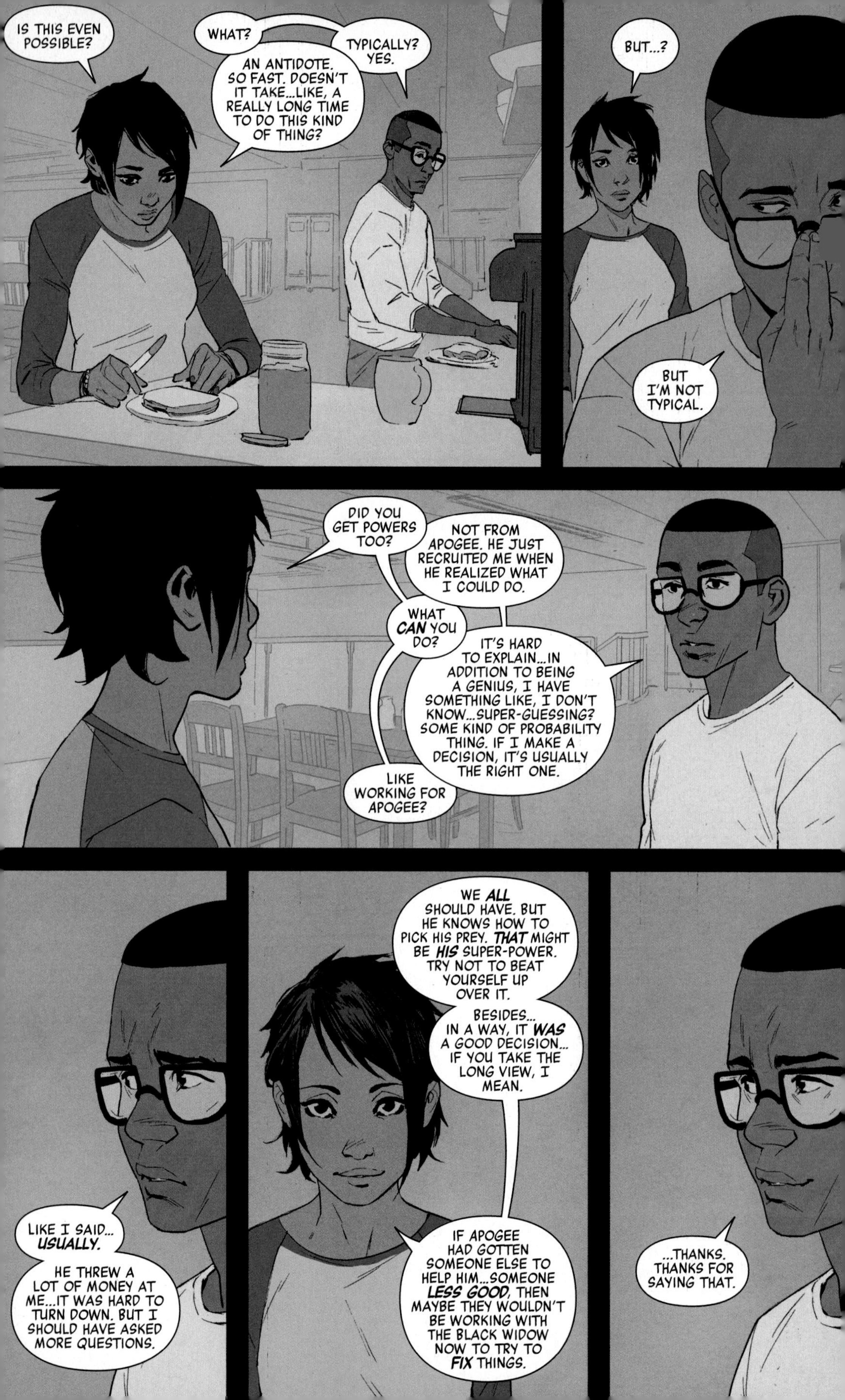
IS THIS EVEN POSSIBLE?
WHAT?
AN ANTIDOTE. SO FAST. DOESN'T IT TAKE...LIKE, A REALLY LONG TIME TO DO THIS KIND OF THING?
TYPICALLY? YES.
BUT...?
BUT I'M NOT TYPICAL.
DID YOU GET POWERS TOO?
NOT FROM APOGEE. HE JUST RECRUITED ME WHEN HE REALIZED WHAT I COULD DO.
WHAT CAN YOU DO?
IT'S HARD TO EXPLAIN...IN ADDITION TO BEING A GENIUS, I HAVE SOMETHING LIKE, I DON'T KNOW...SUPER-GUESSING? SOME KIND OF PROBABILITY THING. IF I MAKE A DECISION, IT'S USUALLY THE RIGHT ONE.
LIKE WORKING FOR APOGEE?
LIKE I SAID... USUALLY.
HE THREW A LOT OF MONEY AT ME...IT WAS HARD TO TURN DOWN. BUT I SHOULD HAVE ASKED MORE QUESTIONS.
WE ALL SHOULD HAVE. BUT HE KNOWS HOW TO PICK HIS PREY. THAT MIGHT BE HIS SUPER-POWER. TRY NOT TO BEAT YOURSELF UP OVER IT.
BESIDES... IN A WAY, IT WAS A GOOD DECISION... IF YOU TAKE THE LONG VIEW, I MEAN.
IF APOGEE HAD GOTTEN SOMEONE ELSE TO HELP HIM...SOMEONE LESS GOOD, THEN MAYBE THEY WOULDN'T BE WORKING WITH THE BLACK WIDOW NOW TO TRY TO FIX THINGS.
...THANKS. THANKS FOR SAYING THAT.

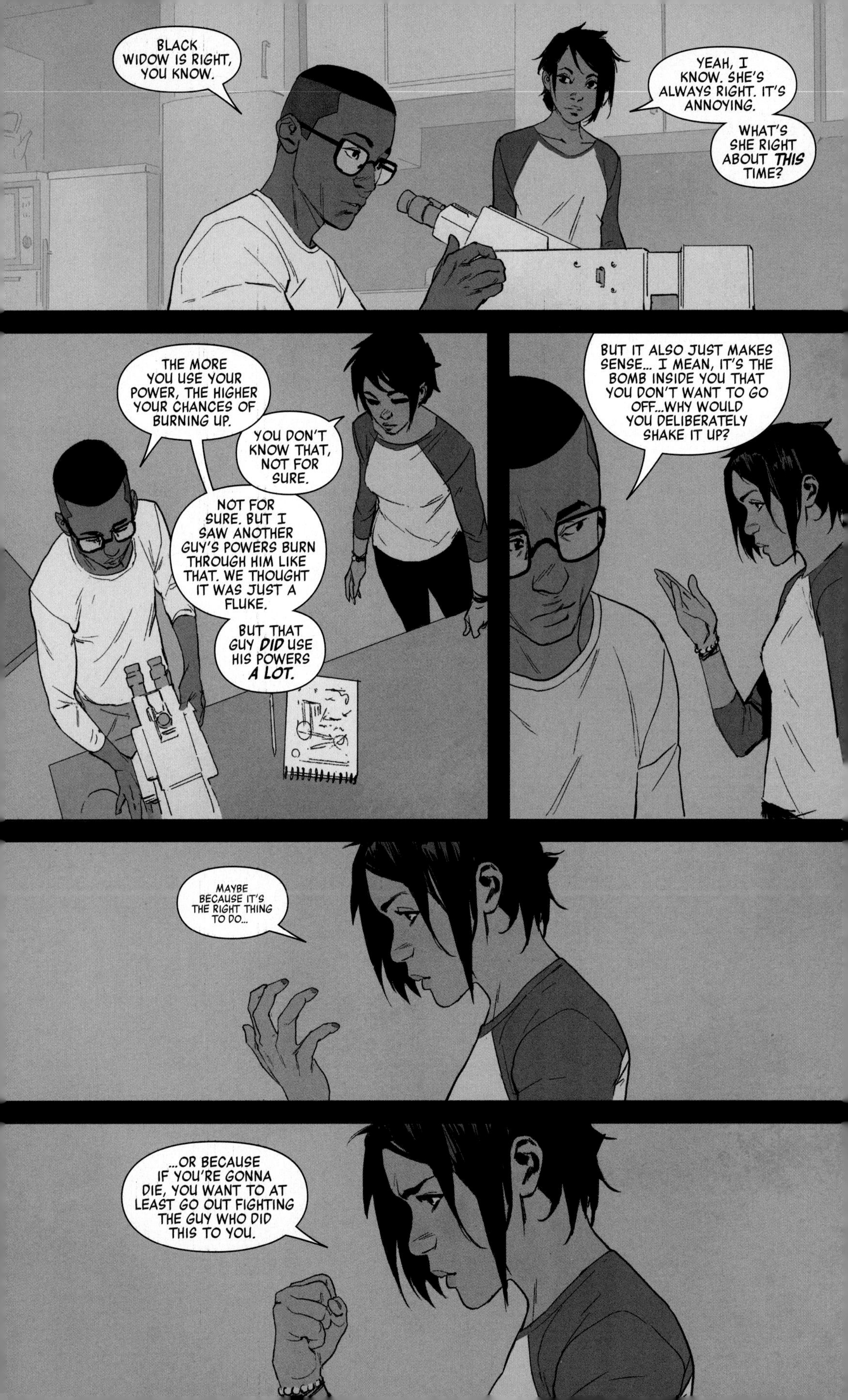
BLACK WIDOW IS RIGHT, YOU KNOW.
YEAH, I KNOW. SHE'S ALWAYS RIGHT. IT'S ANNOYING.
WHAT'S SHE RIGHT ABOUT **THIS** TIME?
THE MORE YOU USE YOUR POWER, THE HIGHER YOUR CHANCES OF BURNING UP.
YOU DON'T KNOW THAT, NOT FOR SURE.
NOT FOR SURE. BUT I SAW ANOTHER GUY'S POWERS BURN THROUGH HIM LIKE THAT. WE THOUGHT IT WAS JUST A FLUKE.
BUT THAT GUY **DID** USE HIS POWERS **A LOT.**
BUT IT ALSO JUST MAKES SENSE... I MEAN, IT'S THE BOMB INSIDE YOU THAT YOU DON'T WANT TO GO OFF...WHY WOULD YOU DELIBERATELY SHAKE IT UP?
MAYBE BECAUSE IT'S THE RIGHT THING TO DO...
...OR BECAUSE IF YOU'RE GONNA DIE, YOU WANT TO AT LEAST GO OUT FIGHTING THE GUY WHO DID THIS TO YOU.

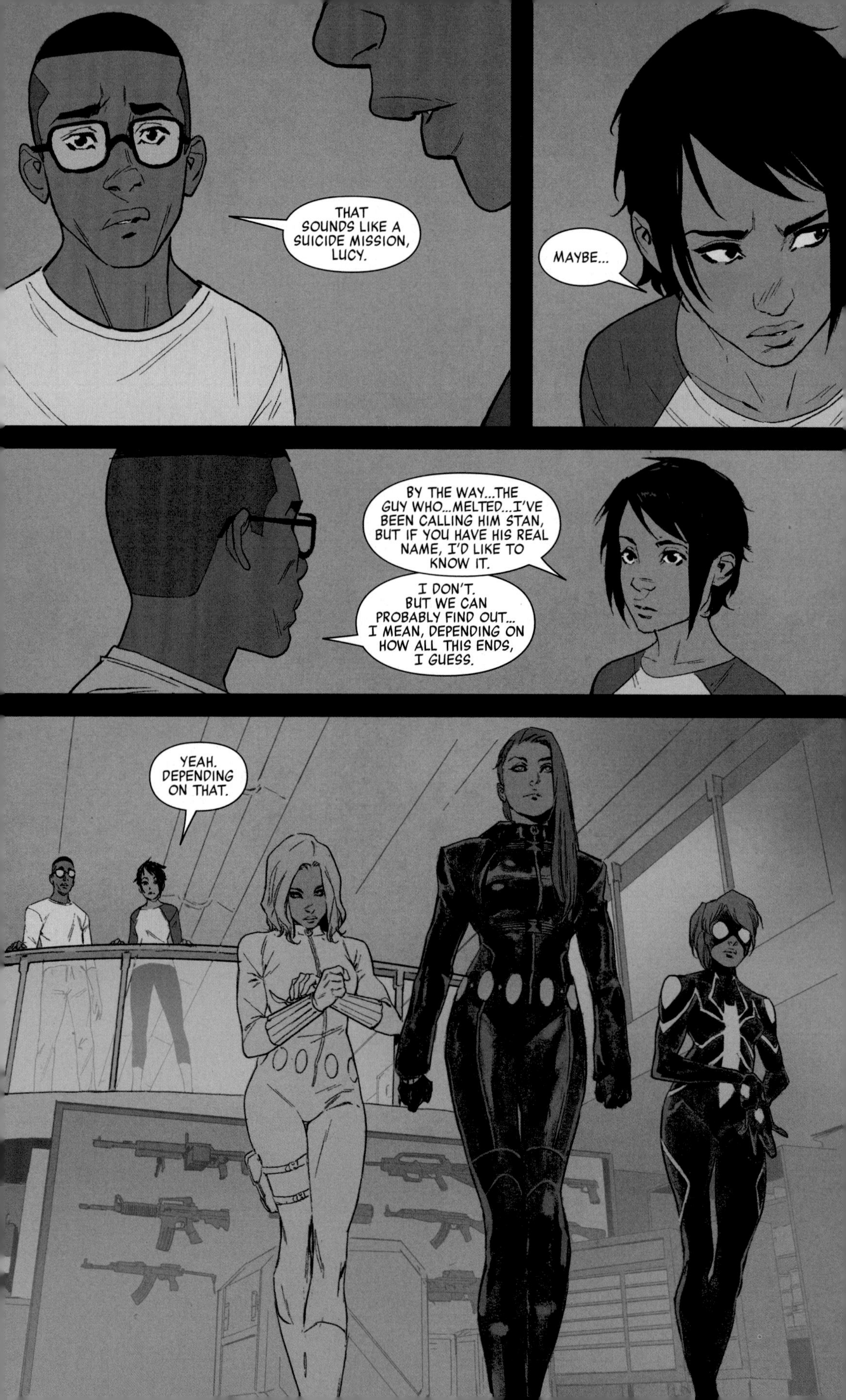
THAT SOUNDS LIKE A SUICIDE MISSION, LUCY.
MAYBE...
BY THE WAY...THE GUY WHO...MELTED...I'VE BEEN CALLING HIM STAN, BUT IF YOU HAVE HIS REAL NAME, I'D LIKE TO KNOW IT.
I DON'T. BUT WE CAN PROBABLY FIND OUT... I MEAN, DEPENDING ON HOW ALL THIS ENDS, I GUESS.
YEAH. DEPENDING ON THAT.

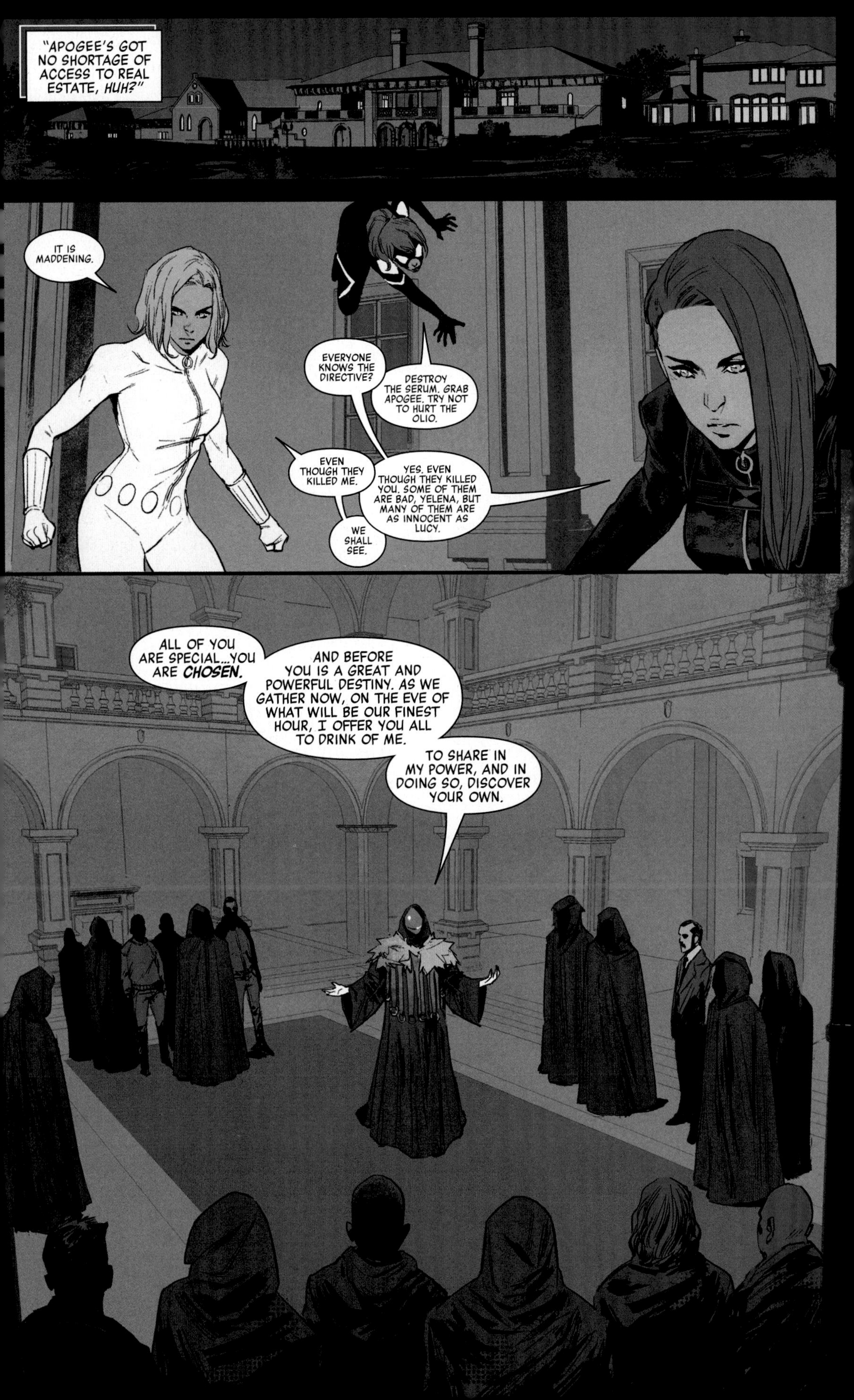
"APOGEE'S GOT NO SHORTAGE OF ACCESS TO REAL ESTATE, HUH?"
IT IS MADDENING.
EVERYONE KNOWS THE DIRECTIVE?
DESTROY THE SERUM. GRAB APOGEE. TRY NOT TO HURT THE OLIO.
EVEN THOUGH THEY KILLED ME.
YES. EVEN THOUGH THEY KILLED YOU. SOME OF THEM ARE BAD, YELENA, BUT MANY OF THEM ARE AS INNOCENT AS LUCY.
WE SHALL SEE.
ALL OF YOU ARE SPECIAL...YOU ARE CHOSEN.
AND BEFORE YOU IS A GREAT AND POWERFUL DESTINY. AS WE GATHER NOW, ON THE EVE OF WHAT WILL BE OUR FINEST HOUR, I OFFER YOU ALL TO DRINK OF ME.
TO SHARE IN MY POWER, AND IN DOING SO, DISCOVER YOUR OWN.

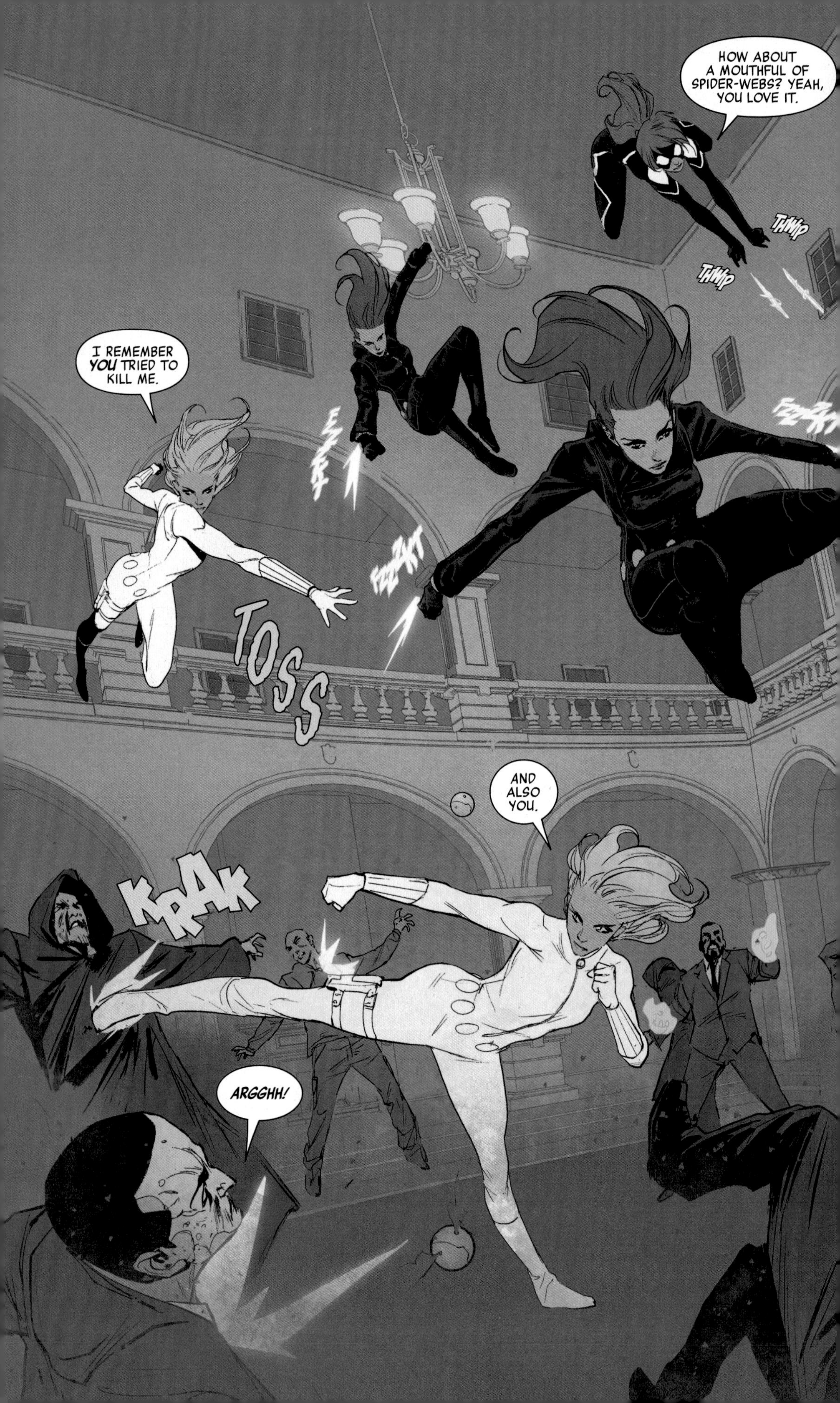
HOW ABOUT A MOUTHFUL OF SPIDER-WEBS? YEAH, YOU LOVE IT.
THWIP
THWIP
I REMEMBER YOU TRIED TO KILL ME.
TOSS
AND ALSO YOU.
KRAK
ARGGHH!

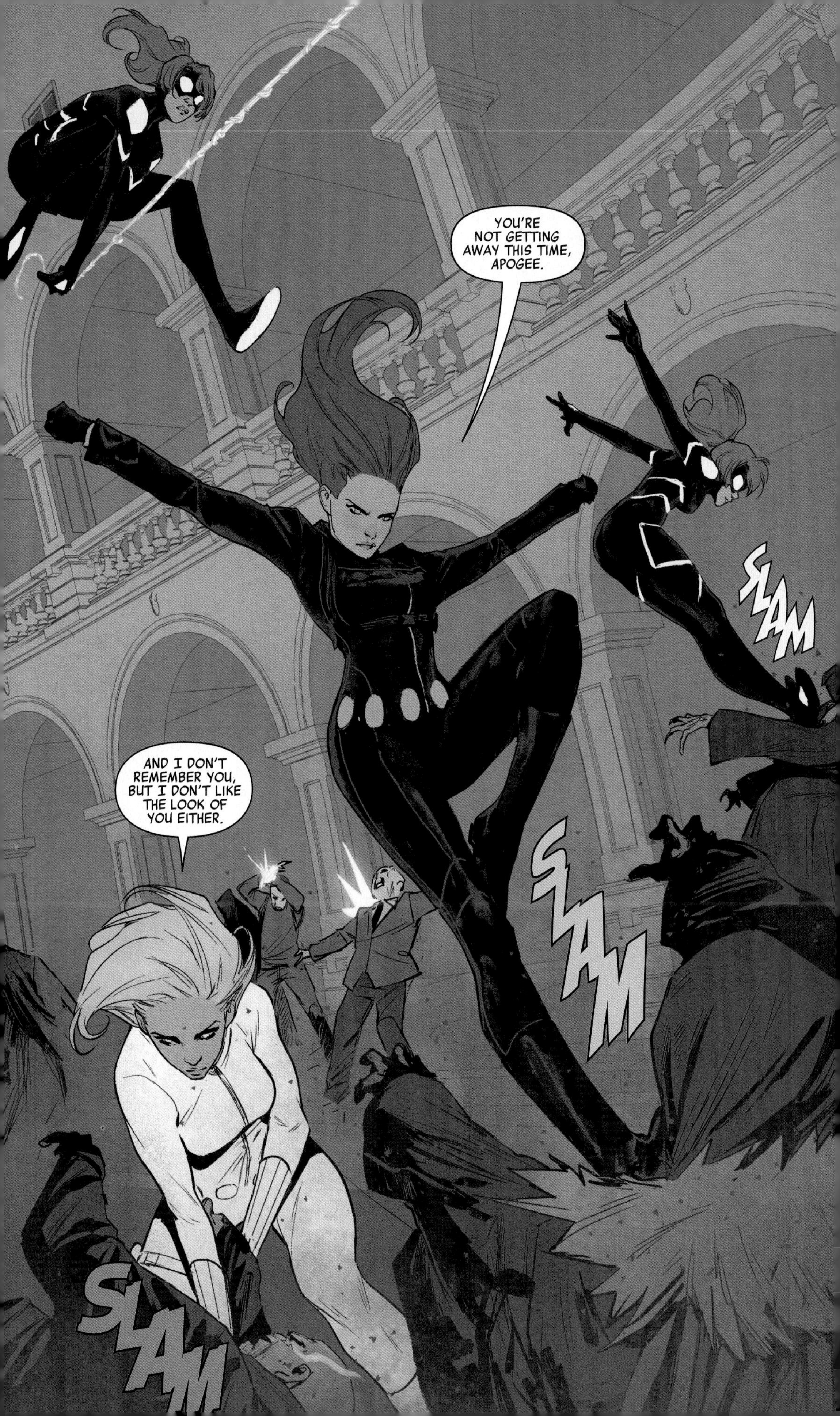
YOU'RE NOT GETTING AWAY THIS TIME, APOGEE.
SLAM
AND I DON'T REMEMBER YOU, BUT I DON'T LIKE THE LOOK OF YOU EITHER.
SLAM
SLAM

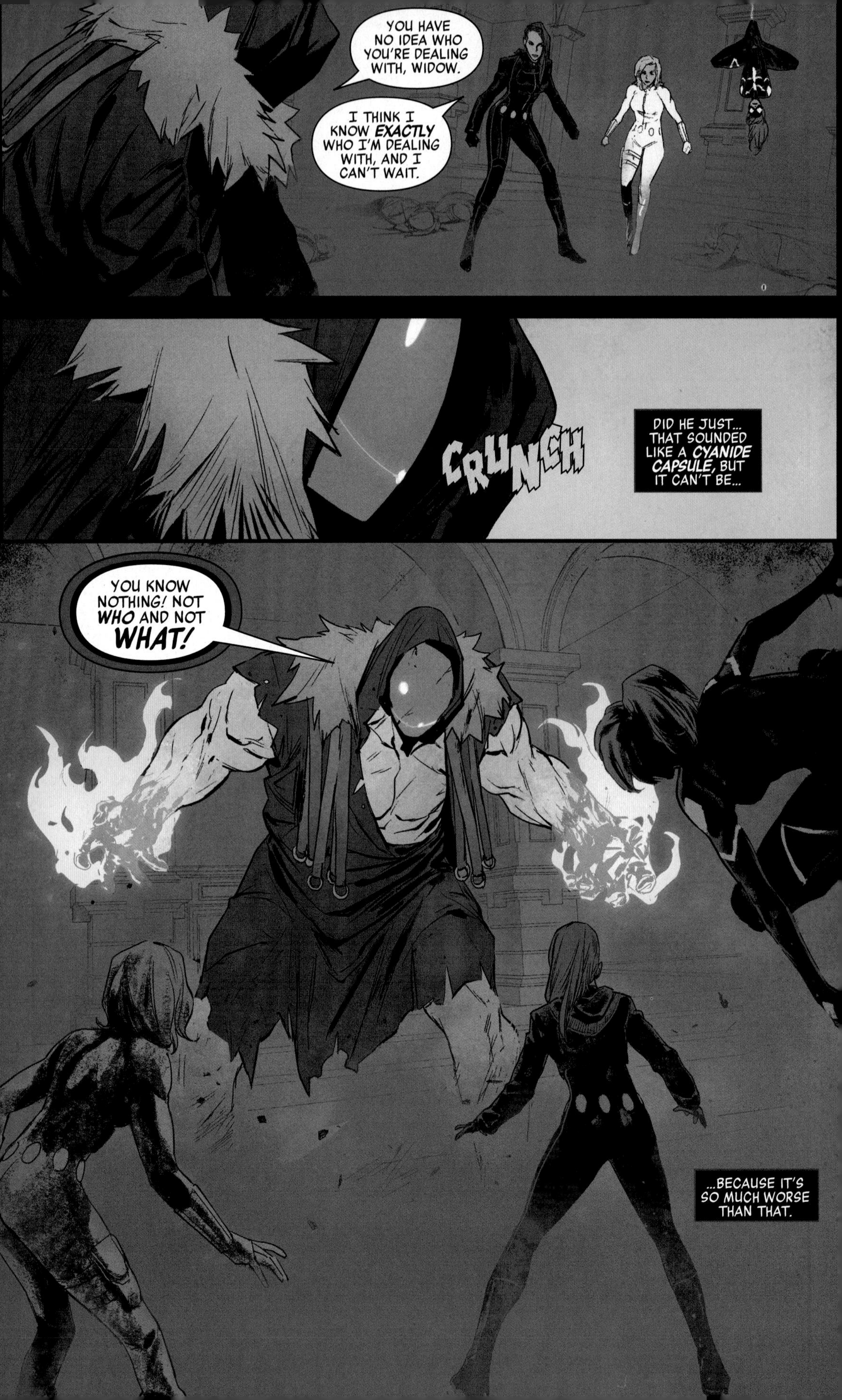
YOU HAVE NO IDEA WHO YOU'RE DEALING WITH, WIDOW.
I THINK I KNOW EXACTLY WHO I'M DEALING WITH, AND I CAN'T WAIT.
CRUNCH
DID HE JUST... THAT SOUNDED LIKE A CYANIDE CAPSULE, BUT IT CAN'T BE...
YOU KNOW NOTHING! NOT WHO AND NOT WHAT!
...BECAUSE IT'S SO MUCH WORSE THAN THAT.

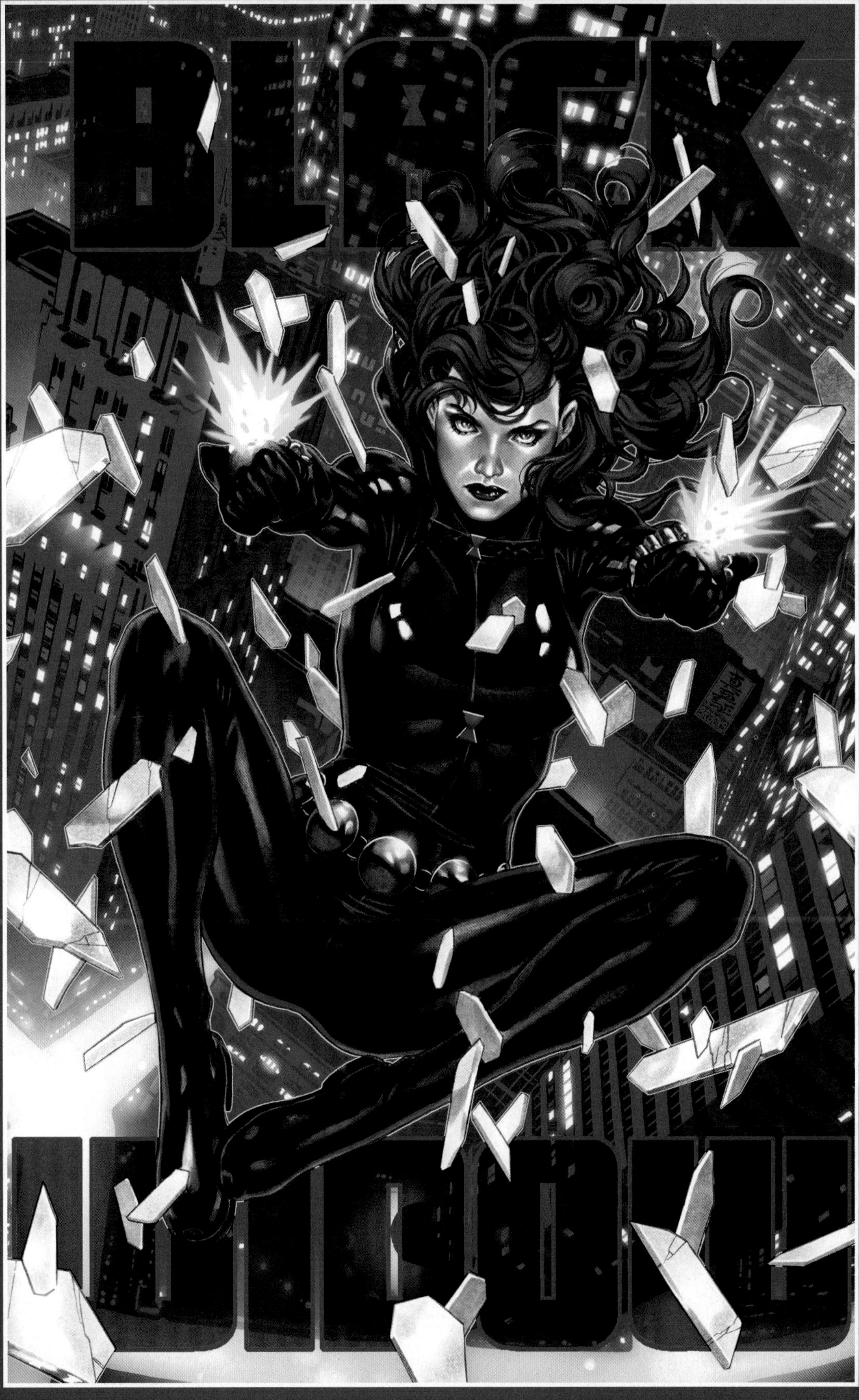
BLACK WIDOW

#10 VARIANT BY MARK BROOKS

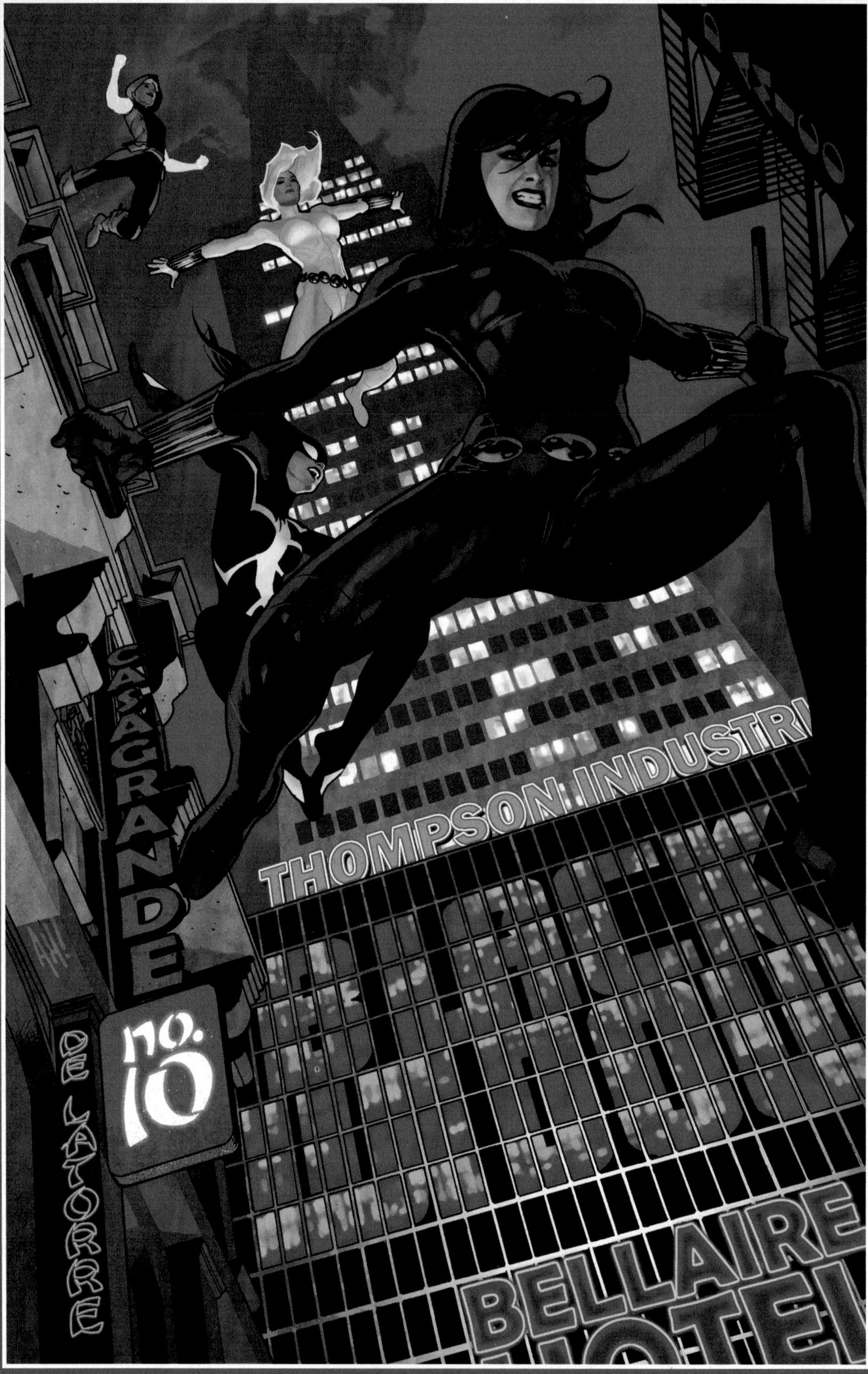
CASAGRANDE
DE LATORRE
no. 10
THOMPSON INDUSTRI
BELLAIRE
HOTE

TEN

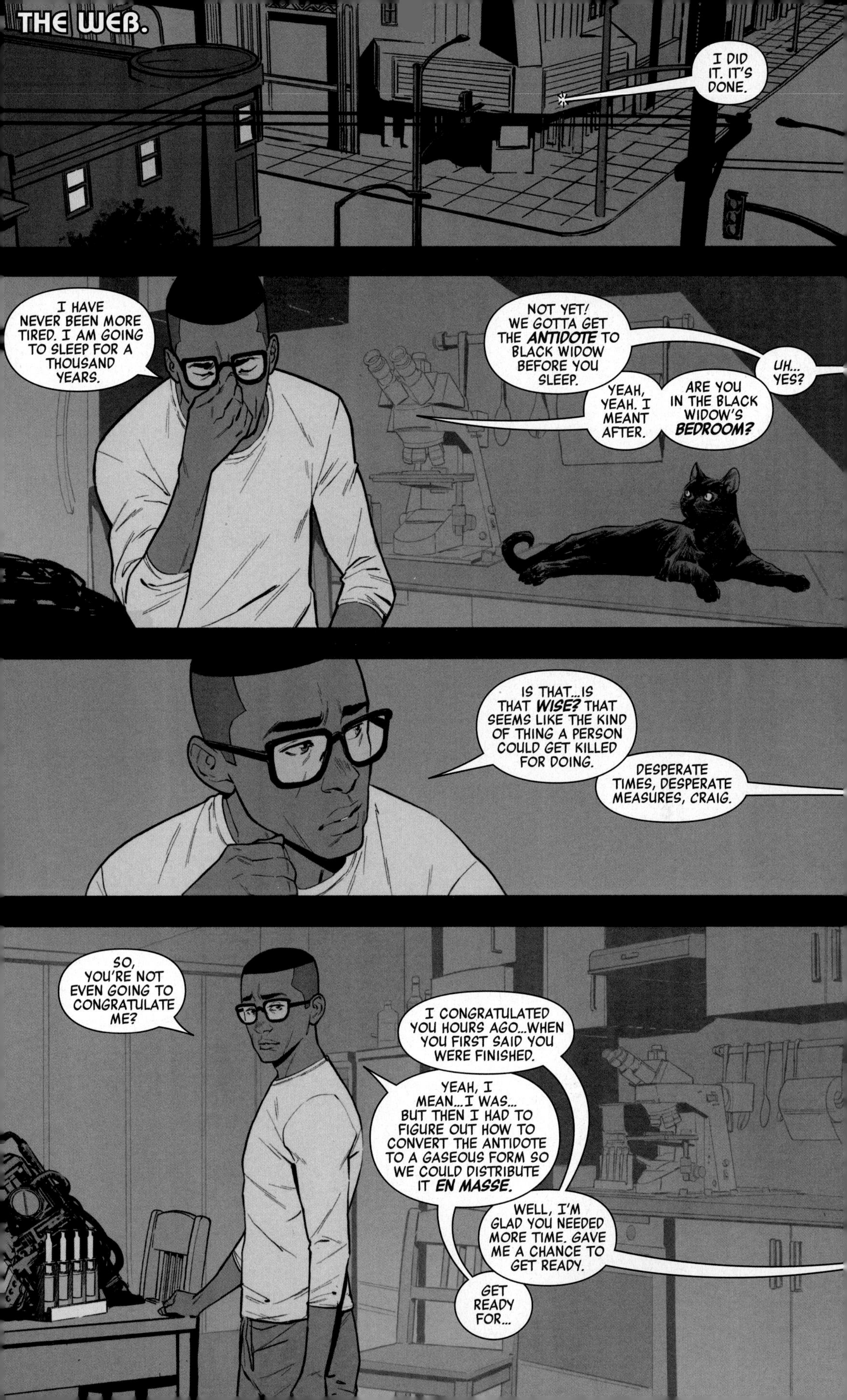
THE WEB.
I DID IT. IT'S DONE.
I HAVE NEVER BEEN MORE TIRED. I AM GOING TO SLEEP FOR A THOUSAND YEARS.
NOT YET! WE GOTTA GET THE ANTIDOTE TO BLACK WIDOW BEFORE YOU SLEEP.
YEAH, YEAH. I MEANT AFTER.
ARE YOU IN THE BLACK WIDOW'S BEDROOM?
UH... YES?
IS THAT...IS THAT WISE? THAT SEEMS LIKE THE KIND OF THING A PERSON COULD GET KILLED FOR DOING.
DESPERATE TIMES, DESPERATE MEASURES, CRAIG.
SO, YOU'RE NOT EVEN GOING TO CONGRATULATE ME?
I CONGRATULATED YOU HOURS AGO...WHEN YOU FIRST SAID YOU WERE FINISHED.
YEAH, I MEAN...I WAS... BUT THEN I HAD TO FIGURE OUT HOW TO CONVERT THE ANTIDOTE TO A GASEOUS FORM SO WE COULD DISTRIBUTE IT EN MASSE.
WELL, I'M GLAD YOU NEEDED MORE TIME. GAVE ME A CHANCE TO GET READY.
GET READY FOR...

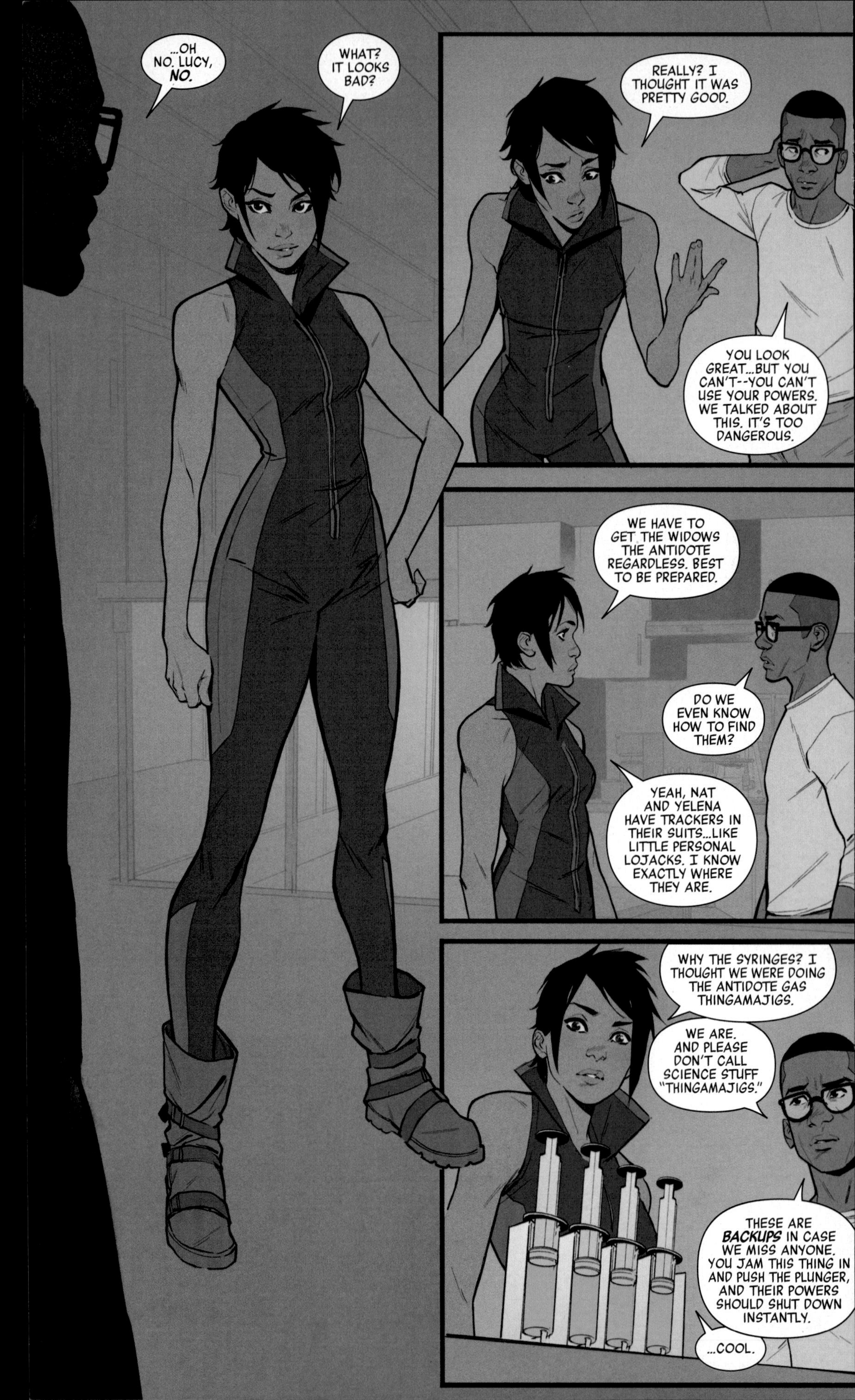
...OH NO. LUCY, NO.
WHAT? IT LOOKS BAD?
REALLY? I THOUGHT IT WAS PRETTY GOOD.
YOU LOOK GREAT...BUT YOU CAN'T--YOU CAN'T USE YOUR POWERS. WE TALKED ABOUT THIS. IT'S TOO DANGEROUS.
WE HAVE TO GET THE WIDOWS THE ANTIDOTE REGARDLESS. BEST TO BE PREPARED.
DO WE EVEN KNOW HOW TO FIND THEM?
YEAH, NAT AND YELENA HAVE TRACKERS IN THEIR SUITS...LIKE LITTLE PERSONAL LOJACKS. I KNOW EXACTLY WHERE THEY ARE.
WHY THE SYRINGES? I THOUGHT WE WERE DOING THE ANTIDOTE GAS THINGAMAJIGS.
WE ARE. AND PLEASE DON'T CALL SCIENCE STUFF "THINGAMAJIGS."
THESE ARE BACKUPS IN CASE WE MISS ANYONE. YOU JAM THIS THING IN AND PUSH THE PLUNGER, AND THEIR POWERS SHOULD SHUT DOWN INSTANTLY.
...COOL.

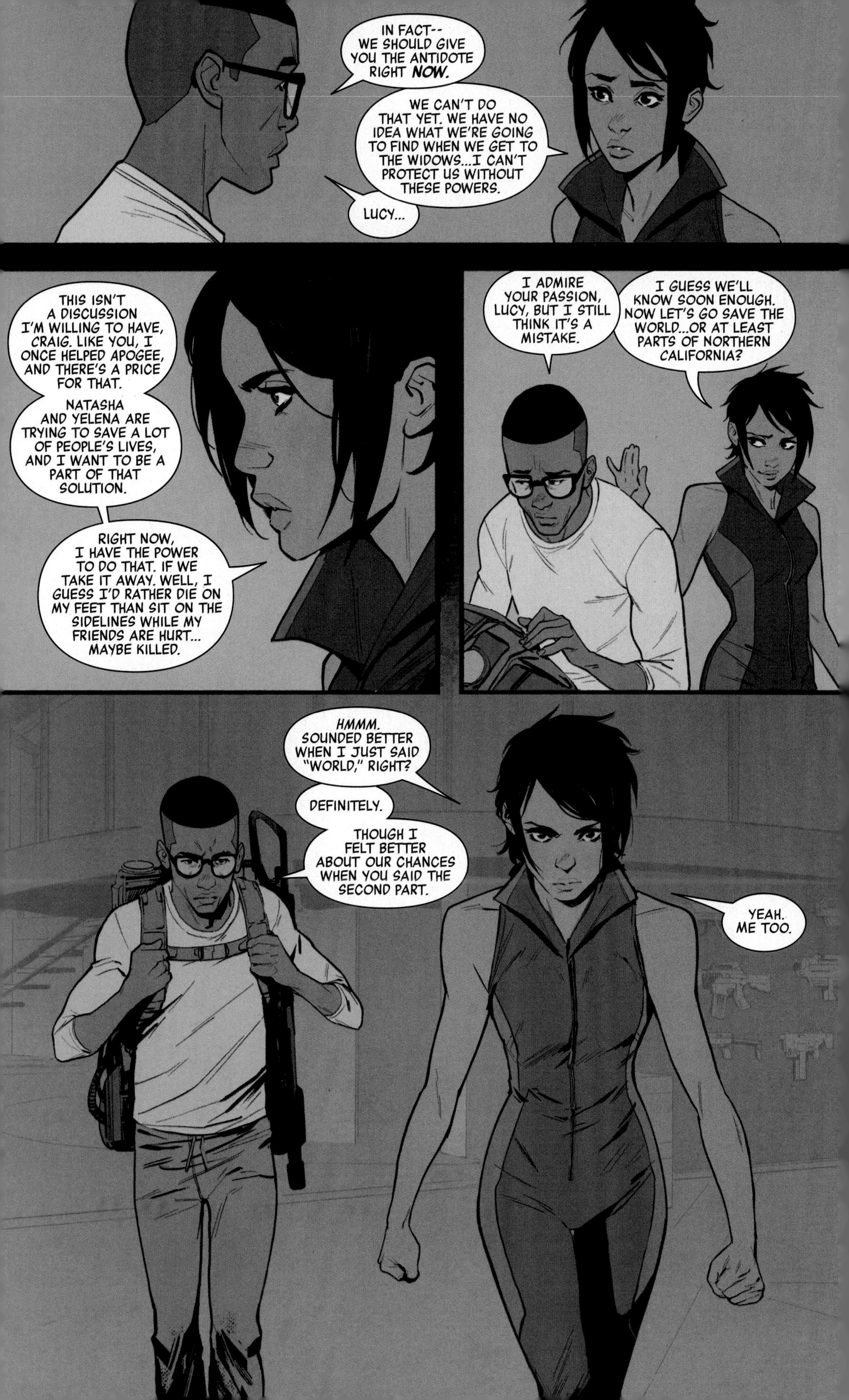
IN FACT-- WE SHOULD GIVE YOU THE ANTIDOTE RIGHT NOW.
WE CAN'T DO THAT YET. WE HAVE NO IDEA WHAT WE'RE GOING TO FIND WHEN WE GET TO THE WIDOWS...I CAN'T PROTECT US WITHOUT THESE POWERS.
LUCY...
THIS ISN'T A DISCUSSION I'M WILLING TO HAVE, CRAIG. LIKE YOU, I ONCE HELPED APOGEE, AND THERE'S A PRICE FOR THAT.
NATASHA AND YELENA ARE TRYING TO SAVE A LOT OF PEOPLE'S LIVES, AND I WANT TO BE A PART OF THAT SOLUTION.
RIGHT NOW, I HAVE THE POWER TO DO THAT. IF WE TAKE IT AWAY. WELL, I GUESS I'D RATHER DIE ON MY FEET THAN SIT ON THE SIDELINES WHILE MY FRIENDS ARE HURT... MAYBE KILLED.
I ADMIRE YOUR PASSION, LUCY, BUT I STILL THINK IT'S A MISTAKE.
I GUESS WE'LL KNOW SOON ENOUGH. NOW LET'S GO SAVE THE WORLD...OR AT LEAST PARTS OF NORTHERN CALIFORNIA?
HMMM. SOUNDED BETTER WHEN I JUST SAID "WORLD," RIGHT?
DEFINITELY.
THOUGH I FELT BETTER ABOUT OUR CHANCES WHEN YOU SAID THE SECOND PART.
YEAH. ME TOO.

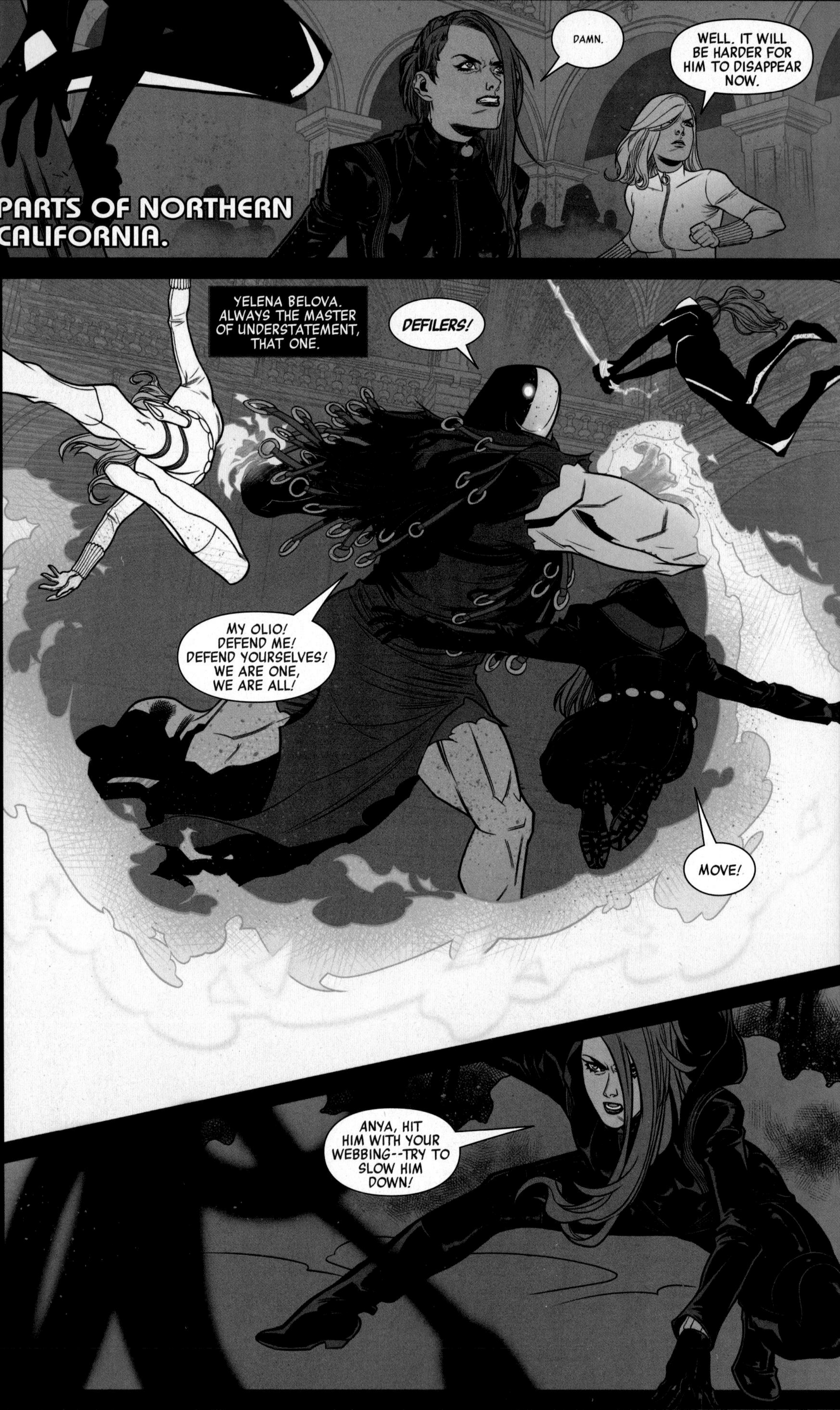
DAMN.
WELL. IT WILL BE HARDER FOR HIM TO DISAPPEAR NOW.
PARTS OF NORTHERN CALIFORNIA.
YELENA BELOVA. ALWAYS THE MASTER OF UNDERSTATEMENT, THAT ONE.
DEFILERS!
MY OLIO! DEFEND ME! DEFEND YOURSELVES! WE ARE ONE, WE ARE ALL!
MOVE!
ANYA, HIT HIM WITH YOUR WEBBING--TRY TO SLOW HIM DOWN!

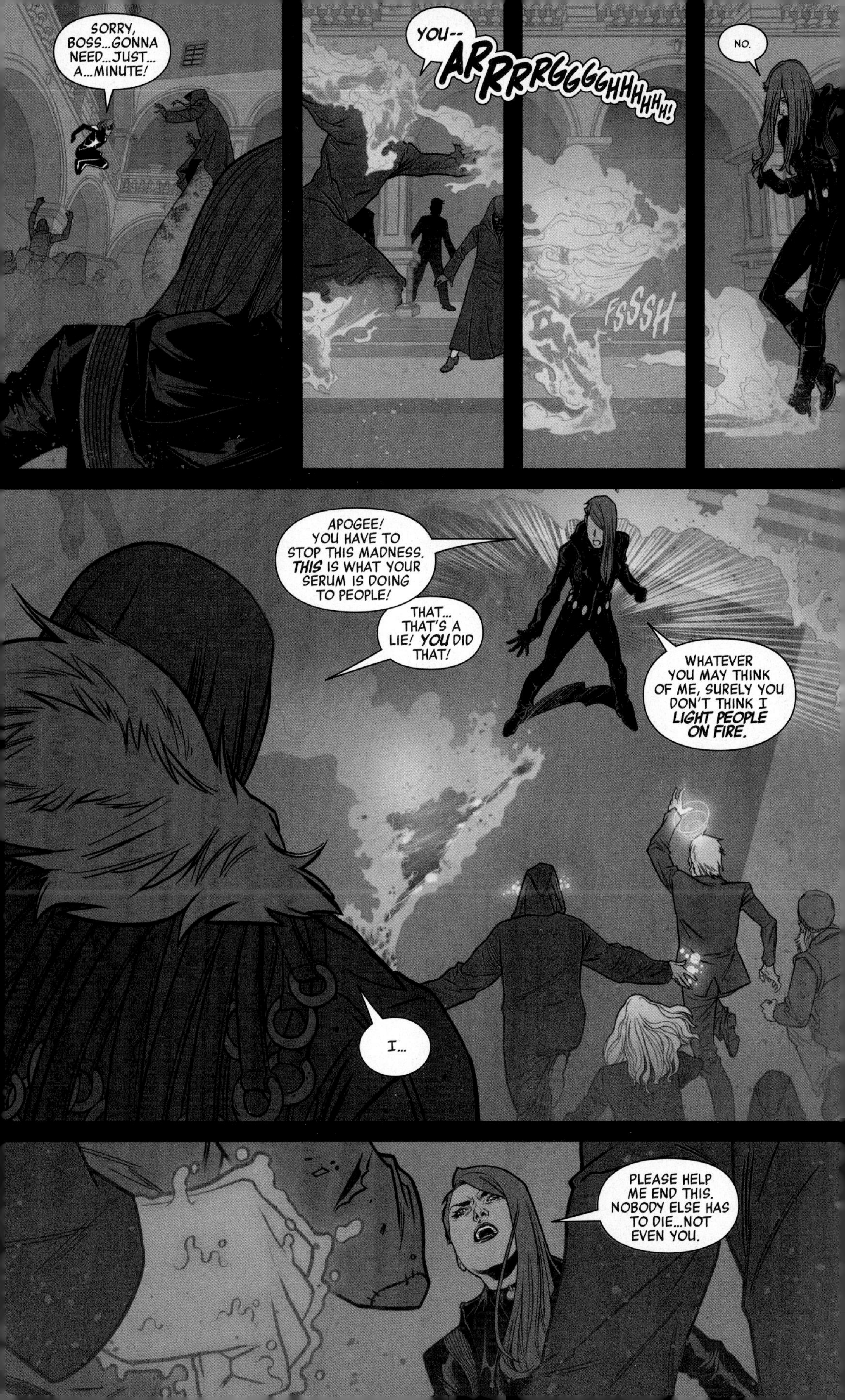
SORRY, BOSS...GONNA NEED...JUST... A...MINUTE!
YOU--
ARRRRGGGGHHHHHH!
FSSSH
NO.
APOGEE! YOU HAVE TO STOP THIS MADNESS. THIS IS WHAT YOUR SERUM IS DOING TO PEOPLE!
THAT... THAT'S A LIE! YOU DID THAT!
WHATEVER YOU MAY THINK OF ME, SURELY YOU DON'T THINK I LIGHT PEOPLE ON FIRE.
I...
PLEASE HELP ME END THIS. NOBODY ELSE HAS TO DIE...NOT EVEN YOU.

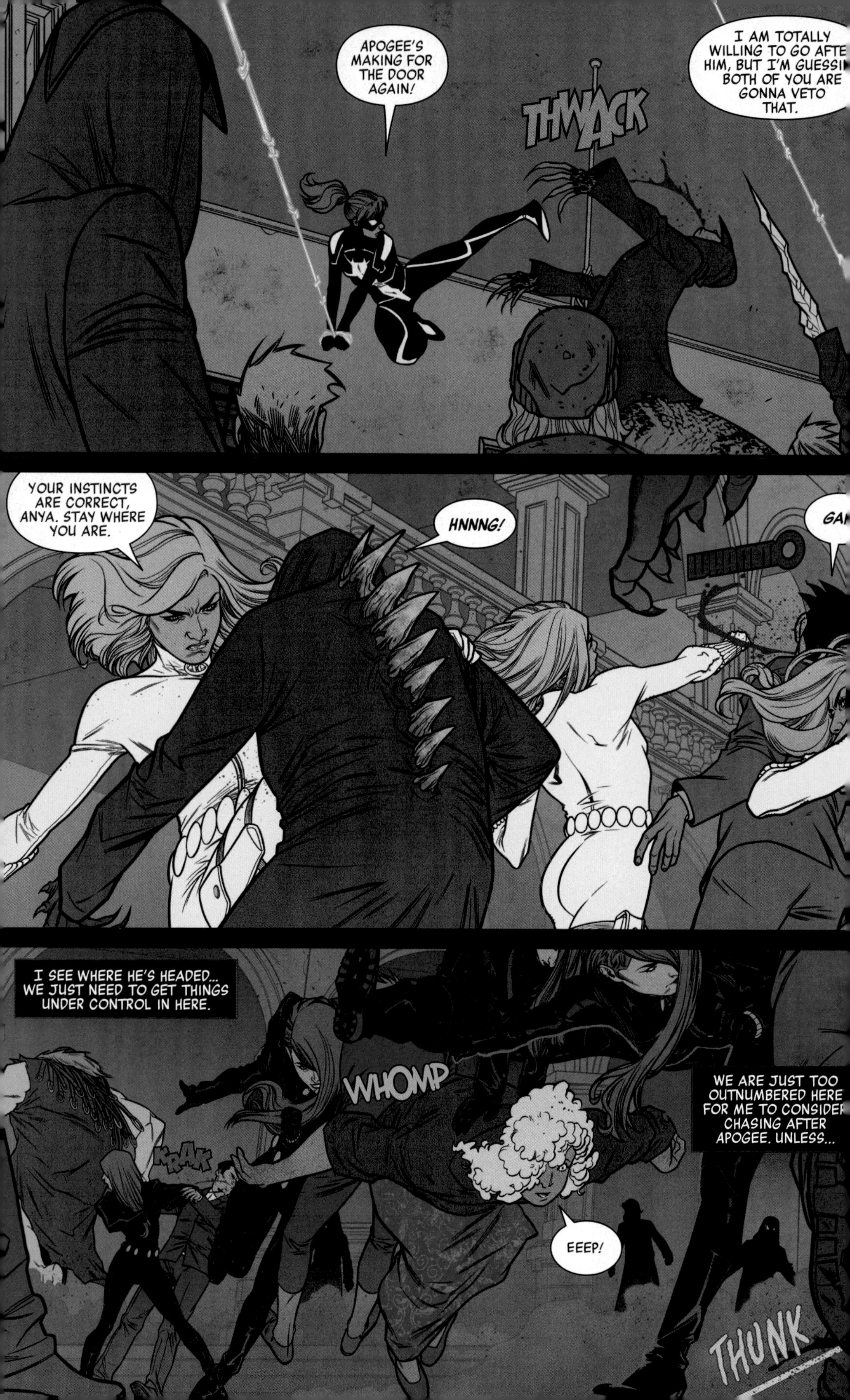
APOGEE'S MAKING FOR THE DOOR AGAIN!
THWACK
I AM TOTALLY WILLING TO GO AFTE HIM, BUT I'M GUESSI BOTH OF YOU ARE GONNA VETO THAT.
YOUR INSTINCTS ARE CORRECT, ANYA. STAY WHERE YOU ARE.
HNNNG!
GA
I SEE WHERE HE'S HEADED... WE JUST NEED TO GET THINGS UNDER CONTROL IN HERE.
WHOMP
KRAK
WE ARE JUST TOO OUTNUMBERED HERE FOR ME TO CONSIDEI CHASING AFTER APOGEE. UNLESS...
EEEP!
THUNK

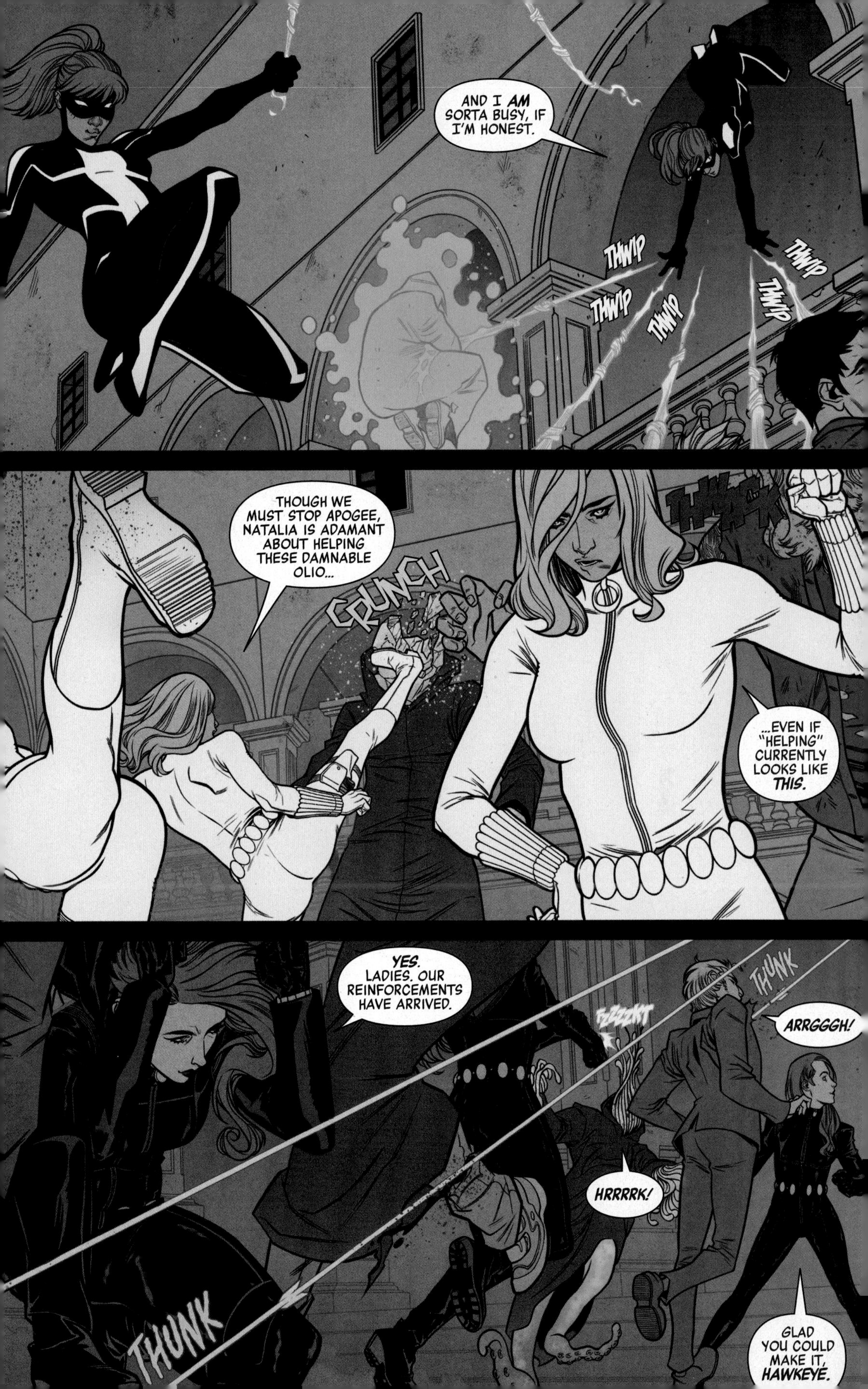

AND I AM SORTA BUSY, IF I'M HONEST.
THWIP
THWIP
THWIP
THWIP
THWIP
THOUGH WE MUST STOP APOGEE, NATALIA IS ADAMANT ABOUT HELPING THESE DAMNABLE OLIO...
CRUNCH
...EVEN IF "HELPING" CURRENTLY LOOKS LIKE THIS.
YES. LADIES. OUR REINFORCEMENTS HAVE ARRIVED.
THUNK
ARRGGGH!
HRRRRK!
THUNK
GLAD YOU COULD MAKE IT, HAWKEYE.

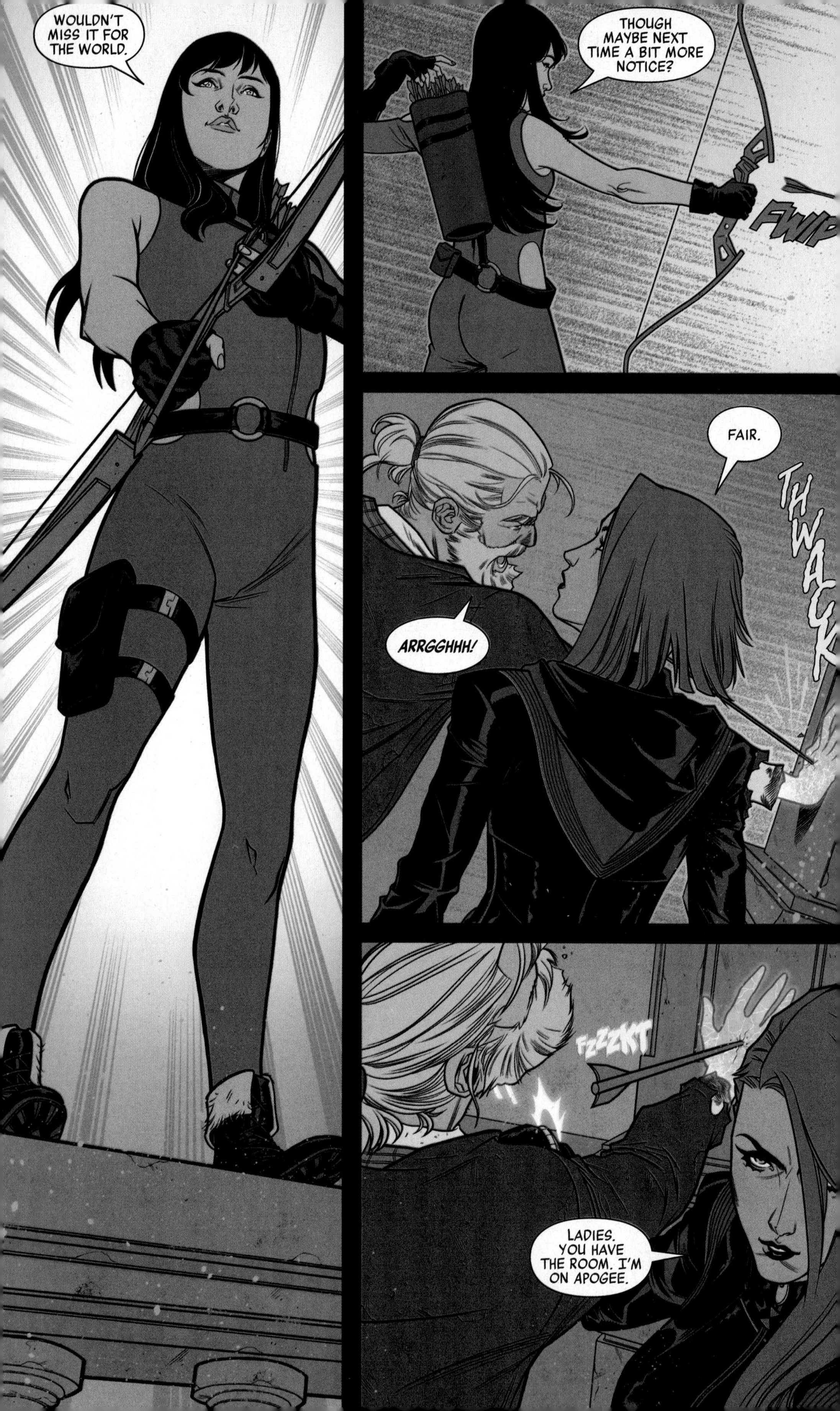
WOULDN'T MISS IT FOR THE WORLD.
THOUGH MAYBE NEXT TIME A BIT MORE NOTICE?
FWIP
FAIR.
THWACK
ARRGGHHH!
FZZZKT
LADIES. YOU HAVE THE ROOM. I'M ON APOGEE.

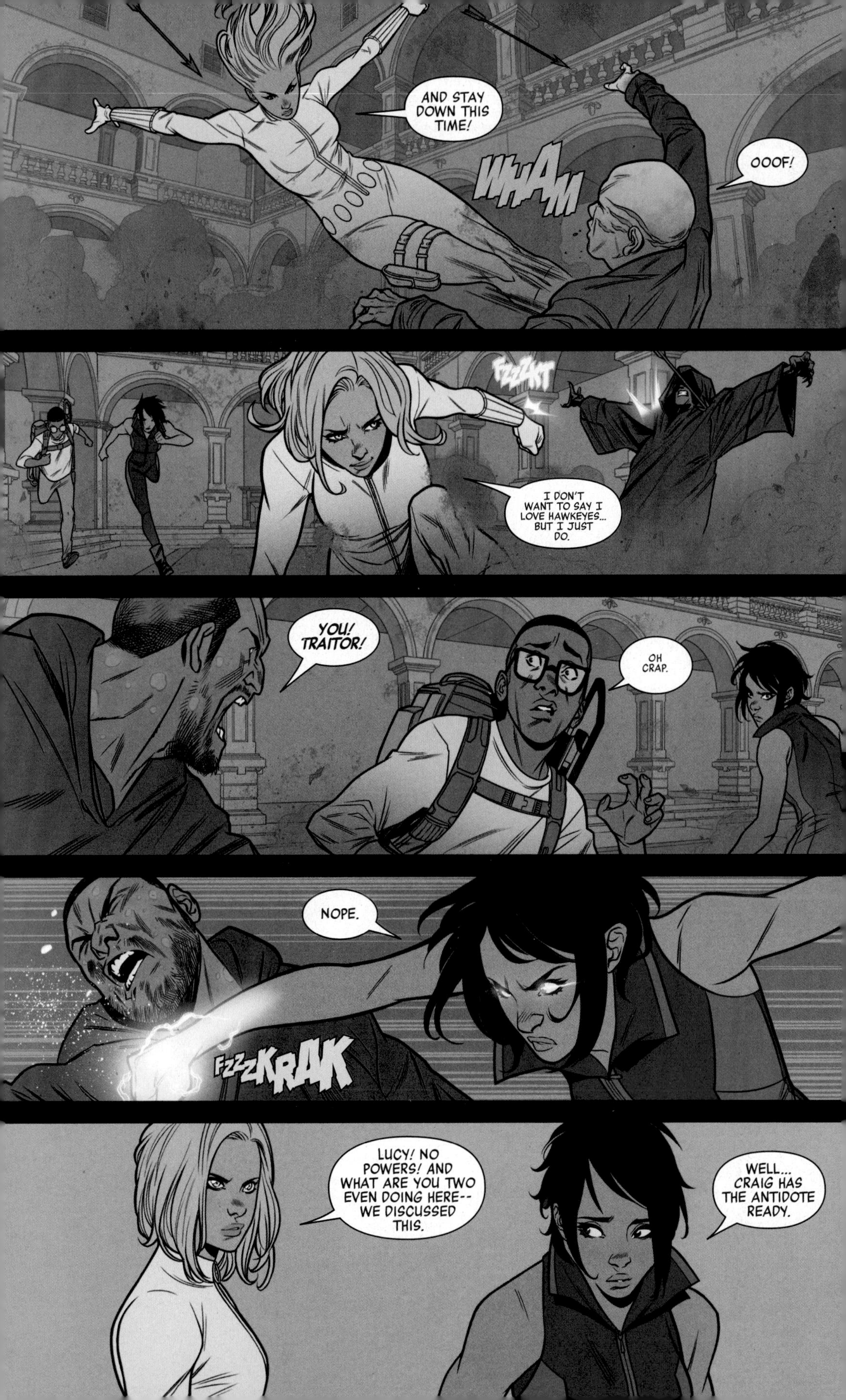
AND STAY DOWN THIS TIME!
WHAM
OOOF!
FZZZKT
I DON'T WANT TO SAY I LOVE HAWKEYES... BUT I JUST DO.
YOU! TRAITOR!
OH CRAP.
NOPE.
FZZZKRAK
LUCY! NO POWERS! AND WHAT ARE YOU TWO EVEN DOING HERE-- WE DISCUSSED THIS.
WELL... CRAIG HAS THE ANTIDOTE READY.

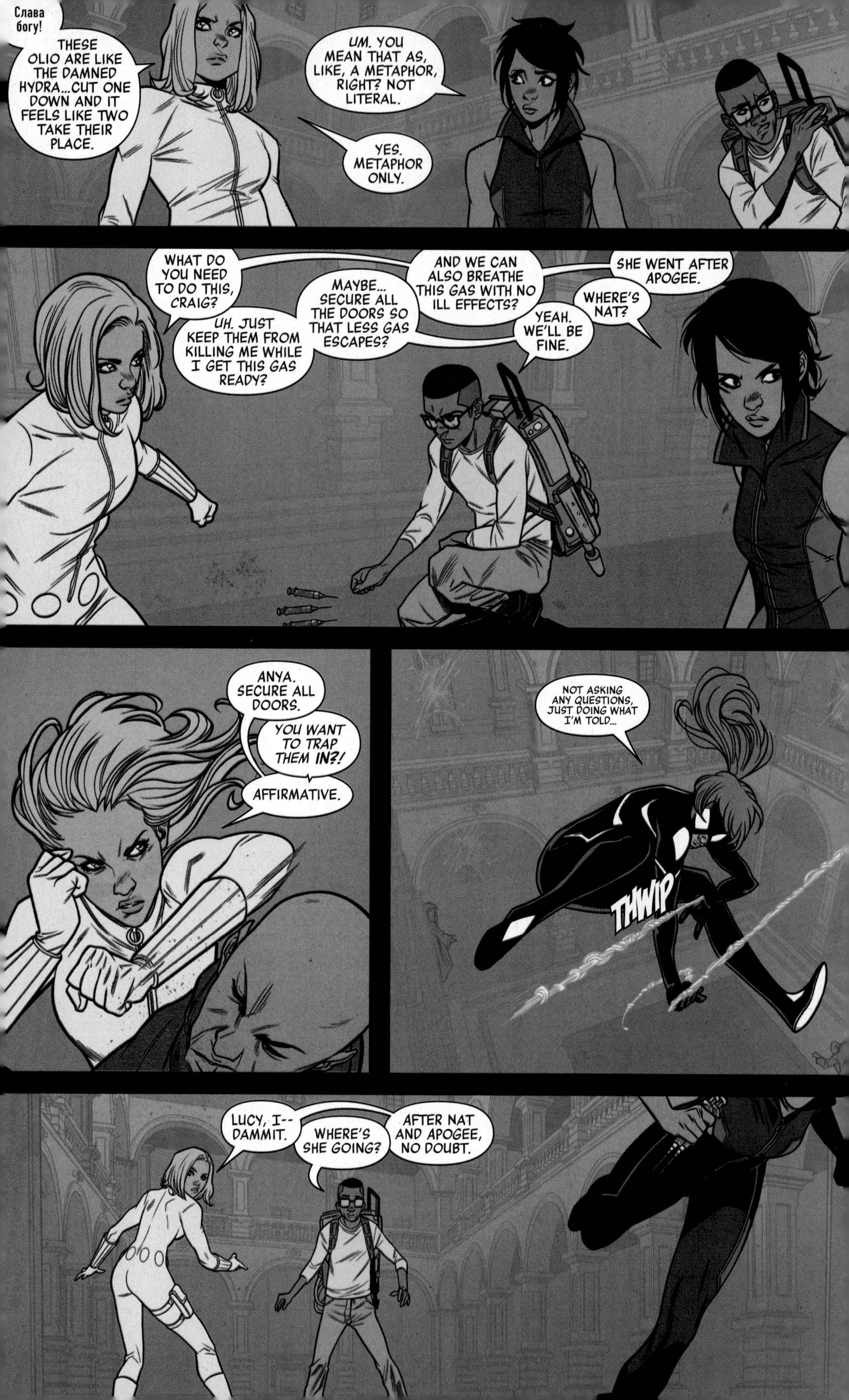
Слава богу!
THESE OLIO ARE LIKE THE DAMNED HYDRA...CUT ONE DOWN AND IT FEELS LIKE TWO TAKE THEIR PLACE.
UM. YOU MEAN THAT AS, LIKE, A METAPHOR, RIGHT? NOT LITERAL.
YES. METAPHOR ONLY.
WHAT DO YOU NEED TO DO THIS, CRAIG?
UH. JUST KEEP THEM FROM KILLING ME WHILE I GET THIS GAS READY?
MAYBE... SECURE ALL THE DOORS SO THAT LESS GAS ESCAPES?
AND WE CAN ALSO BREATHE THIS GAS WITH NO ILL EFFECTS?
YEAH. WE'LL BE FINE.
WHERE'S NAT?
SHE WENT AFTER APOGEE.
ANYA. SECURE ALL DOORS.
YOU WANT TO TRAP THEM IN?!
AFFIRMATIVE.
NOT ASKING ANY QUESTIONS, JUST DOING WHAT I'M TOLD...
THWIP
LUCY, I-- DAMMIT.
WHERE'S SHE GOING?
AFTER NAT AND APOGEE, NO DOUBT.

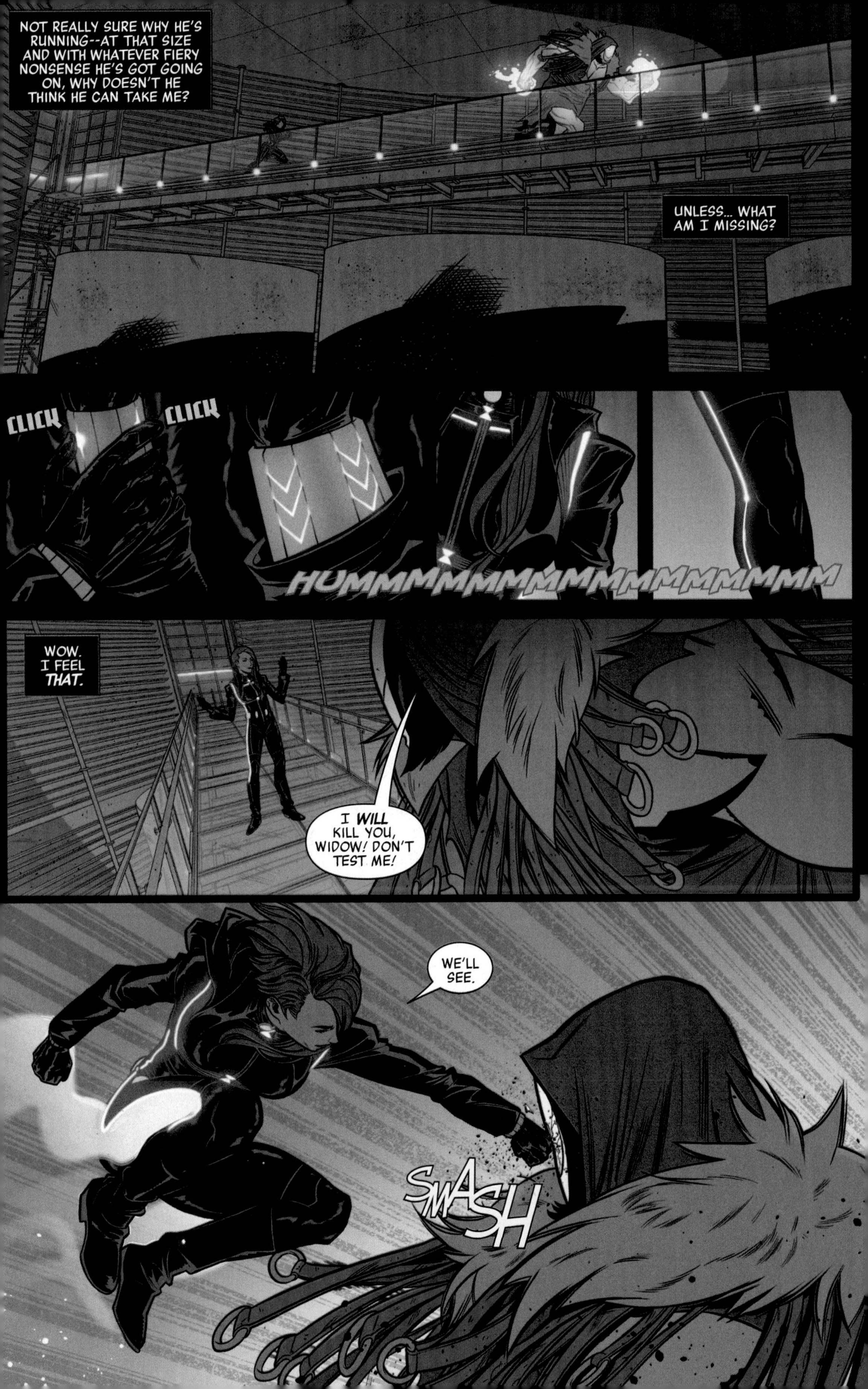
NOT REALLY SURE WHY HE'S RUNNING--AT THAT SIZE AND WITH WHATEVER FIERY NONSENSE HE'S GOT GOING ON, WHY DOESN'T HE THINK HE CAN TAKE ME?
UNLESS... WHAT AM I MISSING?
CLICK
CLICK
HUMMMMMMMMMMMMMMMMMM
WOW. I FEEL THAT.
I WILL KILL YOU, WIDOW! DON'T TEST ME!
WE'LL SEE.
SMASH

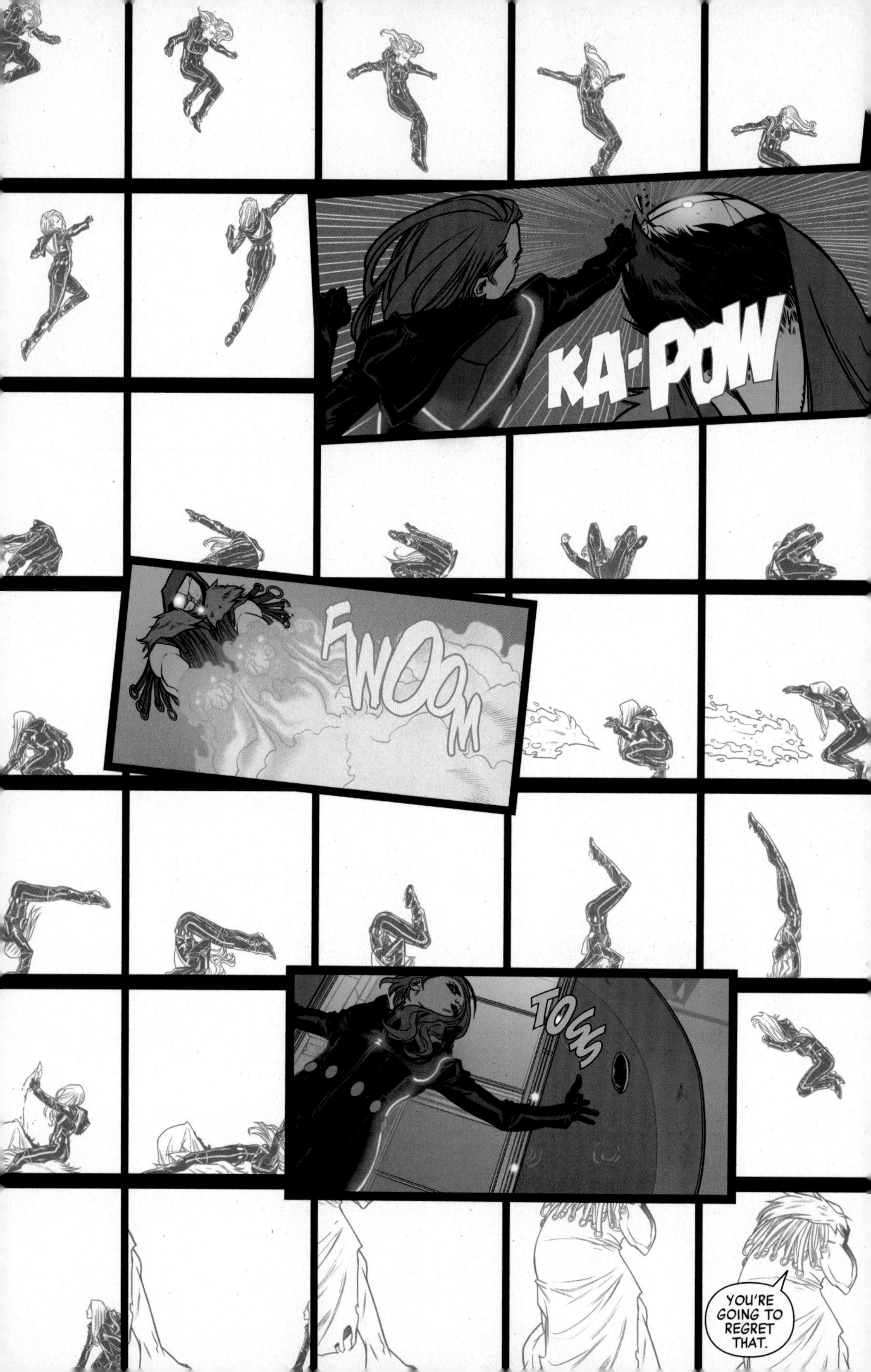
KA-POW
FWOOOM
TOGGS
YOU'RE GOING TO REGRET THAT.

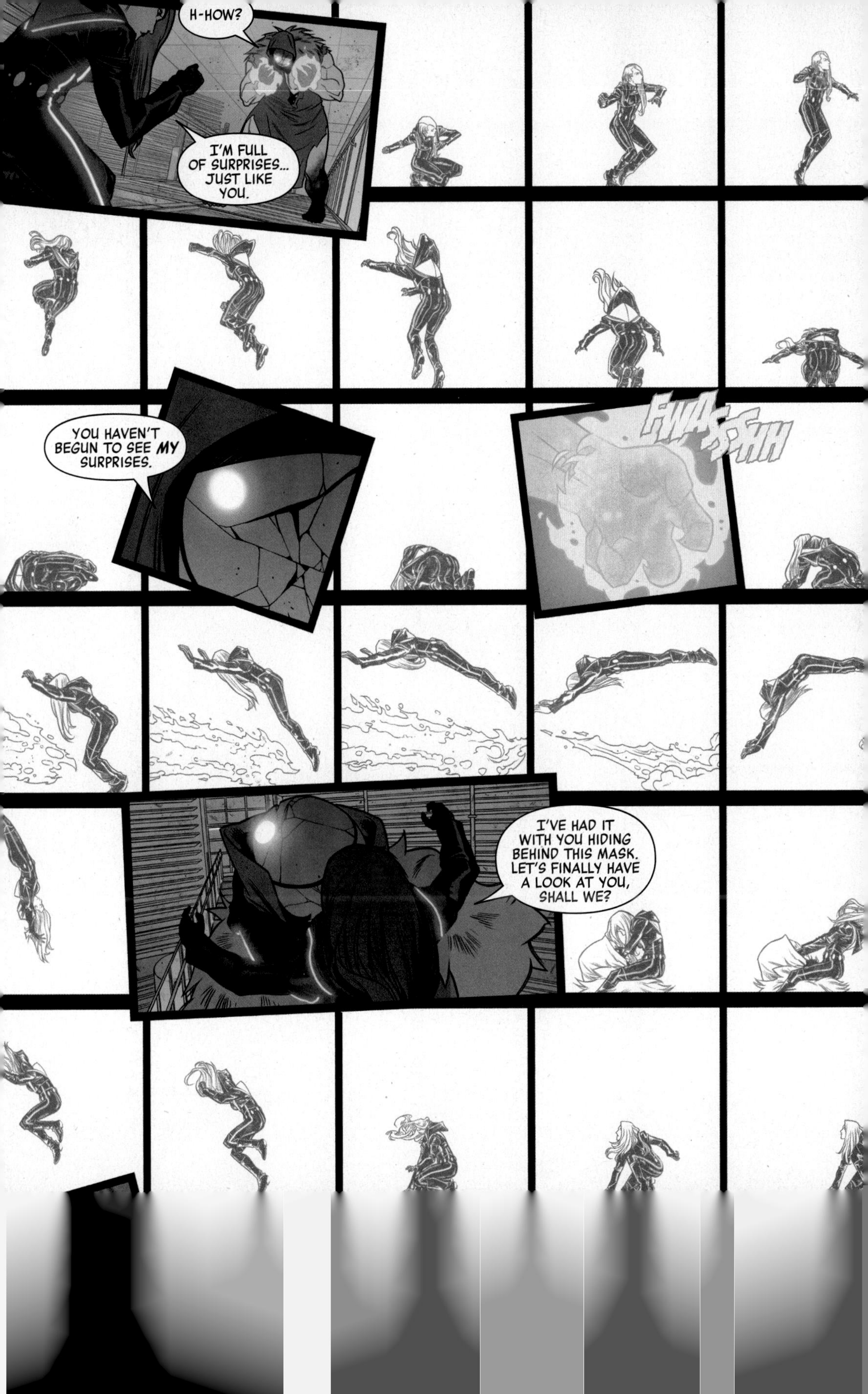
H-HOW?
I'M FULL OF SURPRISES... JUST LIKE YOU.
YOU HAVEN'T BEGUN TO SEE MY SURPRISES.
FWASSHH
I'VE HAD IT WITH YOU HIDING BEHIND THIS MASK. LET'S FINALLY HAVE A LOOK AT YOU, SHALL WE?

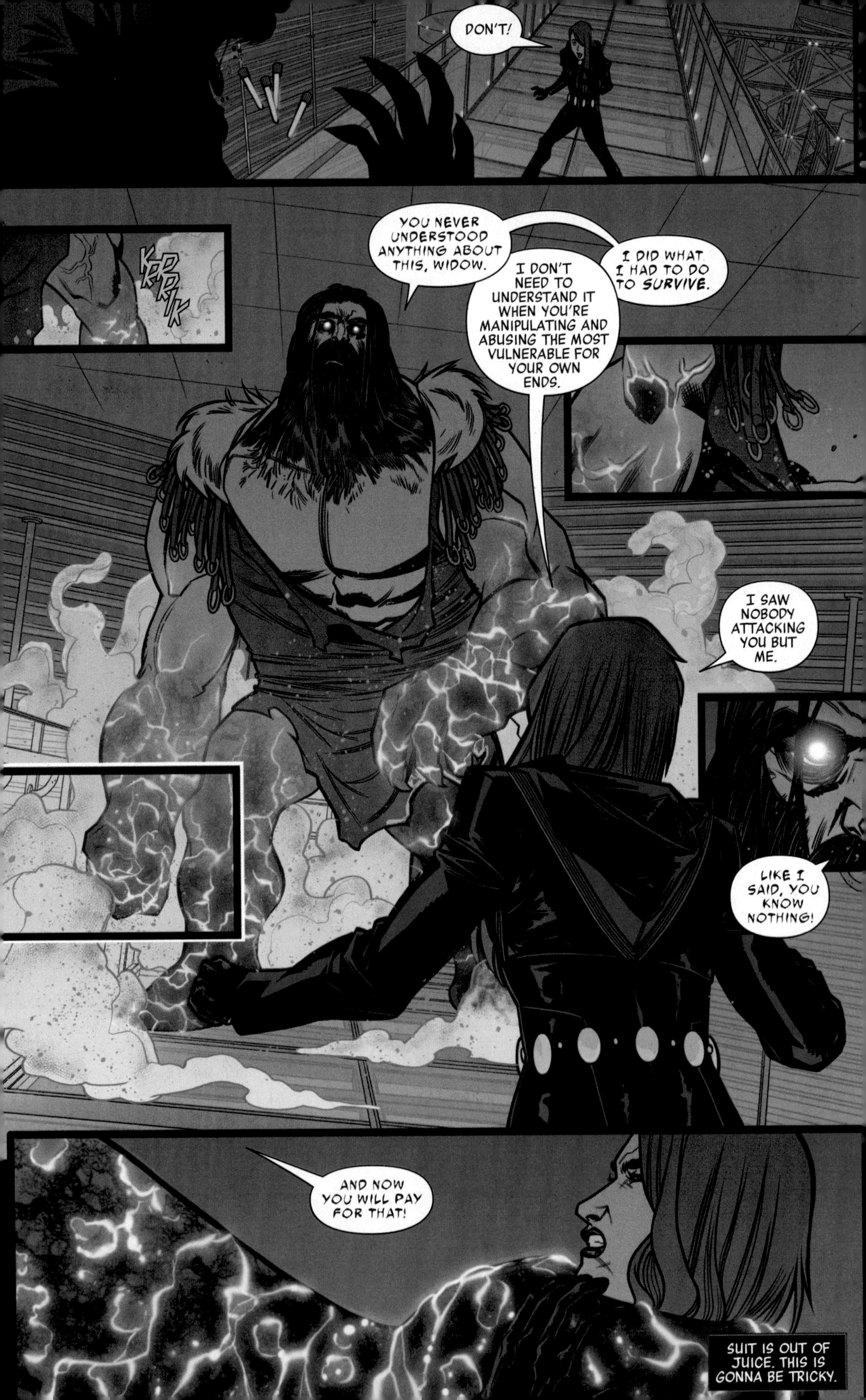
DON'T!
KRRRIK
YOU NEVER UNDERSTOOD ANYTHING ABOUT THIS, WIDOW.
I DID WHAT I HAD TO DO TO SURVIVE.
I DON'T NEED TO UNDERSTAND IT WHEN YOU'RE MANIPULATING AND ABUSING THE MOST VULNERABLE FOR YOUR OWN ENDS.
I SAW NOBODY ATTACKING YOU BUT ME.
LIKE I SAID, YOU KNOW NOTHING!
AND NOW YOU WILL PAY FOR THAT!
SUIT IS OUT OF JUICE. THIS IS GONNA BE TRICKY.

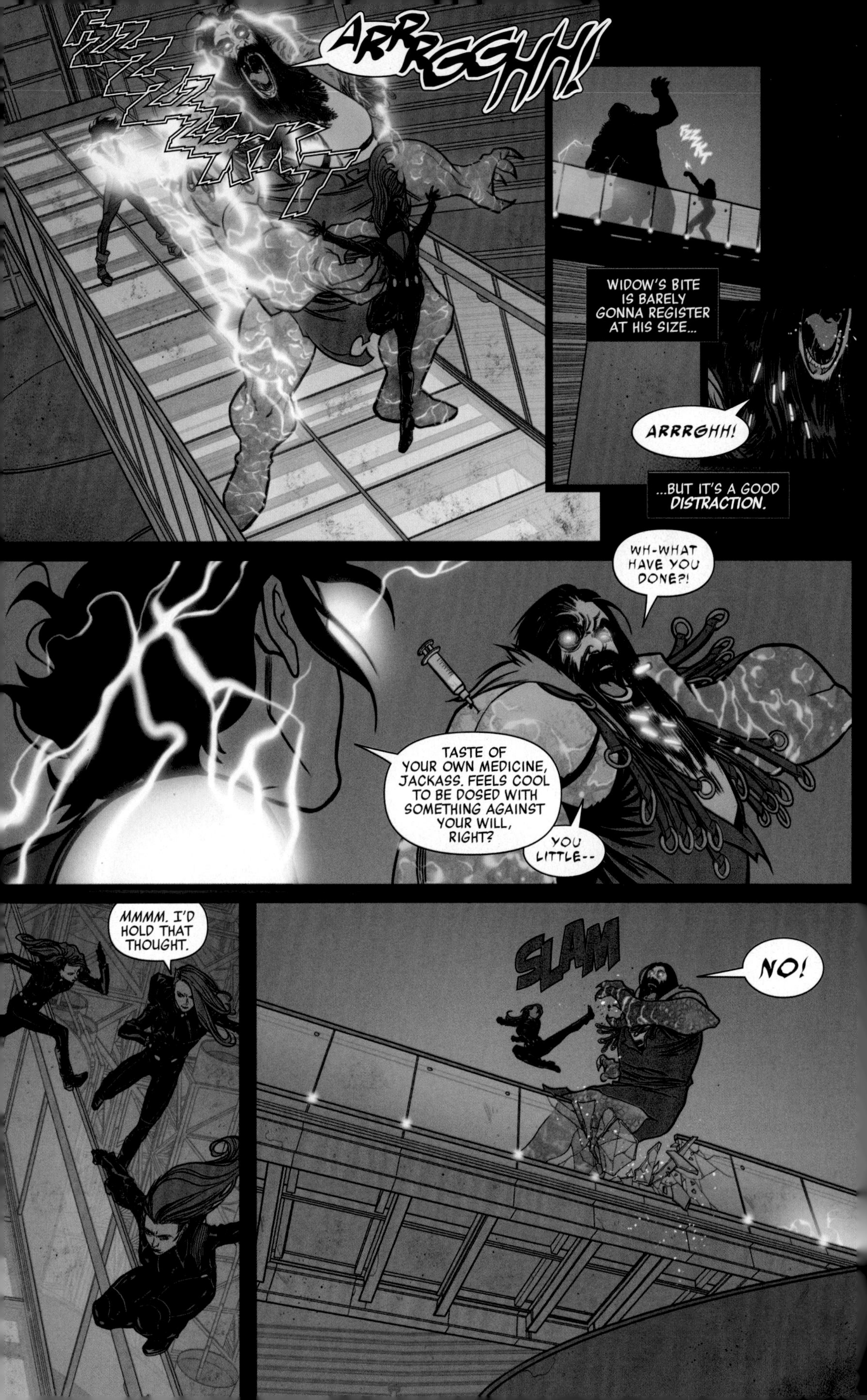
ARRRGGHH!
WIDOW'S BITE IS BARELY GONNA REGISTER AT HIS SIZE...
ARRRGHH!
...BUT IT'S A GOOD DISTRACTION.
WH-WHAT HAVE YOU DONE?!
TASTE OF YOUR OWN MEDICINE, JACKASS. FEELS COOL TO BE DOSED WITH SOMETHING AGAINST YOUR WILL, RIGHT?
YOU LITTLE--
MMMM. I'D HOLD THAT THOUGHT.
SLAM
NO!

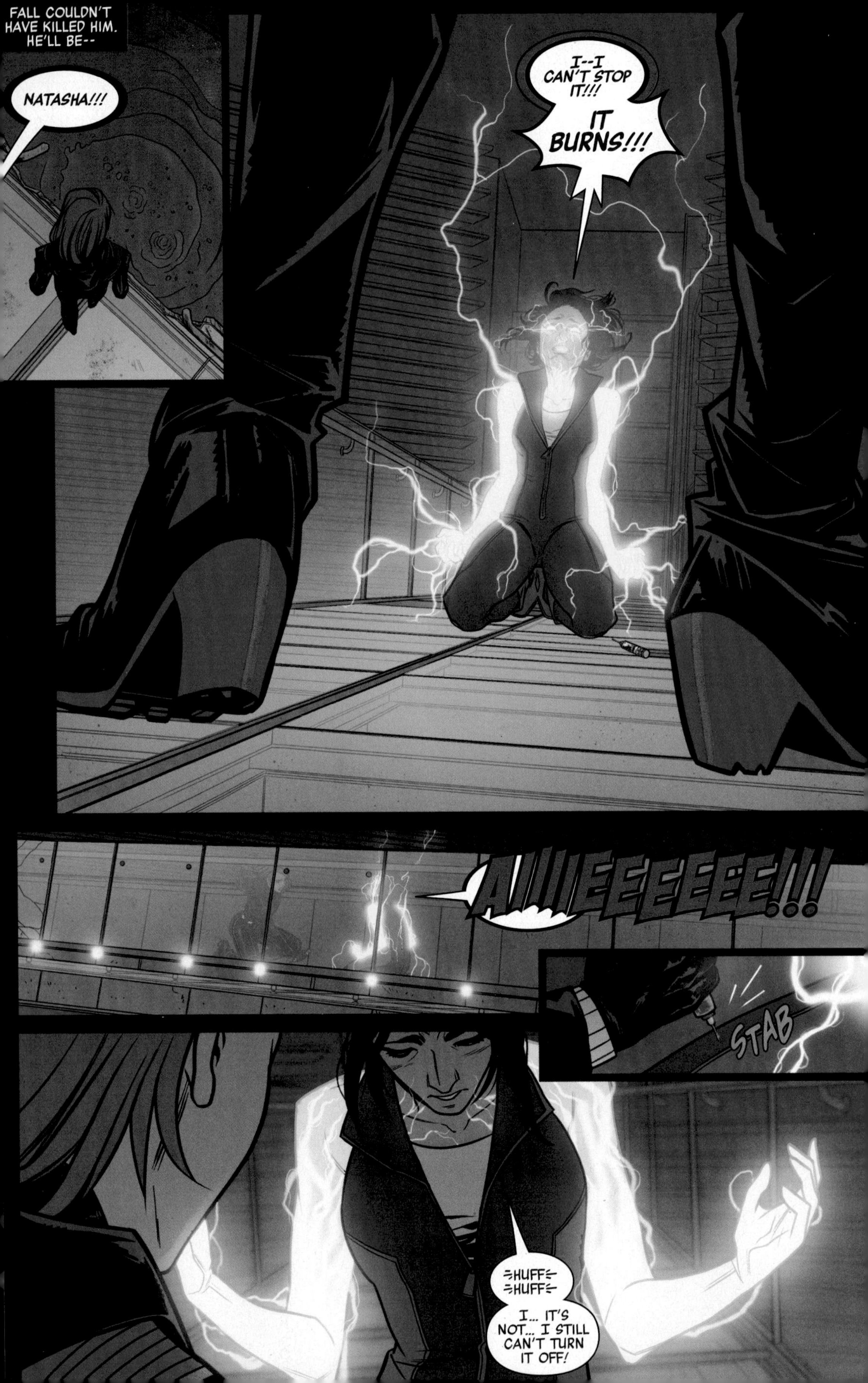
FALL COULDN'T HAVE KILLED HIM. HE'LL BE--
NATASHA!!!
I--I CAN'T STOP IT!!!
IT BURNS!!!
AIIIEEEEEEE!!!
STAB
≈HUFF≈
≈HUFF≈
I... IT'S NOT... I STILL CAN'T TURN IT OFF!

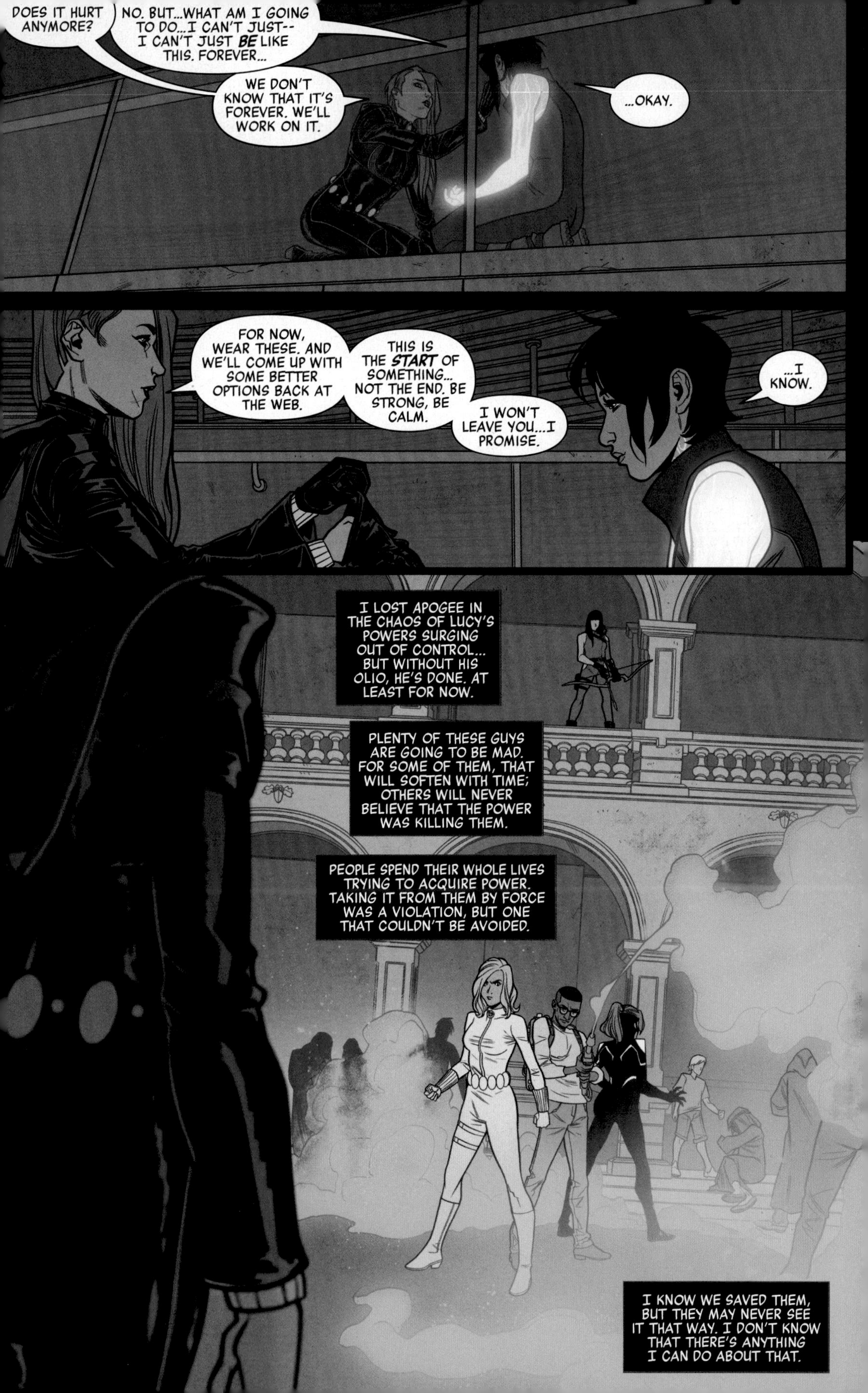
DOES IT HURT ANYMORE?
NO. BUT...WHAT AM I GOING TO DO...I CAN'T JUST-- I CAN'T JUST BE LIKE THIS. FOREVER...
WE DON'T KNOW THAT IT'S FOREVER. WE'LL WORK ON IT.
...OKAY.
FOR NOW, WEAR THESE. AND WE'LL COME UP WITH SOME BETTER OPTIONS BACK AT THE WEB.
THIS IS THE START OF SOMETHING... NOT THE END. BE STRONG, BE CALM.
I WON'T LEAVE YOU...I PROMISE.
...I KNOW.
I LOST APOGEE IN THE CHAOS OF LUCY'S POWERS SURGING OUT OF CONTROL... BUT WITHOUT HIS OLIO, HE'S DONE. AT LEAST FOR NOW.
PLENTY OF THESE GUYS ARE GOING TO BE MAD. FOR SOME OF THEM, THAT WILL SOFTEN WITH TIME; OTHERS WILL NEVER BELIEVE THAT THE POWER WAS KILLING THEM.
PEOPLE SPEND THEIR WHOLE LIVES TRYING TO ACQUIRE POWER. TAKING IT FROM THEM BY FORCE WAS A VIOLATION, BUT ONE THAT COULDN'T BE AVOIDED.
I KNOW WE SAVED THEM, BUT THEY MAY NEVER SEE IT THAT WAY. I DON'T KNOW THAT THERE'S ANYTHING I CAN DO ABOUT THAT.

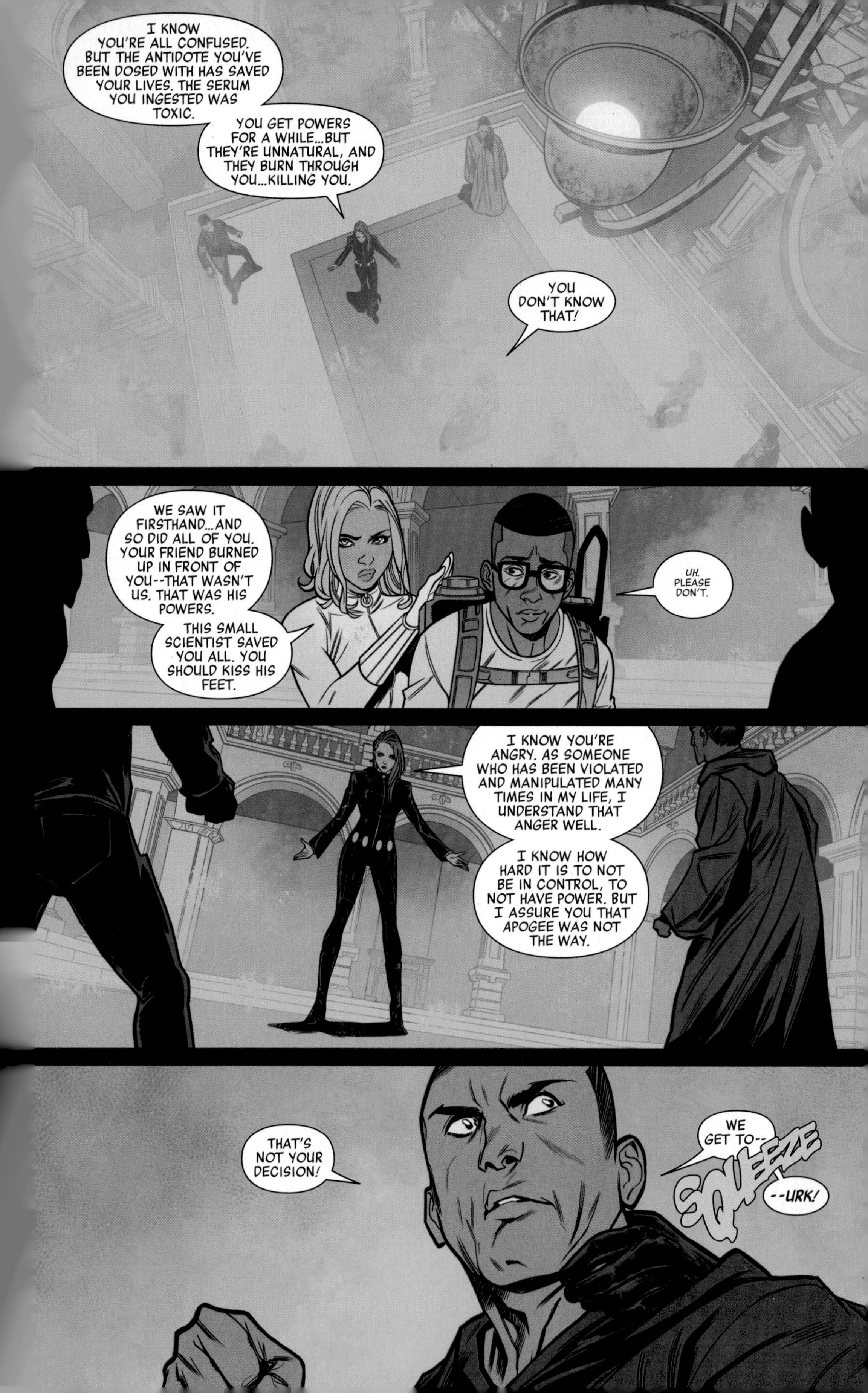
I KNOW YOU'RE ALL CONFUSED. BUT THE ANTIDOTE YOU'VE BEEN DOSED WITH HAS SAVED YOUR LIVES. THE SERUM YOU INGESTED WAS TOXIC.
YOU GET POWERS FOR A WHILE...BUT THEY'RE UNNATURAL, AND THEY BURN THROUGH YOU...KILLING YOU.
YOU DON'T KNOW THAT!
WE SAW IT FIRSTHAND...AND SO DID ALL OF YOU. YOUR FRIEND BURNED UP IN FRONT OF YOU--THAT WASN'T US. THAT WAS HIS POWERS.
THIS SMALL SCIENTIST SAVED YOU ALL. YOU SHOULD KISS HIS FEET.
UH. PLEASE DON'T.
I KNOW YOU'RE ANGRY. AS SOMEONE WHO HAS BEEN VIOLATED AND MANIPULATED MANY TIMES IN MY LIFE, I UNDERSTAND THAT ANGER WELL.
I KNOW HOW HARD IT IS TO NOT BE IN CONTROL, TO NOT HAVE POWER. BUT I ASSURE YOU THAT APOGEE WAS NOT THE WAY.
THAT'S NOT YOUR DECISION!
WE GET TO--
SQUEEZE
--URK!

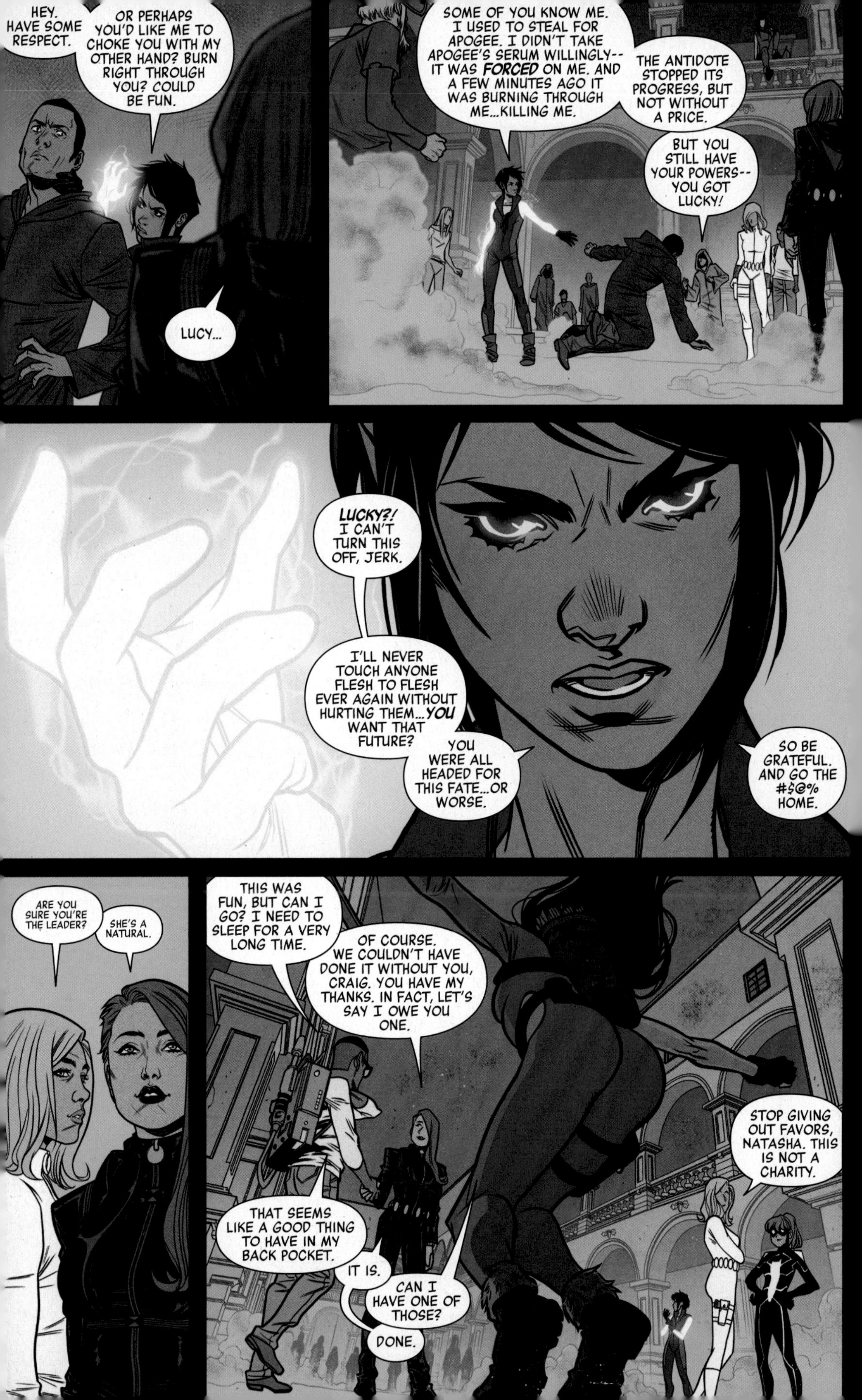

HEY. HAVE SOME RESPECT.
OR PERHAPS YOU'D LIKE ME TO CHOKE YOU WITH MY OTHER HAND? BURN RIGHT THROUGH YOU? COULD BE FUN.
LUCY...
SOME OF YOU KNOW ME. I USED TO STEAL FOR APOGEE. I DIDN'T TAKE APOGEE'S SERUM WILLINGLY-- IT WAS FORCED ON ME. AND A FEW MINUTES AGO IT WAS BURNING THROUGH ME...KILLING ME.
THE ANTIDOTE STOPPED ITS PROGRESS, BUT NOT WITHOUT A PRICE.
BUT YOU STILL HAVE YOUR POWERS-- YOU GOT LUCKY!
LUCKY?! I CAN'T TURN THIS OFF, JERK.
I'LL NEVER TOUCH ANYONE FLESH TO FLESH EVER AGAIN WITHOUT HURTING THEM...YOU WANT THAT FUTURE?
YOU WERE ALL HEADED FOR THIS FATE...OR WORSE.
SO BE GRATEFUL. AND GO THE #$@% HOME.
ARE YOU SURE YOU'RE THE LEADER?
SHE'S A NATURAL.
THIS WAS FUN, BUT CAN I GO? I NEED TO SLEEP FOR A VERY LONG TIME.
OF COURSE. WE COULDN'T HAVE DONE IT WITHOUT YOU, CRAIG. YOU HAVE MY THANKS. IN FACT, LET'S SAY I OWE YOU ONE.
STOP GIVING OUT FAVORS, NATASHA. THIS IS NOT A CHARITY.
THAT SEEMS LIKE A GOOD THING TO HAVE IN MY BACK POCKET.
IT IS.
CAN I HAVE ONE OF THOSE?
DONE.

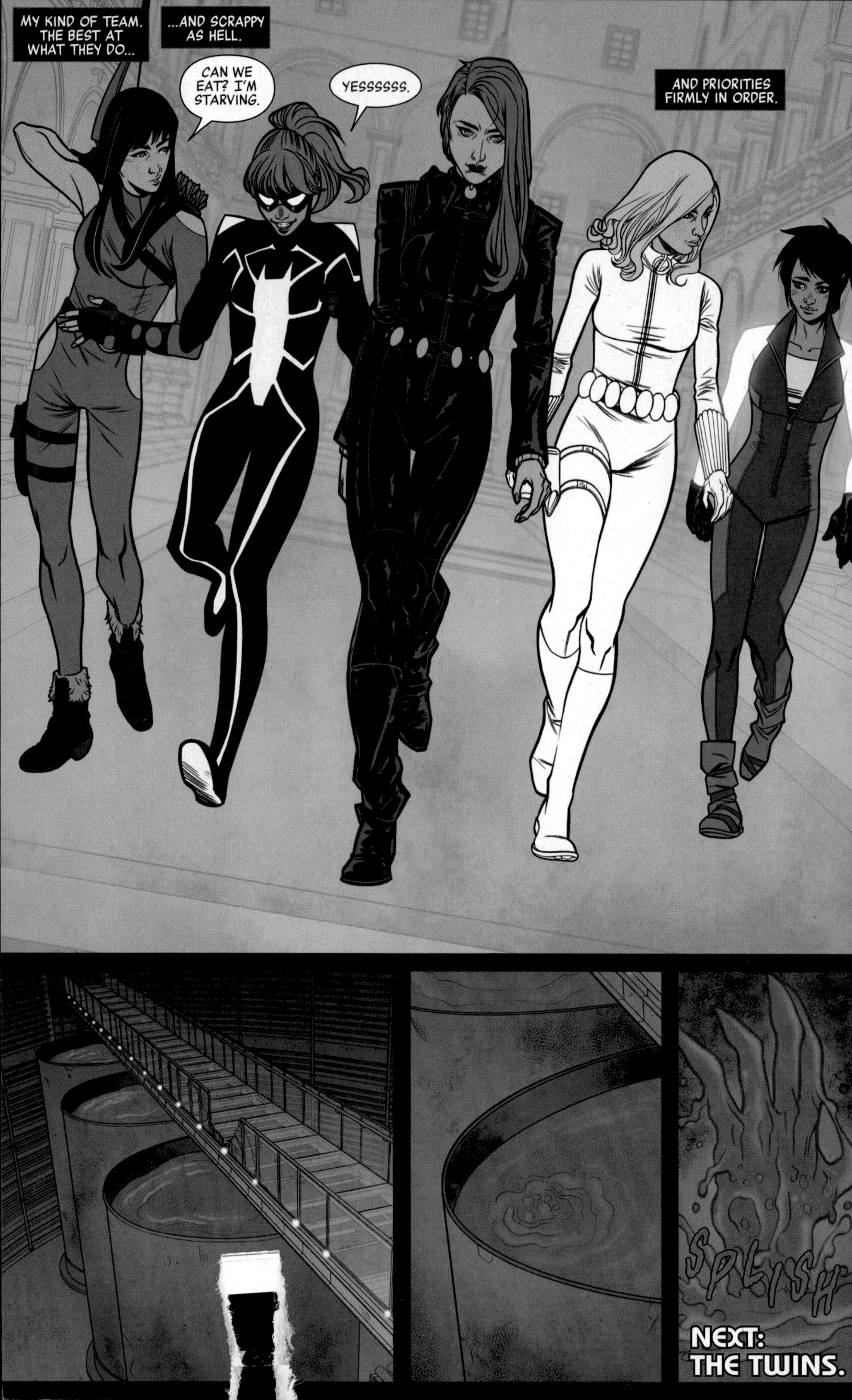
MY KIND OF TEAM. THE BEST AT WHAT THEY DO...
...AND SCRAPPY AS HELL.
CAN WE EAT? I'M STARVING.
YESSSSSS.
AND PRIORITIES FIRMLY IN ORDER.
SPLISH
NEXT: THE TWINS.